What people are saying about
Life Work Transitions.com . . .

"If you do only half of what you find in **Life Work Transitions.com** you can be successful in navigating your career well into the 21st century. To read this book is to sit under the banyan trees with two of the brightest and wisest minds in career counseling today. In a riveting assemblage of wisdom, Knox and Butzel will take you from insight to website and back again. 'Bill Gates meets the Lord Buddha and everyone profits.' Take this advice to heart and your career is in for a transforming experience. You owe it to yourself and your future to buy this book and use it to make the most of your world."
—**Robert J. Ginn**, former Director of Career Services, Harvard University

"Surfing—both of the net and through our work lives—first requires us to be able to stand up to the board. For individuals adjusting to what is still called the 'new' employment contract, and organizations trying to recruit scarce talent, Knox and Butzel provide the foundation for using *meaning* as the center, getting wired and 'hanging ten.' Chapter 2 'Defining Core Competencies' and Chapter 3 'Redefining Your Self' are MUST-reads!"
—**Pennell Locey**, Manager, Executive and Career Development, Polaroid Corporation

"**Life Work Transitions.com** is a visionary leader in the form of a book. It marries the spiritual with the practical and the best that technology has to offer to help people do their best work and make contributions to the world."
—**Cliff Hakim**, Author, *We Are All Self-Employed:*
The New Social Contract for Working in A Changed World

"This book is a must for career offices. Every college student and recent graduate should also own one for constant reference because the career office probably won't be open when you're up at 3am worrying about your job search! **Life Work Transitions.com** is a wise and comprehensive soup-to-nuts resource, able to guide you from total cluelessness to signing the employment contract. Don't try the trip through cyber-search without it."
—**Barbara Reinhold**, Career Director, Smith College, and Content Editor of the Monster Board

"If I were to recommend just one book to those in transition, this is it. It's thorough, comprehensive and an easy read. The information about career websites alone makes this book a must read."
—**Gerry Garvin**, Director, MBA Career Center, Graduate School Administration, Northeastern University, Boston

"Parachute meets the New Age—I loved this book. **Life Work Transitions.com** is spiritual and yet practical, and the kind of book that I wish had been available in the dark days of my career."
—**David G. Jensen**, President, Search Masters International, Inc., Arizona

"*Life Work Transitions.com* is a powerful book that gives job seekers a path to a satisfying career transition. It is especially helpful to those who are surprised to find themselves seeking new employment. Congratulations to Deborah and Sandra!"
— **Ruth Ann (Rickie) Moriarty**, Executive Director,
Operation A.B.L.E. of Greater Boston

"As an outsourced EAP professional I found *Life Work Transitions.com* extremely useful in taking information that I already possessed and laying it out in a clear, concise manner. It provided me with a roadmap to help create my own job destiny."
— **Dianne B. Klayman**, LICSW, MSW

"*Life Work Transitions.com* is a valuable resource for anyone who is going through a major career change, has lost a job through corporate reorganization, or is seeking a new career. It leads you on a journey, helping you find your 'true north' by redefining yourself and discovering the type of work that is truly meaningful and satisfying. But it does not stop there. It gives you a wealth of information and practical, time-saving advice on how to research the world of work using the Internet, visit potential employers' websites to learn more about opportunities, write a convincing resume, and structure the job interviewing process to succeed in getting the job you want."
— **Beth Drysdale**, Executive Director,
Sales and Marketing Executives, Boston

"Finally. A book that harnesses the power of the Internet with the latest in career search techniques. Deborah Knox and Sandy Butzel are two very sensitive and effective career counselors who together have made the leap into 21st century technology—and taken us along for a fascinating journey through innerspace and cyberspace. An INFP and an ENTJ, they complement each other perfectly. And in the process they give us both sides of the career search coin in one volume. I plan to make it required reading for all members of our networking group."
— **George T. Mercer**, Facilitator, Marketing Professionals Network

"In this ever changing job environment, *Life Work Transitions.com* leads the reader to find a firm footing in personal vision, Internet skills, and soul. If you want to know what you love and find a place to be paid for it, the exercises in this book will lead you to that goal. The book's guided exercises will bring you to greater knowledge of yourself, the Internet, and give you the skills to use the Internet to find paid employment that matches who you are and your dreams. The changing job environment gives us the opportunity to get paid for our life's work and our passions. We can go beyond getting a job. Having a job is no longer the path to job security. This book will help you develop the skills and vision to have your security rest in your hands."
— **Rabbi Rim Meirowitz**, Temple Shir Tikvah, Winchester, Massachusetts

"*Life Work Transitions.com* is a wonderful new tool for exploring one's own personality as well as the dynamics of the workplace, all using the muscle of the Internet. It takes the reader by the hand and shows him or her, old or young, step-by-step how to use the ever-expanding resources of the Internet to work through the self-discovery process. Not only do the authors provide clear talk on how to understand and use the Internet, but they provide a highly useable inventory of websites geared to precise topics—e.g., defining one's core competencies, refining interests, researching an industry or specific organization, writing a resume, negotiating a salary, etc. They empower the uninitiated and aid the computer-literate. And they offer real-life practical guides on how to employ the Internet without stress and potential madness."

—Charles Yonkers, former Managing Partner, McKenna & Cuneo

"A career transition is one of the most vulnerable experiences in a person's life. Deborah Knox and Sandra Butzel show how this terrifying time can lead to a spiritual breakthrough and a promising future."

—The Reverend Dr. David A. Killian, Rector, All Saints Parish, and Director of the RUAH Spirituality Program

"*Life Work Transitions.com: Putting Your Spirit Online* is your parachute for the 21st century. Deborah Knox and Sandra Butzel have brought together our yearnings for meaningful (and paying) work with the technologies of the New Millennium. *LWT.com* is an insightful and practical book that not only walks us along a path to honoring who we are and what we really want in our lives, but also gives us practical, on-going real life tools to navigating useful resources on the Internet. This book and their website *http://www.lifeworktransitions.com* is a must for anyone looking for a new career, job, and life."

—Cheryl Gilman, Author, *Doing Work You Love* (Contemporary Books)

"I am grateful to have this work on my bookshelf. So many folks come to talk with me as they grapple with employment that has little meaning. *Life Work Transitions.com* will shape those conversations with useful questions and abundant resources. Living deeply and with balance is the quest for the next century. This book offers a detailed road map and even packs the bags for the soul's journey into the interconnected web of life work planning. It will be good company along the way, for it invites each reader into a conversation with spirit."

—Reverend Martha Niebanck, Waltham, Massachusetts

" 'A Manual for a Fulfilling Life' as well as 'Lifework,' *Life Work Transitions.com* presents a paradigm shift from 'making a satisfactory living' to 'living a satisfying life,' especially useful for anyone facing major transitions and decisions. Highly comprehensive and extremely comprehensible, it is well organized and skillfully integrates spiritual principles of self-actualization with concrete practical 'how to's' in a user-friendly manner. While offering a wealth of resources including a summary of websites by topic and an extensive bibliography, it steers the reader in the right direction with a focus on specific needs rather than overwhelming with information overload. It clearly and simply provides methods for 'learning to navigate,' through life as well as through the Internet, for both beginners and those with previous experience."

—Steffi L. Shapiro, L.I.C.S.W., Holistic Psychotherapist, Spiritual Eldering Seminar Leader

"In the midst of the frightening plethora of information to be sifted when looking for a life career, *Life Work Transitions.com* offers a sensible guide. It supplies actual help in DEFINING a career followed by concrete step-by-step aid in the survival skills needed to utilize the Internet in order to realize success. To make a correct ca-

reer choice, to utilize the Internet as a guide to live a meaningful life thereafter seem to the authors to be the most important things people can do. And HOW to do it is what they have demonstrated very ably in their book. Kudos to them both!"
—**Virginia A. Tashjian**, former Director, Newton Free Library

"If you contemplate a career change Ms. Butzel and Knox have authored a complete primer from conducting a self-evaluation to sharpening interview and search skills. I strongly recommend *Life Work Tranisitions.com* to anyone in career change."
—**Dick Williamson**, former Executive, Polaroid Corporation, and International Consultant

"*Life Work Transitions.com* is invaluable and truly interactive. It is a wonderful resource that brings the job search/career transition experience into the new millennium by providing a step-by-step, user-friendly guide to harnessing the power of the Internet."
—**Kathy Burnes**, Research Associate, National Center on Women and Aging, Heller Graduate School, Brandeis University

"This impressive book combines psychological and spiritual approaches to self-understanding and self-development; extensive exercises for self-discovery, identifying your values, skills, and desired work environment; a thoughtful analysis of the changing world of work; and comprehensive information and guidance on how to use the Internet to access a wealth of career- and job-related websites in *whatever* area of work is of interest to you."
—**Barbara Brandt**, Sustainable Living Activist and Author, *Whole Life Economics*

"Reading *Life Work Transitions.com* was an empowering experience as it seamlessly incorporates traditional and non-traditional assessment and evaluation resources in concert with electronic resources. The connections between life and work experiences are inseparable and interdependent just as our reliance on information resources in hardcopy and electronic format. *Life Work Transitions.com* is a tool for those just beginning to think about a career, for seasoned veterans and everyone in between working with the whole person not a fragmented part."
—**Nancy Johnson**, Supervisor, Reference Department, Newton Free Library

"*Life Work Transitions.com: Putting Your Spirit Online* is an innovative journey into your psychospiritual paradigms for work and meaning combined with the opportunities of technology to help you find your dream. Knox and Butzel offer a fresh approach to career and life work planning with insights for each stage of the lifecycle. They brilliantly cover all the bases...log in and you will find what you have been seeking. This is the quintessential career guide for the new millennium. It must be experienced."
—**Gail McMeekin**, Career and Creativity Consultant and Author, *The 12 Secrets of Highly Creative Women*

LIFE WORK TRANSITIONS.COM

Life Work Transitions.com
Putting Your Spirit Online

DEBORAH L. KNOX AND SANDRA S. BUTZEL

Boston   Oxford   Auckland   Johannesburg   Melbourne   New Delhi

Butterworth–Heinemann supports the efforts of American Forests and the Global ReLeaf program in its campaign for the betterment of trees, forests, and our environment.

Library of Congress Cataloging-in-Publication Data
Knox, Deborah L.
      Life work transitions.com : putting your spirit online / Deborah
  L. Knox and Sandra S. Butzel.
          p.   cm.
      Includes bibliographical references.
      ISBN 0-7506-7160-2 (pbk. : alk. paper)
          1. Work—Psychological aspects.   2. Self-actualization
  (Psychology)   I. Butzel, Sandra S.   II. Title.   III. Title: Life work
  transitions dot com.
  BF481.K6   1999
  158.6—dc21   99-31481
                                                                            CIP

British Library Cataloguing-in-Publication Data
A catalogue record for this book is available from the British Library.

The publisher offers special discounts on bulk orders of this book. For information, please contact:

Manager of Special Sales
Butterworth–Heinemann
225 Wildwood Avenue
Woburn, MA 01801–2041
Tel: 781-904-2500
Fax: 781-904-2620

For information on all Butterworth–Heinemann publications available, contact our World Wide Web home page at: http://www.bh.com

10 9 8 7 6 5 4 3 2 1

Printed in the United States of America

Contents

Preface

Questioning. Creating. Evaluating. Doing. Where are you in the process of managing life work transitions and change? How are you honing and developing your survival skills? There is a tremendous need to know how to live well and to know what living well means for you, for it is different for every one of us. You need to be able to define yourself so that the core of you, that inner part that remains relatively constant, can lead you in the critical act of decision-making through all of life's changes.

In order to make sense of the massive amounts of information surrounding us, we need to be clear on what information we need and how to use it. It's important to learn how to manage newly generated information to remain on the cutting edge of your field. Knowing what you do best, what you value and how you can make a difference allows you to select the information you need to achieve your goals. Not knowing can paralyze you with fear and uncertainty, create a lack of confidence, and prevent congruence with your true self.

The focus of this book is on finding and redefining "right livelihood" as a vehicle for self-realization, and economic independence. It offers you a process for thinking about work so that you will instantly be able to find your center amidst a world of constant change. It includes a comprehensive, reliable guide for defining your career and life work success and a basic guide for beginners to access the Internet for information and connection with the world of work. Through the combined activities of introspection and the use of the Internet you will develop the confidence to gather important information to make decisions and effectively manage change.

This career and life work discovery process was first created and developed by the genius, John Crystal, coauthor with Richard Bolles of *Where Do I Go From Here With My Life* in the early 1970s. Based on his own personal experience as a former spy during World War II, John was able to capture the essence of the survival skills he developed with the following truths: Know yourself and know how to gather information about the world you are entering; make decisions, accomplish your goals, and move on. He applied these principles to his process of finding right livelihood (although he didn't call it that) after the war. Since then the field of career exploration has matured and we have continued to reflect on and draw from our own personal experience to deepen and expand the process, bringing it to this current manifestation. We have written from our combined experiences with clients from the business sector, men and women in midlife transitions, and artists and entrepreneurs whose lives are authentic and financially viable expressions of their core values. Our unique contributions come from an unerring loyalty to our own authentic self-expression over the past twenty years as well as during the creative collaboration of writing this book.

Many of our clients want to discover balance in their lives. They want to be able to draw boundaries around "what is enough?" You may be wanting to change your lifestyle or your life work. Defining what is enough can result in a downsizing of material goods that might mean painful choices for some people. But what replaces the "stuff" often has more lasting value. Time, relationships with family and friends, opportunities for personal growth or spiritual practice, and creative learning experiences are a few of the important values surfacing as a result of changes in us and changes in our society.

If you are of the "boomer generation" you may have helped reinvent the culture of the 60s. Now there is a counter-revolution underway in reinventing the world of work. As the major decision makers in many of our organizations and institutions, as well as chief operators of solo enterprises, many of us are in unique positions to redefine the business world and cocreate this transformation with younger people who will inherit the new workplace. What the new millennium provides is an opportunity for all of us to come together around new paradigms including: industry with compassion; being true to your inner core and respecting others; quality services coupled with a realization that we must work in concert with future generations; opportunities to contribute unique talents, abilities, and vision to achieve holistic organizational goals; the balance of managing existing resources with the needs of workers; awareness of global markets and the satisfaction of customers; valuing diversity as a key to creative problem-solving; and bringing your whole self to work and balancing your personal/family needs.

What many of us are seeking is authenticity in our vocations. In order to acquire and practice "right livelihood" we must transform our understanding of work and how we bring ourselves to the workplace. This book is organized into four parts that speak to the need, the process, and the revolutionary means of connection available through the Internet.

Part One, "Putting Your Spirit to Work in the Twenty-First Century," provides an overview to the issues facing individuals in transition. In addition to incredible changes in the motivations and needs of individuals on the brink of the new millennium, there are dramatic changes occurring in the workplace. The New Employment Reality is presented with the skills required to succeed in that new reality. Individual changes and market driven realities call for a new definition of work that will provide inspiration and hope. And, finally, one of the greatest opportunities for bringing humanity and technology together lies before us in terms of the Y2K challenge.

The process for managing change and transition begins with the individual becoming empowered to make authentic choices that lead to healthy living. We have reviewed and integrated the work of four theoreticians and practitioners who offer guideposts and encouragement for achieving self-actualization in the workplace. First we will examine the work of contemporary William Bridges, who has exemplified the three stages of a transition and the feelings frequently associated with it. Understanding where you are and how to move through a transition will be facilitated by using the processes outlined in this book.

We are thrilled to share the work of Robert J. Ginn, Jr., formerly with the Career Office at Harvard University, as he offers a road map for the stages of career development that will provide insight into your process of achieving balance and authenticity through your work. Next we will visit Abraham Maslow's hierarchy of needs to show the importance of being physically and psychologically grounded in our experience in order to achieve self-actualization. And finally we'll explore Carolyn Myss's brilliant synthesis of the symbolic meaning of the chakra energy system as it relates to the Christian, the Jewish, and the Hindu belief systems for an understanding of how healing a transition can be. These models will not only help you understand where you are in managing your career life work transitions, they will provide valuable reference points by which to determine the next steps of your journey.

In Part Two, "The Beginners' Guide to the Internet," you will learn how to master this twenty-first-century survival skill by getting online and navigating the Web to visit sites while going through the career life work process. Think of the Internet as the key to infinity; it represents access to knowledge and new market opportunities. Now think of yourself as the search engine that can navigate anywhere and learn anything. But in order to make efficient use of our time and this tool, we must learn to focus our attention and establish our priorities in order to achieve the results we desire. Thus, this guide is offered with a time saving philosophy—get in, find it, and get out. Another principle of Internet use is find it, evaluate it, and act on it. To facilitate this process *Life Work Transitions.com* offers a seamless interface with the Internet and our own web site with links to every Internet site listed in the text.

In Part Three, "Finding Your 'True North': Creating a Personal Mandala," we present our model for the career and life work planning process in its entirety. The components of the process are presented so that you will learn how to use this simple model for diagnostic purposes as well as to develop a comprehensive life work profile that can be adapted to your changing circumstances and needs. The heart of this process reflects the basic teachings of John Crystal, with additional exercises and approaches drawn from our experience in the fields of creativity, adult learning, and our ongoing search for meaning and purpose. Each of the five chapters, with comprehensive exercises (which are also posted on our web site *(www.lifeworktransitions.com)* also includes relevant Internet sites to augment our self-assessment process and highlight other models of career development. As a result of completing this process you will be able to create a personal mandala (a one-page profile) that provides direction, focus, and centering to help you discover your "true north." We then teach you how to translate this profile into a comprehensive life work objective while beginning to explore the world of work.

In Part Four, "Putting Your Spirit to Work in the Marketplace, Making the Connection," you will learn to target and focus a specific life work objective and research the world of work using the Internet. You will be introduced to a three-part model for researching the world of work. They include: Getting the Lay of the Land, Verifying Your Interest and Applying for and Getting the Job. Each stage gets you closer to your new job and introduces you to interviewing strategies. The Internet streamlines the outer exploration process as you learn to explore career fields of interest, discover actual hiring requirements, and verify opportunities. In fact, you will find yourself online in an active and participatory way as you become involved in the process and the seamless interface of text and Internet provided at our web site *(www.lifeworktransitions.com)*. You'll learn the best ways to present yourself **in person,** through interviews and networking; **in print**, developing effective resumes and other written correspondence; and **online**, using email to apply for jobs and communicate with others in your field of interest. You'll learn important tips for conducting a job search online and for maintaining records of contacts and follow-up. Entrepreneurs, pro-retirees and anyone else not yet comfortable with this survival tool for the twenty-first century, will find Part Two, "The Beginners Guide to the Internet," a powerful learning tool. We hope you enjoy the process.

Acknowledgments

This book could not have been written by either one of us alone. The marriage of spirit and technology required a true collaboration of working experience, knowledge, and commitment. The other real collaborators are our clients who inform us everyday of the importance and need for making healthy, effective life work transitions in response to an ever changing marketplace. We are grateful to Karen Speerstra for putting our spirit online.

Deborah:

I am deeply grateful to Sandy for undertaking and completing this project with me. I would never have done it alone. It is a better product because we each brought our individual strengths, talents, and perspectives to the process, which we have found fully engaging.

I have had many mentors, teachers, and colleagues who influenced my thinking and the resulting business over the past 20 years. In my early 20s, I felt called to find a life work that would allow me to express and become my true, authentic self. I am grateful to Susan Zalkind who was there during those turbulent years. The model introduced to me by John C. Crystal became the foundation for helping others find their right livelihood, while I continued to learn and grow with them. Since that time, different teaching opportunities with clients from the public and private sector, artists, entrepreneurs, as well as corporate men and women, have revealed how universal this process can be in helping others.

Since the early 1980s, the field has grown and I am proud of the community of practitioners who have shaped the field. We are the cutting edge of the new employment contract, which has now become a way of life for so many. To my friends and colleagues who have helped with this great work, I am forever grateful. To my Sophia sisters everywhere—thank you.

Sandra:

Thank you, Deborah, for introducing me to career counseling and for being my mentor the last fifteen years. I also want to thank you for nudging me to write this book. This is our second collaborative writing experience and the results have been fulfilling, creative, and a lot of fun. It has also given me an opportunity to share with a wider circle the strategy and the style of my work behind closed doors with individual clients.

I also want to thank Bob Ginn, my other steady, helpful, and inspiring mentor who has coached me through the years and collaborated with me with many clients. He makes sure I keep my own career in perspective and carefully tended so that I am most effective.

Most of all, I want to thank my clients who have taught me all the really important things about life and work. One in particular, Jim Damiano, introduced me to the Internet. I have always had a computer in my office and taught and shared technology with my clients. But when Jim bought me a new powerful MAC, a huge monitor, and a modem, everything changed for me and my clients and for the better.

I cannot leave out my homegrown group of cheerleaders: John, Steven, David, and Jessica. Thank you for supporting the long hours, my preoccupation with the Internet, and for all the meals for Deborah and me while writing this book. Both of us thank Steven for the beautiful design of "My Personal Mandala."

I

PART ONE

Putting Your Spirit to Work in the Twenty-First Century

Are you yearning to know and express your unique talents in response to some critical need in society? Do you feel you have something special at your core that can guide and lead you on the path of right livelihood, if you only knew how to begin that journey? Would you like to be proactive and self-directed in managing life work transitions? The universal search for purpose and belonging that calls you has been studied by mystics and theologians from time immemorial. Today, this quest is taking place in the work world and in the spaces that exist between employment opportunities.

As we approach the millennium, more individuals are hearkening to that call to know and understand why they are here. Because of technological advances bringing the global village into our backyards, there is an expanding universe of work that needs doing. Finding, expressing, and putting spirit to work is the most critical challenge facing those who want to make a difference in the twenty-first century.

In addition to this internal drive, the new work ethic of the twenty-first century and the new workplace will be defined and driven by those individuals who possess personal vision, a strong sense of professional responsibility, and the technical expertise to access a global market-place. This book provides a unique opportunity and guide for a spiritual and technological exploration of your life and career resulting in a clearly stated, yet comprehensive, career and life work objective that is flexible, lasting, and deeply personal. You will also learn how to manage the information that leads to knowledge and wisdom by assessing, se-lecting, and prioritizing important criteria. One of the greatest chal-lenges facing us at the end of the twentieth century is to create work that will provide meaning as well as the means of earning a livelihood. Many individuals have been downsized from corporate America in the prime of their careers. Others are being forced to retire early and, on losing the long-sought pension plan, must find alternative means of employment. This may come in the form of a similar job in a related field. Others will feel called to address the deeper issues of finding meaningful work that mirrors the inner desire and the outer realities facing us on the brink of the new millennium.

THE INDIVIDUAL IN TRANSITION

If you are convinced that there is more to work than earning a living, this book is for you. If you feel a certain power/force guiding you and you yearn to connect with it, this book is for you. If you believe in karma/destiny and want to look for the miracles in the everydayness of your work world, this book is for you. If you believe there is a unique spark of the divine in each of us and you want to participate in workplaces that hold and practice that belief, this book is for you. If you feel driven to speak your truth about some deeply held personal belief and find it sud-denly attached to a cause far greater than yourself, this book will help you focus your energies.

Perhaps, after working in one field, you find the expectations and re-wards have shifted dramatically. Perhaps money is no longer the sole motivator and customer feedback is less fulfilling. You may lack a vision about the relevance and purpose of what you do. Or perhaps your heart grows dim when you perceive a situation of waste, neglect, or abuse. You desperately want to make a difference, but lack the confidence or knowl-edge to proceed. You can find meaning and purpose by defining and creating a personal vision statement that will give you a focus and direc-tion. The need to know what we are called to do can catapult us onto the path of discovery.

If you are in between employment opportunities, by choice or necessity, it is important to understand where you are in your transition cycle, in order to maximize the energy you have available. Likewise, if you are dealing with a major life transition, such as losing a job, having to move, or experiencing a major illness, you will be able to better handle the transition by becoming aware of the feeling stages associated with such a loss. William Bridges, in his excellent guide *Transitions: Making Sense of Life's Changes*, has identified three stages involved in a transition that individuals will experience when undergoing change. These stages serve as a guide for undertaking the journey, and the associated feelings are a road map for you to stay informed about what you may be experiencing. They include:

Endings	Dealing with Loss	Anger; Blame; Fear; Shock
Neutral Zone	Transitional Period	Anxiety; Confusion; Uncertainty
Beginnings	Setting New Goals	Integration; Reinventing yourself

Most of us, when dealing with change, may not fully realize the devastating feelings of loss associated with **Endings**. In addition to the obvious, there can also be a tremendous loss of identity, friends/community, or sense of belonging. Acknowledging the loss by naming it and fully exploring it will encourage the healing to begin. If you are ready to explore the loss and begin to move through the stages of a transition, ask yourself the following questions:

1. What do I miss the most from my previous workplace? Is it the relationships, the environment and routine, the availability of resources, or the rewards? Or perhaps it is a sense of purpose or belonging that has kept you there even after the meaning has left.
2. What am I glad to release and leave behind? What creates a smile on your face when you realize you won't have to put up with that anymore? Perhaps it's the impossible deadlines or the ever changing priorities. Or is it a boss or colleagues who truly drove you crazy? What you are glad to leave behind can be translated into positive criteria as you begin to think ahead to what is next.
3. What am I most proud of having accomplished while there? What are my major regrets? And what will I do differently as a result of this inventory in my next immediate position? You can answer these questions now and move on or go to our web page where you will find more information that will help you deal with this first

stage of the transition. However you choose to proceed, remember that none of these stages are dealt with in such an orderly and logical fashion. You may have to revisit loss again and again until you are finished with the associated feelings. But finished you will be at some point.

When some of the devastating feelings of loss have been acknowledged, one enters the **Neutral Zone**—this middle ground where the ending has been acknowledged but you may still be in the void. My favorite description of this phase is how Linus must feel when his blanket is in the dryer. All of the familiar anchors—in terms of role, status, self-definition—are rearranged. During this stage, one often feels anxious and uncertain about what really will happen. In this middle phase, it is a wonderful idea to begin to journal using your word-processor to record thoughts and ideas that are being stirred within you, or buy a beautiful journal and dedicate it to your healing process. The power of journaling, recording your innermost thoughts and concerns, is at the core of the Career and Life Work Process presented in Part Three. In writing and naming we objectify our thoughts, define our reality as none other knows it, and proceed with our healing process. For more information on the benefits of journal writing go to *http://www.nzdances.co.nz/journal/ benefits.htm*. The distance and objectivity acquired through journaling will help you learn to manage and trust the feelings of uncertainty, and will lead to a natural sense of energy and curiosity. "What am I going to do?" is one of the most healthy, life affirming questions we can ask. In order to answer that question, a more thorough process of self-assessment can be successfully undertaken once the grief has been experienced. Although you may visit this nebulous space again, realize that the juice for the journey is there and ready to be tapped.

The **New Beginning** phase is marked by increased clarity about values and more focused goals. The journaling helps keep the creative energy alive while dealing with the inevitable feelings of uncertainty that will continue until your new self-definition is clarified. Processing your feelings consciously, plus acquiring the self-knowledge that comes from completing the numerous exercises, will lead you to reinvent yourself. The process presented in Part Three will allow you to make the most of the learnings to be gained during this transition process as you prepare yourself for finding your true life work.

Think of this exploration process as both internal and external. Internally you are seeking the core truth that will allow you to find and express your true voice. Externally, in our society, the disappearance of traditional jobs and career ladders, the restructuring of the workplace, and the increased use of technology will provide new opportunities for finding and creating meaningful work. In order to survive we must have work. Yet, in order to thrive we must have meaningful work. For more information check *http://www.gbod.org/quest/bookreviews/transitions.html* for a review of Bridges' book and *http://www.gwi.net/chutch/when.htm* for a summary of *When Smart People Fail*. Our web site also has a summary of this material as it relates to job loss.

IS THIS THE PATH FOR YOU?

Is there within you a need to express purpose and wisdom? Is there a longing to find your true expression and have work you love? The truth will reveal itself as a result of your persistence in following the journey outlined in Part Three. It all begins with intention. If you are seeking to find true meaning, purpose, and passion in your life work, then you will find it. Therefore you decide to take this journey now, because if you don't, you will never ever know and the world may not gain what you have to offer. The power of that concept is reflected in the words of Martha Graham:

> There is a vitality, a life-force, an energy, a quickening,
> which is translated through you into action.
> And because there is only one of you in all time,
> this expression is unique, and if you block it,
> it will never exist through any other medium,
> . . . and the world will not have it.

One of the most profound results of undertaking this journey is becoming aware of the serendipitous events in your life, as you learn to recognize and trust the natural unfolding of your life's pattern. James Hillman, in *The Soul's Code*, refers to the acorn image to illustrate the entire potential of our life's destiny in a tiny seed. How we grow the tree and utilize and develop that potential is one of our most basic and blessed responsibilities. Undertaking this journey of career exploration, while learning our life lessons, will help develop the insight and personal responsibility required in the new world of work. If you hope to have this kind of knowing and find your right livelihood you may have realized there are many false prophets and paths beckoning to you. As Frederick Buechner wrote in *Wishful Thinking: A Seeker's ABC:*

> There are all different kinds of voices calling you to do all different kinds of work, and the problem is to find out which is the voice of God, rather than that of society, say, or the superego, or self-interest. By and large, a good rule for finding this out is the following: the kind of work God usually calls you to is the kind of work: a/that you need most to do, and b/that the world needs most to have done. If you really get a kick out of your work, you've presumably met requirement a/, but if your work is writing deodorant commercials, the chances are you've missed requirement b/. On the other hand, if your work is being a doctor in a leper colony, you've probably met requirement b/, but if most of the time you're bored and depressed by your work, the chances are that you've not only bypassed a/, but probably aren't helping your patients much either. . . .*The place God calls you to is the place where your deep gladness and the world's deep hunger meet.* [Italics added by author.]

Finding work you love is the discovery of your deep gladness. By thoughtfully clarifying your skills, goals, values, rewards, and interests through this journey of self-discovery you will discern your deep gladness, the full expression of yourself. By defining your passions and your concerns you will identify areas where the world is hungry for service or attention. The place God calls you to in the world, where you can exchange skills and energy, is your marketplace.

THE TWENTY-FIRST CENTURY WORKPLACE

In the early 1970s, John Crystal, coauthor with Richard Bolles of *Where Do I Go From Here With My Life?*, introduced the concept to us that work was originally created to meet unmet societal needs. He was talking about creating work, not necessarily finding jobs. In 1989 Charles Handy introduced the concept of "portfolio work" to replace the concept of linear career progression, in his groundbreaking book *The Age of Unreason.* The illustrative example he used to demonstrate this concept was of the actor/director in theater who would take on any role that came along in order to survive and thrive in the field, all the while accumulating skills and experience for the one blockbuster event. This innovative concept has since been employed by entrepreneurs, consultants, and crafts people who developed successful business strategies that consisted of using multiple portfolios of skill sets to address different customer needs and alternative reward systems, while pursuing a larger vision. The current downsizing of corporate America establishes the portfolio career as an emerging trend for the future. No longer will we be employed by one company, let alone remain in one career or one job. (See *http://www.globalideasbank.org.*)

We need to see ourselves as self-employed and responsible for developing our own portfolios. As Handy says: "Portfolios accumulate by chance. They should accumulate by choice. We can manage our time. We can say no. We can give less priority, or more, to homework or paid work. Money is essential, but more money is not always essential. Enough can be enough. Without deliberate choice, portfolios can become too full." The process of career and life work planning involves you in making deliberate choices. This practice sets the stage for discernment leading to right action and right livelihood.

THE NEW EMPLOYMENT REALITY

Before you begin the journey of self-discovery, and of your rightful place in the universe, let us look at the current state of work as we move into the twenty-first century. There is a new employment contract which stresses flexible employment opportunities and preparedness rather than job security. This new focus on individuals taking personal responsibility for managing their work lives will actually create more employment opportunities. The resulting flexibility and mobility comes from being able to rearrange multiple skill sets to fit changing work structures and target a vast array of markets that can utilize your skills and knowledge base. The New Employment Contract requires you to develop and maintain the following practices in order to acquire mastery. You will have the rest of your life to fine tune them!

1. Know yourself as "Me, Inc.," possessing a portfolio of multiple skill sets, which can be applied in a variety of settings.
2. Know the appropriate skill sets and functions in your fields of interest. Look for "what needs doing." Forget job titles. Seek projects.
3. Know your field. Stay current through professional associations, networking and knowledge management.
4. Know your current skill sets (and your desired future) and identify a training process for developing competencies and knowledges that will increase your "value added" and your overall marketability.

5. Know your customers and the changing demands of the market-place. Demonstrate curiosity and initiative to learn about their real needs and changing values.
6. Know your department or specialty and the changing demands of the marketplace, internal and external customers, vendors, and the politics of your industry.
7. Know your competition and collaborators. Develop relations that foster mutual learning and respect and encourage the brokering of services rendered. Think of yourself as a cocreator of valued goods and services.
8. Know how to lead change. Develop a proactive attitude. Take responsibility for managing personal transitions and anticipating change.

The New Employment Reality requires you to learn to manage your career. Cliff Hakim, in his book *We Are All Self-Employed*, first introduced the concept of the "career lattice" as opposed to the career ladder that formerly defined traditional career growth and development. The latter was based on a natural progression of jobs largely defined by the hierarchical workplace of the 1960s and 70s. Good performance often resulted in promotions, increased wages, and opportunities to grow within the organization. The organization was responsible for fulfilling this structure. Hakim's lattice approach (similar to Handy's portfolio) applies to the new organizations that structure themselves with less hierarchy and more of a team environment, where lateral moves are encouraged to develop skill sets. For those individuals who remain outside the formal employment system, the portfolio skill development approach places the responsibility for ongoing career development in the hearts and minds of the individual seeking new projects.

The 1980s brought full employment, cross-functional teams, and multidisciplinary training, urging the hierarchy to disassemble itself. The incredible flush and productivity of that era was replaced quite dramatically by the downsizing of the 90s, which has left literally thousands out of the traditional workplace. Middle management jobs were some of the first to go in those industries that had been the mainstay of our economy. They were replaced by a generation of computers giving managers direct access to all information without reports being funneled through middle management. Individuals must now find opportunities within their organization or department where they can make a real contribution. Lateral moves rather than promotions become attractive because they offer new opportunities to learn important skills and expand the possibilities for employment.

The new employment reality teaches us to focus on projects and tasks at hand. This may mean seeking out new projects, relationships, and knowledge in order to expand opportunities. The notion of continuous learning is key for the worker of tomorrow. In order to continue to learn and thrive individuals must conduct self-assessment exercises and update their portfolios regularly in order to move forward.

CAREER MANAGEMENT COMPETENCIES

Knowing yourself as possessing a portfolio of multiple skill sets will allow you to take advantage of multiple career opportunities. Learning and developing the career management competencies to implement the new employment contract will ensure you lifelong learning and earning possibilities. Learning and developing these competencies is the cornerstone of successful career mastery. Increasingly, the successfully employed individual needs to not only possess mastery in a technical/functional or knowledge area, but must also possess the skills for communicating, marketing, and demonstrating that expertise. For now, become familiar with these competencies, and for further assessment and the opportunity to develop a personalized training program turn to Chapter Two.

Career Assessment: conduct frequent skill/knowledge assessments; create learning goals to remain current and informed; identify and communicate with a network of individuals from many diverse areas.

Self Management: commitment to raising one's consciousness, the ability to demonstrate initiative and progress through adversity; work independently with increasing awareness of the larger community.

Interpersonal and Facilitation: demonstrate insight into motivating human behavior, develop and practice team building, conflict management, and mediation.

Project Management: manage and acquire information and resources; broker services through partnering and collaboration; trouble-shoot and plan.

Creativity and Visioning: the ability to "act on something so compelling that it's right in front of you"; intuitive knowing what can and must be done; initiate, develop and maintain ideas; synthesize, adapt, and improve.

Planning and Decision-Making: the ability to plan and set goals; establish a structure that encourages individual responsibility; review, select, and prioritize criteria.

Leadership: the ability to act as a leader and develop the discipline of building community; be committed to aligning various courses of action that will empower individuals; be willing to cocreate and share the results.

Computer Technology: knowledge and practice of online resourcing such as Internet and email community accessibility, database management and retrieval, word processing.

Growth and Development: creation of a plan and identification of resources to realize your goals of continuous learning to become all you can be and realize your potential.

Portfolio Careers and the demands of Workforce 2000 speak to the need for individuals to think of themselves as being self-employed. By not relying on one single employer, let alone the naive belief that one career will last a lifetime, we are required to become more independent and resourceful. By developing and practicing the career management competencies outlined above the individual will be able to successfully navigate the uncharted waters of the twenty-first century.

REDEFINING WORK

There is plenty of work to be done even if the jobs are disappearing and the traditional workplace is changing. There will be more giant organizations resulting from ongoing mergers and many new entrepreneurial ventures resulting from individual vision and initiative. Matthew Fox, in his *Re-invention of Work*, encourages us to think about redefining work to be more inclusive, humane, and dignified. This twentieth-century radical priest says that "to live well is to work well." Having meaningful work is about meeting unmet societal needs, engaging in self-expression, and creating mutual exchanges of energy and value. Work should allow us to make a difference in the moments of our daily life, as well as on a global level. Work needs to be about creating and caring for community. Creating your life work requires your unique expression. Individually each of us needs to exercise personal responsibility if we are to ensure our collective survival.

Since the workplace is temporal and defined by current reality, we cannot ignore the forces or the effects of the current downsizing and elimination of jobs. Indeed, if you are reading this, you may well be one of the ones who is existing in the space between work. Somehow you are managing, but you feel a strong lack of purpose and meaning. At the same time, you see an emergence of many new fields, companies, and opportunities. By exploring what needs doing in your world and being attuned to the ever-changing marketplace of the twenty-first century, you will be engaged in the all important process of redefining, reinventing, and revaluing work and self. As individuals assume responsibility for this, we will find ourselves realigning our societal values and definition of work. No government agency can do this for us and the employers need workers to lead the way.

As we learned during the 1960s, and still find true today, "the personal is political." Being personal at work, means discovering our "deep gladness." When we experience congruency between values, beliefs and behaviors we produce enhanced results. By defining your criteria that ensure the full expression of who you are, you will be redefining and reinventing work—for yourself first and then for others, by example.

Another perhaps inevitable lesson from the 1960s is the knowledge that "if the people lead, the leaders will follow." This was true for those who protested the Vietnam War before it became popular to do so, and it was true with the environmental movement. As a friend recently observed at a meeting of the Conscious Business Alliance, an organization committed to promoting spiritual awareness in the workplace, the environmental movement was born the day the first person picked up a piece of trash with conscious awareness. By assuming personal responsibility for our beliefs we can make a difference.

The impetus for change grows daily, according to Jeremy Rifkin in *The End of Work*. Because of restructuring and merger-mania, many jobs have actually disappeared and he sees no real growth areas for wage work. The prescription for change lies within each of us, even in the low-paying service sector, where individuals who consciously follow this process to identify meaningful personal criteria will fare better than those who are unaware of the power of personal choice. By defining what is essential and important to you in your work, your life becomes a laboratory for social change as you assume personal responsibility for your actions. Your work becomes your passion because it is the place where you are always learning, growing, and redefining what is essential and important. (Yes, my friends . . . even in the law department)

Y2K: THE CHALLENGE OF THE TWENTY-FIRST CENTURY

Perhaps the ultimate challenge facing us and calling for new ways of working is the Y2K problem. When the calendar clicks from '99 to '00 there will be a true millennial shift and we will begin to experience our computer-dependent world in an entirely new way. John Peterson, Meg Wheatley, and Myron Kellner-Rogers, in a widely distributed article entitled "The Year 2000: Social Chaos or Social Transformation," discuss the implications of this problem caused by technology that they feel can only be solved by new social relationships. The Y2K challenge is defined as:

- A technological problem that now cannot be solved by technology
- The first-ever, nonnegotiable deadline
- A systemic crisis that no one can solve alone
- A crisis that dissolves boundaries and hierarchies
- A unique opportunity to evoke contributions from individuals, organizations, and communities
- The greatest opportunity to simplify and redesign major systems

We have created not only a computer-dependent society, but an interdependent planet. What better opportunity for individuals who are committed to solving problems in a collaborative proactive style? This is clearly work that needs doing by many different organizations—public as well as private.

The social problems that might be triggered can only be solved by humans effecting new social relationships. Our book helps you develop the confidence and the tools to make a contribution. According to the writers of this compelling article, "All of us need to become very wise and very engaged very fast and develop entirely new processes for working together. . . ." The evolution of the new employment contract is reinforced when we understand the implications of our learning to work together and bring forth our best ideas and solutions.

Whatever community, organization, or business we are involved in we must begin to address how it will perform its essential task of delivering goods and services in the absence of present systems. We must ask ourselves what simplified systems can be developed now to replace existing ones that will ensure the smooth flow of operations with open and full access. As an individual worker or contributor, each of us must demonstrate personal wisdom, functional understanding, and expertise to address those aspects of the problem that are uniquely ours.

Whether the crisis exceeds or meets our expectations, it provides an opportunity for individuals to be more and do more than ever before. The human spirit has demonstrated a remarkable ability to respond to crises with the following truths:

- Shared purpose and meaning bring people together
- People display amazing levels of creativity and resourcefulness
- People want to help others—individual agendas fade immediately
- People learn instantly and respond at lightning speed
- The more information people get, the smarter their responses
- Leadership behaviors (not roles) appear everywhere, as needed

For the individual who is on purpose with his or her work, the Y2K challenge and the changing nature of the workplace both provide ample opportunities for expressing their deep gladness and meeting the world's hunger. The opportunity for individuals to spiritualize their work and the environment provide real challenges for self-actualization. For more information on this issue, use the web to keep up-to-date (*http://www. Year2000.com*. For a copy of the article, e-mail your request to *mjw@ berkana.org.*).

OTHER MODELS OF INFLUENCE

The career life work planning process for mastering change that is presented in Part Three is closely aligned with several other developmental models. These theoretical models may serve as guideposts on your journey, offering assurance and reference points if you feel lost. In addition to the first model of transition presented earlier, this next model looks at the typical stages of career development. You can use this model to assess where you are in relation to developing authority and autonomy in your life work. The other models that follow will help you as you journey to develop more of your potential in the spiritual and personal areas of your life. In addition to the brief summaries included, we invite you to visit the specific web sites to gather more information.

Nine Stages of Career Development

The nine stage model was originally researched and defined by William Perry and Lee Knefelkamp in the 1970s. We are grateful to Robert J. Ginn, Jr., for allowing us to share his insights from "Discovering Your Career Life-Cycle," a manuscript and keynote address presented at the

Radcliffe Career Services 80th Anniversary. In this manuscript, he further developed the original nine stages based on his 25 years as a career counseling practitioner. According to Bob, "the model speaks clearly to the fear and hysteria which is becoming more and more the daily bread of workers in these last years of the 20th century." You may find yourself resonating with more than one of these stages based on your current circumstances, your chronological age, and the amount and variety of work experience to date. You can find the complete text of "Discovering Your Career Life-Cycle" at our web site: *http://www.lifeworktransitions.com.*

Let us begin this "Journey Toward Hope and Life and Vision" with the following words of introduction by Robert J. Ginn, Jr.: "Unless we understand the forces that shape the way we think and act in our vocations, it is difficult to gain control over our career path. When we learn to direct our life energy toward achieving personal growth and vocational authenticity we resist the loss of identity associated with joblessness and we stop wasting the abilities with which we are gifted. We also retain the wonderful joy we churn out of the process of growing in vocational self understanding."

Developing an awareness of the nine stages will help you develop spiritually and personally as well as vocationally. The reference points depicting the various stages include some behaviors that may indicate "stuck" or rigid styles of thinking, as well as awareness of new behaviors and insights that will create growth and development. See if you can find the truths that you have experienced in the past, and where you might be now as a prelude to creating your life work.

Stage One: Absolute Reliance on External Authority

- Two main assumptions: there is a right career and there is an authority that knows what the right career is; therefore, one will not leave a career unless what they are leaving is bad and there is hope of something better.
- Fewer employers are willing to provide the kind of security that people at this stage feel is necessary. They want adaptive specialists who can manage their own career and move quickly from one area to another as companies respond to rapid changes in the economy.

Stage Two: Awareness of the Possibility of a "Wrong" Decision

- Still feels an external authority in life will define the correct career choice.

- Begins to trust in a process of understanding one's past, abilities, and motivators. A willingness to explore and clarify the impact of genetic programming, social situation, and a complex self. Knowing these biases is the prerequisite to personal freedom.
- Realize whatever shatters their world view is telling them that wrong choices are possible and no one's fault.
- Often arises from the broken pieces of a shattered world view; for example, jobless Ph.D.s or the disillusionment of layoffs through downsizing.

Stage Three: Substitution of the Process as Authority

- Deals with disillusionment from discovery that career development is not as simple as previously thought.
- Shift from belief that one authority exists to belief that the right decision-making process will yield the right career. The process becomes the authority.
- Continued allegiance to the concept that one right career exists leads to following the "right" process to avoid making mistakes.

Stage Four: Awareness of Multiple "Good" Decisions

- Abandonment of the constructs of one authority and right career.
- Discovery that one can be involved in the process of one's career development.
- Big cognitive flip: the individual rather than the authority authors lists of priorities. She is able to look back on her life story and see the ways vocational self-concept is flowing, growing, and changing.
- May begin feeling the oppression of freedom, too many options.

Stage Five: Emergence of Self as Decision Maker

- Develop internal sense of self as the decision maker and responsible for the choices of life.
- Experiences the reality that vocational identity is determined internally by a moral consciousness based on decision and values clarification and to a much lesser extent by socially defined roles.
- Acceptance of being in charge; this exhilarating, exploring, and doing phase recognizes multiple possibilities and the need to create personal order and clarification.
- Accepts the need to be clear about what needs to be done and the need for feedback about how well one is doing.

Stage Six: Awareness of the Chaos of Free Choice

- "Pride goeth before a fall." Learn about luck, accident, and illness. Temptation to trade authenticity and integrity for security.
- All the alternatives feel like a burden and that life is in chaos.
- Discrepancy between what is desired and what is actually happening creates an inner tension; resolution of tension is the basic barometer of maturity and mental health.
- Challenges and crises promote growth but are often painful.

Stage Seven: Beginnings of Integration of Self and Career Role

- Second cognitive flip: end of polarized career identity. Choosing a traditionally defined role is abandoned in favor of seeing career as a form of self-expression.
- Look at careers as events with certain regularities and with enormous variations and freedom. Responsible for vocational actions, living in light of potential.
- Career is an expression of identity rather than the reverse, where identity is derived from career role or institutional affiliation. Discover the core of vocational freedom. "We are more than what we do."
- Requires some clarity about what one stands for. Realization that life is constructed by us out of our own existential commitments to values, to people, to the kind of self we would be, to our part in the unfolding complexity of life, to the acquisition and exercise of certain skills consistent with all of the above.

Stage Eight: Experiencing Commitment

- Taking responsibility for the creation of career means also taking responsibility for the undesired outcomes.
- Begin to see that powerlessness, loneliness, fear, pain, and rejection are part of life. Following your bliss is not always blissful, and doubts can come in.
- Learn that life becomes serene and enjoyable precisely when you have become detached from a professional identity defined by others.
- Careers have no reality apart from personal participation in them. Judging success in a career can only come from the perspective of your future integrity.

- Focus is on the task, not the reward. Truth from experience guides expansion of self-created career roles.
- Celebration of self, vocational power, authenticity, integrity, and even sanctity.

Stage Nine: Expansion of Self-Created Roles

- Learn that working is a form of self-expression limited only by the demands of justice, harmony, and mutuality.
- Not owned by career. Truly focused on task not the reward.
- Begin to love the self we are and the self we want to give the world.
- Learn the magic of believing, going with the flow, the harmony of the universe.
- Major problem: *What is* always has the edge on *what might be*. Easier to settle for reality than truth.
- Joy of doing, of accomplishing, of trying and achieving, is always active. It is accompanied by the joy of transcending ego boundaries to being and becoming part of something greater than ourselves.
- Resisting personal growth means sustaining great losses and living at one's own peril.

In Part Three you will find an exercise for writing your spiritual autobiography. This exercise will help you discover times when you experienced the "joy of transcending ego boundaries." You will then be able to identify the conditions that support your being and becoming part of something greater than yourself. Your own self-assessment will help you analyze your current beliefs in relation to the nine stages of career development.

Attaining Self-Actualization in the Workplace

The work of Abraham Maslow, who in the late 1960s began looking at the self-actualized adult, offers us a model for wholeness and well-being that can finally be realized in the emerging world of work. Both organizations and individuals will benefit from this. Self-actualization is defined in various ways but there is a solid core of agreement around the following definitions:

1. acceptance and expression of the inner core or self
2. actualization of latent capacities and potentialities resulting in "full functioning"

3. availability of human and personal essence, and
4. minimal presence of ill health, neurosis, or diminution of the basic human and personal capacities (Maslow, *Toward a Psychology of Being*, p. 197).

Maslow says that "capacities clamor to be used, and cease their clamor only when they are well used. That is capacities are needs. Not only is it fun to use our capacities, but it is also necessary for growth. The unused skill or capacity or organ can become a disease center or else atrophy or disappear, thus diminishing the person" (p. 201). The pursuit of finding and fulfilling oneself though one's work is thus key to a healthy and spiritual lifestyle. This state of full functioning is similar to the **flow** identified by Mihaly Csikszentmihalyi. To learn more and discuss these ideas with others on the net go to *http://www.flownetwork. com*. Maslow's focus was on human needs that indicate potentialities within a framework of development and growth. He speaks of five levels of need arranged in hierarchical order. The most basic needs must be relatively well satisfied before the individual is able to function at a higher level. A brief summary of Abraham Maslow's hierarchy of needs follows.

1. **Physiological Needs** include hunger, sex, and thirst as well as the need for sleep, relations, and bodily integrity.
2. **Safety Needs** are centered around the requirements of a predictable and orderly world. The individual will attempt to organize the world to provide the greatest degree of safety and predictability.
3. **Belonging Needs** indicate the ability to carry on affectionate relationships with other people and belong to a wider group. The person is able to function well in interpersonal situations.
4. **Esteem Needs** constitute the desire for achievement and competence, for independence and freedom, for reputation and prestige. When the satisfaction of all the lower needs has occurred, the final level will be achieved.
5. **Self-Actualization Needs** are met when the individual reaches full use and exploitation of talents, capacities, and potentialities.

Maslow's focus on the healthy person and his intense investigations of a group of self-actualized people found the following characteristics to be evident in those who have achieved self-actualization (See *http:// www.maslow.com/* and *http://www.cfil.com.*):

Figure Pt. 1.1   Maslow's Hierarchy of Needs

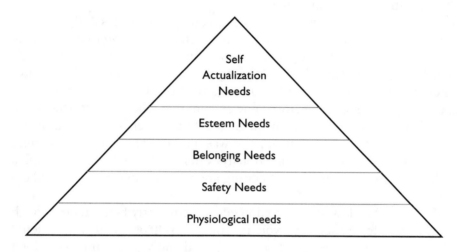

1. They are realistically oriented.
2. They accept themselves, other people and the natural world.
3. They have a great deal of spontaneity.
4. They are problem-centered rather than self-centered.
5. They have an air of detachment and a need for privacy.
6. They are autonomous and independent.
7. Their appreciation of people and events is fresh rather than stereotyped.
8. Most had had profound mystical or spiritual experiences (not necessarily religious).
9. They identify with mankind.
10. Intimate relationships with a few specially loved people tend to be profound.
11. Their values and attitudes are democratic.
12. They do not confuse means with ends.
13. Their sense of humor is philosophical rather than hostile.
14. They have a great fund of creativeness.
15. They resist conformity to the culture.
16. They transcend the environment rather than just coping with it.

This list of characteristics might fit every employers' profile of the "ideal candidate" or serve as a working goal for the self-employed person.

Working at this level of self-actualization would surely result in more pleasure, harmony, and peace.

One of our clients realized that her career was successfully meeting her safety needs, while at the same time, because she had found her true vocation was also realizing her actualization needs. However, she experienced a gap in meeting her belonging needs which were satisfied later when she chose to work within an organization. Likewise, her needs to experience more of her personal power were met when she left that same organization to start her own business. Thus when she arrived at another level of self-actualization, she was able to experience many more of the characteristics listed previously. This kind of awareness, coupled with maturing, results in a deepening appreciation of one's personal experience.

Which of Maslow's identified needs are currently being met through your work life? Where are you in your overall personal assessment? Check the characteristics of self-actualized individuals and see which ones you manifest. As you proceed with the process presented in Part Three and reflect on your life work you may become more aware of times when you reflected these criteria.

Personal Healing and Energy Centers

In order to further focus our attention on understanding how to realize a healthy and spiritual life style through one's work, we turn to the work of Carolyn Myss. In her brilliant works *Why People Don't Heal and How They Can* and *Anatomy of the Spirit* she has reinvented an astonishing and insightful model that integrates the chakra system of the Hindus with the Judaic Tree of Life and the Christian sacraments. The concept of understanding that our "biology is our biography" is especially applicable to healing the wounds received from the workplace and will occur for you as you begin to tell your story.

The seven chakras can best be thought of as energy centers connecting the body and the spirit. Like a computer disc, these energy centers are imprinted with information and energy needed by your physical/spiritual body to perform your life work. By familiarizing yourself with the energy system reflected in each of the chakras, you can acquire the grounding needed to be fully present to yourself and today's marketplace. For more information go to her web site at *http://myss.com*.

Here is a brief description of some of the belief patterns associated with each of the chakras, in ascending order. The mental/emotional

Figure Pt. I.2   The Human Energy System: Correspondences (From *Why People Don't Heal and How They Can* by Carolyn Myss. Copyright © 1997 by Carolyn Myss. Reprinted by the permission of Harmony Books, a division of Crown Publishers.)

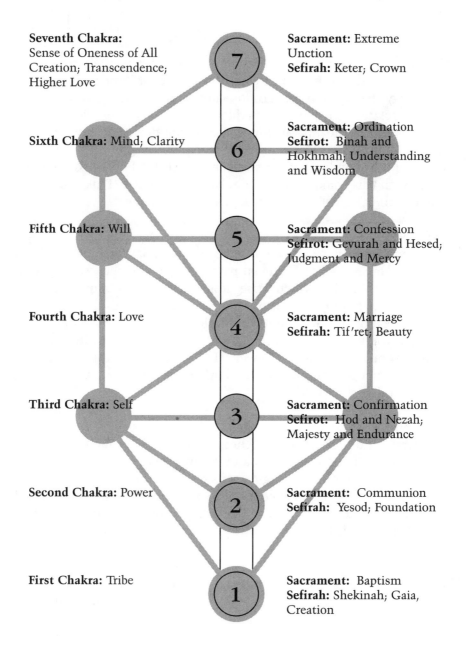

Seventh Chakra: Sense of Oneness of All Creation; Transcendence; Higher Love

Sacrament: Extreme Unction
Sefirah: Keter; Crown

Sixth Chakra: Mind; Clarity

Sacrament: Ordination
Sefirot: Binah and Hokhmah; Understanding and Wisdom

Fifth Chakra: Will

Sacrament: Confession
Sefirot: Gevurah and Hesed; Judgment and Mercy

Fourth Chakra: Love

Sacrament: Marriage
Sefirah: Tif'ret; Beauty

Third Chakra: Self

Sacrament: Confirmation
Sefirot: Hod and Nezah; Majesty and Endurance

Second Chakra: Power

Sacrament: Communion
Sefirah: Yesod; Foundation

First Chakra: Tribe

Sacrament: Baptism
Sefirah: Shekinah; Gaia, Creation

issues associated with each chakra activate the chakras' energies and spiritual lessons in sequence from bottom to top. We have also correlated this information with Maslow's needs to help you identify where you are currently in your own personal journey to discover right livelihood.

First Chakra

This energy center contains the belief patterns most strongly connected to our biological family and our early social environment. Thus this *tribal* energy shows up in concern for safety and security. It is connected to how we relate to the physical world and our ability to provide for life's necessities and stand up for ourselves. To the degree that we are "at home" with our bodies is the degree to which we are grounded—a major requirement for conducting our work in the world. The affirmation associated with this chakra: **All is One. Key word: Tribe.** This stage is associated with the physical needs identified by Maslow.

Second Chakra

From group control we move to one-on-one relationships, such as friendships, business and financial partnerships, and the use of power. Negative relationships which arise around issues of blame and guilt, money and sex, power and control, inevitably must be resolved. But this is also the seat of creativity, and the development of ethics and honor in all our relationships. The affirmation associated with this chakra: **Honor Others. Key Word: Power.** The safety needs identified by Maslow are met by honoring self and others, and thus include the second and third chakra development.

Third Chakra

This energy center relates to the belief patterns we hold about ourselves. It is the center of our self-esteem and is concerned with issues of trust, care of oneself and others, being responsible for our decisions, and experiencing personal honor. Self-confidence and self-respect are generated at this level as the ego matures. The affirmation associated with this chakra: **Honor Self. Key Word: Self.**

Fourth Chakra

This heart chakra serves to connect the lower three chakras (the tribal energies) with the upper three (the individual and symbolic energies) and has the power to create or destroy. The issues associated with this chakra include love and hatred, resentment and bitterness, grief and anger. The healing that must take place from the wounds received in today's world of work will be addressed as people deal with the issues of loneliness and commitment, forgiveness and compassion, and ultimately, hope and trust. The affirmation associated with this chakra: **Loving is Being. Key Word: Love.** This chakra represents the belonging needs identified by Maslow that will be addressed through our interactions with others.

Fifth Chakra

This is the center of willpower, where we make choices and personal commitments and learn to speak our truth. It has to do with finding your voice and following your dream. The energy of this chakra helps you to use personal power to create and learn the important issues of self-control, rather than control over others. The affirmation associated with this chakra: **Surrender to God. Key Word: Will.** The esteem needs identified by Maslow are met through developing the appropriate use of personal power to create an authentic life and are mirrored in the fifth and sixth chakras.

Sixth Chakra

This energy center runs the power of the mind and thus carries tremendous authority. By developing insight and intuition we learn to see beyond the visible and are empowered to reconsider our beliefs. The pursuit of truth and the ability to be self-reflective enhances our openness to the ideas of others and encourages us to learn from experience. The affirmation associated with this chakra: **Seek the Truth. Key Words: Mind, clarity.**

Seventh Chakra

The energy of this chakra is like a magnet that draws us upward into divine perception. It is the connector with our spiritual consciousness that urges us to trust life and see our lives in the context of a larger pattern. This chakra encourages us to live a life of values, ethics, courage, and humanitarianism. It generates the transforming spiritual quests and questions such as: Why was I born? What is the deeper meaning of my life? Manifesting the energies of this chakra comes through development of one's faith and spiritual awareness. The affirmation associated with this chakra: **Presence. Key Word: Oneness/ transcendence.** Our self-actualization needs are met when we are doing the work we love and love the way we are doing it. Use the review in Box 1.1 to assess your current energy pattern.

BOX 1.1   ENERGY SYSTEM REVIEW

Use the following questionnaire to understand and identify work-related issues associated with the chakras. If, according to Myss, "our biology is our biography," how might the wisdom of the chakra system be used when we are stuck or constricted by a particular life work situation? How do the chakras interplay with the body and the emotions? For more on these ideas, see "Bodymind" by Ken Dychtwald. Discover how your energy may be blocked. Consider some of the suggestions for moving the energy. You may want to review the chakra system at *http://www.myss.com* for more insight.

First Chakra Affirmation: All is One   Keyword: Tribe

1. What activities make you feel most grounded? Think of a time in your life when you were really present and describe what was going on. Where is your bodies' energy now while you are reading this book? Do you feel connected to the earth/ground? This lowest chakra reflects survival needs and material concerns, and when blocked can result in a holding on to feelings and a lack of spontaneity.

Second Chakra Affirmation: Honor Others   Keyword: Power

2. Think of a situation when you felt fully empowered with and by another. Describe what was going on. Who was the person? What was the nature of the relationship? What did you create together? This chakra relates to issues of separation vs. openness in our relations to others. Is there a relationship in your life work now that contains issues that need resolving? How can you approach it with new insight?

Third Chakra Affirmation: Honor Self   Keyword: Self

3. Do you, as a rule, take responsibility for your actions and decisions? Is this true in all areas of your life and business, e.g., health-related concerns, recycling waste products, honoring professional commitments (no matter how overloaded you are), and being available with your truest self? Would completing the process outlined in Part III, "Finding Your True North," be some-

thing you would be able to commit to, in order to honor your self? This third chakra relates to basic issues of control and consumption. How are you feeding and nurturing yourself?

Fourth Chakra Affirmation: Loving Is Being   Keyword: Love

4. Are you carrying wounds from the workplace that need to be healed in order to continue this journey? Is there anger, bitterness, and/or disappointment holding you back? Can you feel your heart opening to new opportunities to connect with others and begin anew? Acknowledge the loss and prepare to move on to a new beginning. The heart chakra must be both open and properly protected as a channel that lets love flow in and out.

Fifth Chakra Affirmation: Surrender to God   Keyword: Will

5. By surrendering to what is, we are able to take appropriate action. By being present in the moment we are able to bring our future into being. What is in your future now? The throat chakra allows you to communicate with thought and feeling, by saying "I am." What choices are you making on a daily basis that allow your authentic self to be present to all that is in your life? A deeper understanding of self is stirring and drives of spiritual awakening can occur.

Sixth Chakra Affirmation: Seek the Truth   Keyword: Mind, Clarity

6. As you begin a new project, or approach it on a daily basis, do you remember to center your energy and allow your intuition to be your guide? Are you able to surrender to the outcome, rather than control what is happening? When you face disappointments, are you able to learn from your mistakes? This sixth chakra is known as the third eye, and for many correlates with what is known as our sixth sense. It involves a higher form of self awareness, that excludes over intellectualizing. The ultimate result is being more interconnected with the larger world.

Seventh Chakra Affirmation: Presence   Keyword: Oneness/transcendence

7. In order to further your healing from wounds received in the workplace (or life, for that matter), learn to rely on the spiritual beliefs that speak to you personally. Do you trust life and are you able to see your life in the context of a larger pattern? Are you living your life on purpose and fulfilling your destiny? How do you know that? If you are not, visit the chakra center that needs your attention. At the crown chakra, your full potential is tapped. Tensions dissolve, unity and transcendence are experienced.

Remember there is a progressive nature and necessity as we follow the energy of the chakras (much like Maslow's hierarchy of needs). You can't jump straight to the top, but have to move up the ladder of consciousness and development. The chakras hold challenging patterns of energy along the path toward self-realization.

By aligning these two models—one of meeting basic needs and the other of personal healing—we can arrive at a fully functioning, healthy place in earning our livelihood. The outcome of self-actualization can be met through discovering one's life work, and the experience of oneness, or transcendence can be practiced through our daily work routine. Whether you are in the process to discover your life work or to develop mastery in your current area, these models serve as a guide map for achieving and healing. Likewise, when you are feeling stuck, confused, or lack motivation, it can be a good idea to review these models to determine the challenges you are facing. This process of review and reflection is essential if we hope to continue our active, creative involvement in the world of work.

GETTING STARTED

A final review of the nine stages of career development with the three stages of transition will help you ascertain your preparedness for the personal exploration presented in Part Three. If you have recently experienced a loss, or you are finally realizing you have to change your work, you will be working through the issues associated with the first two of the nine stages of career development. Your previous reliance on an absolute authority has been challenged and the realization that wrong choices are possible may have begun. By opening yourself to trusting in a process, such as the one offered in this book, you will discover greater clarity and experience profound personal growth.

The Neutral Zone, that murky confusing area where everything is in change and nothing is constant, can be tempered and become richly rewarding if one is fully engaged in this process of career and life work mastery. This process becomes the authority as you increase your self-awareness and become aware of your ability to make good decisions and implement them. You in fact become the authority in your life by going through stages three, four, five, and six as you realize there may be multiple "good" options and that you are in charge of your choices.

And finally, having gathered all the information about yourself and having targeted and negotiated your place in the world of work that this process requires, you will be ready for your new beginning. Career becomes a form of self-identity and self-expression. One is able to assume personal responsibility for the good and bad that inevitably occur. One is truly focused on the task, more than the rewards, and experiences the joy of doing and accomplishing while being part of something greater than ourselves. This level of functioning is, of course, experienced as we learn the magic of believing, going with the flow, and experiencing the harmony of the universe.

This journey toward hope, light, and vision is the journey of self-actualization and personal healing. Finding "your true gladness" and matching it with "the world's deep hunger" can be realized through our process of career and life work mastery. We welcome you now to begin the journey of becoming all you can be.

But first, in order to develop one of the major survival skills of the twenty-first century, turn to Part II, "The Beginner's Guide to the Internet." You will learn the fundamentals of using the Internet and computer technology to visit the many sites specific to the career development process. One always learns more easily when the activity is focused around high motivation. If your desire is to find your life's work, use our web site to complete the exercises included in Part Three, or purchase a three-ring notebook to write your responses in your own hand; high-tech, or high-touch, the choice is yours.

II

PART TWO

The Beginner's Guide
to the Internet

Welcome to cyberspace and the Internet as an invaluable tool in helping you at every stage of the career development process. When I first introduced the Internet to my clients, I was primarily teaching them how to find job postings through a few job posting sites. Then, almost overnight, major newspapers had their classified ads online, and universities, hospitals, and companies developed Internet home pages with internal job postings listed. With the aid of the Internet, finding the hidden job market became easy. Very shortly, the Internet became an endless resource for every topic covered in my career counseling practice. Career specialists were eager to share their ideas and techniques on the Net for anyone who was interested, for free. And now it is our turn to contribute to the growing and sharing network of career information. This guide is appropriate for readers with their own computers or readers who are using a computer with Internet access in a library or One Stop Career Center.

Margaret Riley (now Dikel), while a librarian at the George C. Gordon Library at the Worcester Polytechnic Institute, volunteered to begin working with the Internet in 1993. She discovered a recruiting site, *career.com*, which she posted for students and soon had 300 email messages requesting more. That was the beginning of a handout and web site called *Employment Opportunities and Job Resources on the Internet*, better known as "The Riley Guide," in which she organized sites on the Web relating to job search. In a very short time, the word spread that her web site was the preeminent site for career resources and job search. She maintains that reputation today and is the author of a book published by the Public Library Association, titled, appropriately enough, *The Guide to Internet Job Searching*. Her site, *http://www.rileyguide. com*, is the one we recommend as your ultimate backup. When in doubt, go to the "The Riley Guide."

Life Work Transitions.com also has its own web site, *http://www. lifeworktransitions.com*, and there you will find the addresses (which are also links) for every web site mentioned in this book. For your convenience, the sites are presented by chapter and are arranged in the order they appear in the text. Please turn on your computer, connect to the Internet, go to *http://www.lifeworktransitions.com* and experience a seamless interface between this text and the web sites recommended.

The Internet is often characterized as a "moving target." The Net, like the world of work, is constantly changing. Home page editors want to keep their pages interesting and current and inevitably reorganize things, which sometimes changes the Internet address. However, when you use our web site, you will not have to worry about address changes. The sites listed in our web site are updated regularly, and excellent new sites are added from time to time. In addition to links to sites recommended in the book, *http://www.lifeworktransitions.com* also has career related articles, interactive exercises from the book that you can print out in 8 1/2" x 11" format, and information on how you may contact the authors.

However, in addition to utilizing our site, we want to make sure that you are familiar with the basics necessary for surfing the Web independently. You will not need to panic if a link takes you to a dead end because you will learn how to find the destination on your own with the search tools taught in this chapter.

We understand that some of you may be approaching the Internet for the first time and others may have tried the Internet but felt overwhelmed. (For those of you who are old hands with the Net, proceed to the next chapter.) In this chapter you will learn efficient methods of Internet search and retrieval which will, hopefully, free you from any hesitation you might have. At the same time you will be accumulating valuable skills for the workplace. You will be able to add "Internet literacy" to your resume.

This guide provides just enough background so the Internet will make sense to you. It will not make you an expert; you do not need to be an expert. The goal is to make the Internet a simple tool so that you will not hesitate to use it for your own benefit. After all, most of you are not experts in the mechanics of a car, but almost all of you know how to drive a car and make use of its benefits. The same analogy applies to the Internet. Although the focus of this book is career development, the tools you learn will apply to any subject of interest.

FREQUENTLY ASKED QUESTIONS (FAQS) ABOUT THE INTERNET

What Is the Internet?

The Internet is a technological marvel that connects people all over the world through computers and the information they store. The architecture of the Internet, in the simplest of terms, is as follows. It is an information highway with several lanes. The World Wide Web (WWW) is the multimedia lane; if you are on the WWW lane, you will see pictures, drawings, fancy fonts, sometimes sound and video, and wonderful borders and frames accompanying the text. If you are on the other lanes of the highway, you will see typewriterlike text only.

The on-ramp to the highway, or the connection from your computer to the highway, is called an Internet Service Provider (ISP) and can be regular phone wire, T1 and T3 connections, ISDN lines, or cable (as in cable TV or broad band). Once you are on the highway you need a bus to take you to locations and back again, and that bus is called a browser; the most famous browsers are Netscape and Internet Explorer. The map or directory is called a search engine and gives the browser the location or address of information you want. There are many and some of the most well-known are Yahoo, Infoseek, Lycos, Excite, and AltaVista.

In summary:

- An Internet Service Provider (ISP) enables you to connect your computer to the information highway.
- A Browser goes on the highway, gets the information you need, and delivers it to your computer.
- A Search Engine is the directory or map to the information sites.

You are probably wondering, "Well, what is America Online (AOL)?" AOL and its competitors such as Compuserve and Prodigy, combine or bundle the functions of the on-ramp/ISP, the bus/browser, and the map/search engine. In addition, they bundle a lot of information on the Internet in a very easy picture format (graphical interface), summarizing locations they feel their customers will use most often. In reality, AOL has contracts with companies to host sites and receives payment for this service. However, AOL will allow you to skip its preformatted Internet sites and go straight to the Internet. You can even use the search engine of your choice. For example, you can use the Yahoo Directory even though you connected to the Internet via AOL.

Now that you have a conceptual framework to understand the basics of the Internet, it is time to go for a ride. For teaching purposes, we assume that you are familiar with the basics of word processing and that you have access to a computer with an Internet connection. We will start by explaining how you make a bookmark. Then we will compare four major search engines and follow their categories to career sites. This will be followed by an exercise using search windows for finding more specific or refined career-related information.

What Is a Bookmark?

Bookmarks are key to using your time online efficiently. They allow you to keep a list of the sites you have visited and return to them at a later date without going through the steps of searching.

Regardless of the browser you are using, there will be some mechanism for saving Internet addresses in a personal list. If you are using one of the Netscape browsers, the top menu bar will either have the word *Bookmark* on it or an icon that looks like a ribbon. If you are using Internet Explorer, it will be the word *Favorites*. With AOL it is a little red heart for My Favorite Places. Put your cursor on the word or icon, drag down to Add a Bookmark or Add to Favorites, and it is done. When you want to return to that address, all you have to do is click on Bookmark/icon, drag down to the address you want, let go, and the site will appear on the screen.

You can also organize your bookmarks in topic folders such as Search Engines, Job Posting Sites, Goal Setting, or Professional Associations. Each folder can have an unlimited number of bookmarks in it, and the folder can be either opened with all the bookmarks in it showing, or closed with all the bookmarks hidden in the folder. If you feel the name of the bookmark does not give a clue about its contents, you can rename

Figure Pt. 2.1   Illustration of Bookmark Folders.

a bookmark. For each browser the procedure for making folders and editing names is a little different. The procedures for AOL and Internet Explorer are quite intuitive.

For Internet Explorer, open your bookmarks by clicking the file icon labeled Favorites. To rename a bookmark, single click on the bookmark you want to edit, and type in what you want to name it. To create a new folder go to the word Favorites in the top bar, drag down to New Folder, and it will appear highlighted in your list of bookmarks. Click on the words Untitled Folder and give your new folder a title. Drag and drop the appropriate bookmarks in it creating a topic folder for a number of bookmarks.

For AOL, open your bookmarks by clicking on the file icon with a heart on it. To rename a bookmark, highlight the listing and click <u>Modify</u> at the bottom of the list of bookmarks; type in the new name of the bookmark. To create a new folder, click on <u>Add Folder</u> at the bottom of the list of bookmarks, type in the name you want it to have and it will appear on your list of bookmarks. Drag and drop the appropriate bookmarks in it creating a topic folder for a number of bookmarks.

If you have a Mac and use Netscape, open your bookmarks by typing "apple" plus "b." To edit a bookmark, highlight it in your list of bookmarks, type "apple" plus "i" and then type in its new name. To create a folder, open your bookmarks, and go to the File Menu, drag down to new folder, type in its title and it will appear in your list. Drag and drop the appropriate bookmarks on it.

If you have a PC and use Netscape, type "control" and "b" to open the bookmarks window. To edit a bookmark, right-click on the bookmark, and pull down to "Bookmark Properties." Let go, and the editing window will appear. Make necessary changes, and close the window. To create a folder for bookmarks, again open the bookmarks window. From the File menu of this window, pull down to "New Folder" and let go. Give the folder a name and close the window. Drag and drop the appropriate bookmarks onto it.

For a tutorial using graphics to explain bookmarking, see *http://www. learnthenet.com/english/html/17bookmark.htm*

How Do You Use a Search Engine to Locate Sites on the Internet?

Search engines index and catalog web site addresses so that the browser in your computer knows where to find information that you want delivered to your computer. Every search engine is organized slightly differently, and each reflects the personalities of its creators. Each one, however, offers a list of general categories or channels for searching the Internet as well as a direct search option. The categories are very much like the subjects in an enormous card catalog. For example, if you went to geography as a topic in a card catalog, you would then look for the continent you were interested in, the country, the river, and so on. The logic of a category (sometimes called channels) search on the Net is similar. We will be using four popular search engines—Yahoo, Infoseek, AltaVista, and AOL Netfind—so that you can get a feel for the differences and begin to sense which one you like best.

http://www.yahoo.com
http://www.infoseek.go.com
http://www. altavista.com
http://www.aol.com/netfind/

Start your computer (if you haven't already done so), connect to the web via your ISP, and start your web browser, Netscape, Internet Explorer, or AOL. (If you are using AOL, you need to click on the word or icon for Internet in the top bar and drag down to Go to Netfind.) In Netscape, Internet Explorer, and AOL, there will be a long narrow rectangle with an Internet address in it starting with http://www at the top of the page. That address is called a Uniform Resource Locator (URL). (Don't confuse it with the Search Window. See Figure Pt. 2.2.) The word in front of the URL window is "Location" for Netscape, "Address" for Internet Explorer, and "Find" for AOL. Regardless of the browser, move your mouse to the rectangle, click and drag over the whole address, let go of the mouse, and press delete. The box will be cleared; type in *http://www.yahoo.com* and press the return key.

You are now looking at the most popular search engine/map/directory on the Net. Make it a bookmark or a favorite place because you will be using this site often. Notice the categories for searching provided by Yahoo that start with Arts and Humanities and end with Society and Culture. **Words that are underlined mean they are "linked"** with more information. If you move your cursor over the underlined word, your **cursor will turn into a little hand**; that is always the sign that something is a hot link. If you click your cursor on the underlined word, it will light up, turn red, and take you to that location. The category most useful to you at this point is named Business and Economy.

Click on the words <u>Business and Economy</u> and another set of categories appears, starting with Business Libraries and ending with Usenet. Click on the word <u>Employment</u> and you will see another list starting with Booksellers and ending with Workplace Violence. By now, you should be beginning to see the logic of the hierarchical organization of

Figure Pt. 2.2   Illustrating URL and SEARCH Windows

Figure Pt. 2.3   Yahoo and Search Channels.

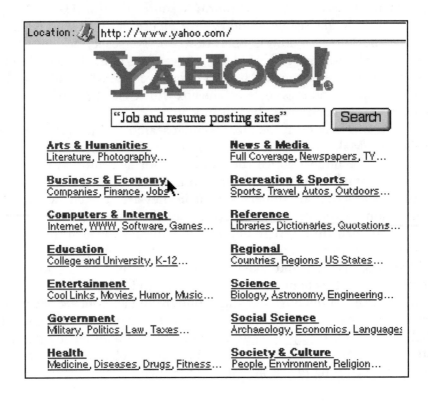

this search engine. Please resist the temptation to click on any of the other options until we have visited our three other "case-study" search engines. If you don't resist doing so, you could be on Yahoo all day, and it is important for you to visit other search engines and see how their logic of organization differs from Yahoo's.

Clear the long rectangle at the top of the page and type in the URL address, *http://www.infoseek.go.com*, and press return. As with Yahoo, please bookmark this site or add it as a favorite place. You will be using these bookmarks later, and they are shortcuts that will save you time. Notice that Infoseek also provides categories for searching but they are quite different from Yahoo's. They start with Automotive and end with Women. Click on the category <u>Careers</u> and you will see a page very different from the one that came up by clicking Employment on Yahoo. Infoseek's premier career site, Career Path, is prominently featured at the top of the page. Infoseek also provides two lists, Resumes and Jobs, with links that take you to web sites on those topics.

Proceed to the next "case-study" search engine called AltaVista. Clear the URL address rectangle, and type in *http://www.altavista.com*. Press return and you will see a very conservative looking site with yet another list of search categories. Bookmark this site or favorite place. The list of search categories for AltaVista starts with Automotive and ends with Travel & Vacations. In AltaVista you will also see a category called Specialty Searches which lists such things as Health, Entertainment, Careers and Maps. Click on Careers in the Specialty Searches and you will arrive at AltaVista's career site called Careers with Worklife with lists of links in several windows. It's Featured Link in the right-hand column is excellent.

Click the Back arrow at the top left-hand corner of your browser page and go back to the home page of AltaVista. Click on Business & Finance and then click on Jobs & Careers, and you will see a list starting with General Guides and ending with Workplace Issues.

Again, clear the URL window and type in *http://www.aol.com/ netfind*. Scroll down the page to Web Centers. The categories of choice begin with Autos and end with Travel. Click on Business and Careers. You will see a page with Departments starting with Jobs and ending with Business Computing; click Career Advice. Several lists appear for search opportunities as well as a connection to the Monster Board for job search.

You have now experienced "doing the Internet" and hopefully realize that the process is neither scary nor magic, well a little magic. At this point you might want to play for a while with any of these search engines. Go to your bookmarks or favorite places, click on one of our three search engines, and click on categories to your heart's content. You might also want to create a search engine folder for your search engine bookmarks.

In order to **go back to a site** you have been to in this session on your computer, click the back arrow on the upper left-hand corner of the browser page. Another avenue for returning to sites recently visited is to click the word GO on the very top bar on your computer screen for Netscape and Internet Explorer. You will see a list of the sites you have recently visited. Drag down to the site to which you want to return and you will do so. For AOL, go to the pop up arrow at the right-hand end of the URL address box. Click on it, and it will give you a history of locations you have visited. Drag down to the site you wish to see again, and it will happen.

Whatever you do, do not let yourself get discouraged. You are still in charge of your own life and can simply turn the computer off until the next time.

How Do You Use the Search Window?

The next basic for using the Internet is learning how to use the search window in a search engine. We will revisit our four "case-study" search engines and use their search windows rather than their preselected categories for finding career sites.

There are two very basic tips to help you refine your search words and increase efficiency.

1. If you are searching for something containing more than one word, put the words in quotation marks, for example, "The Riley Guide." The search engine will consider the three words as a string, or words in that exact sequence, and give you only sites with the words "The Riley Guide." Otherwise, the search engine would present every file with the word "Riley" in it and every file with the word "guide" in it. You would see hundreds, perhaps thousands, of sites available to you; that is why so many people feel overwhelmed by the Internet. Using search refinement techniques saves emotional and physical energy.

2. The other basic technique utilizes the use of the word "and" or (+) and "not" or (–) signs. For example, if you want employment opportunities in Los Angeles, you could type in "Employment Opportunities" + Los Angeles or "Employment Opportunities" and Los Angeles. Be sure you type in the quotation marks. The search engine would present you employment opportunity sites with the word Los Angeles in them. If you want to look for Marketing Associations, not Sales Associations, you would type "Marketing Associations" – sales or "Marketing Associations" not sales in the search window. The word not and the minus sign before "sales" means that the word "sales" would **not** appear in any of the sites presented.

These simple search techniques have worked very well for me in my extensive research on the Net. If you want to refine your search and become more sophisticated, click on such words as How to Search, Advanced Search, Help, or Search Tips located near the search window on every search engine's home page.

Figure Pt. 2.4 Using URL and SEARCH Windows.

There are also some terrific sites on the Web for learning **all** the tricks of searching on the Internet. "A Tutorial for Web Surfers" by Yahoo is excellent at *http://howto.yahoo.com/*. Click on <u>Searching Yahoo</u> and you will find a clear presentation of search tips. Infoseek has a Tutorial for Beginners using search tips at *http://www.go.com/Help?pg=SearchTips. htm*. Print it out for future reference or bookmark it. An excellent site for evaluating search engines and for explaining simple and advanced search techniques is a tutorial offered by the University of California Library at *http://www.lib.berkeley.edu/TeachingLib/Guides/Internet/FindInfo.html*.

(Are you remembering to bookmark your sites? You could place all the search tip sites listed in the above paragraph in a bookmark folder, called "Search Tips.")

In order to get a sense for the different kinds of search results produced by each of our case study search engines, you need to type the same search words in each search engine's search window and compare the results. Either use your bookmarks to get to each engine or type in their URL addresses in the URL window: Yahoo (*http://www.yahoo.com*), Infoseek (*http://infoseek.go.com*), AltaVista (*http://www.altavista.com*), and AOL (*http://www.aol/netfind.com*).

Please type these phrases in the Search Window of each search engine:

The first phrase is:	career and interview or career + interview
The second phrase is:	"Job resume posting sites"
The third phrase is:	"Physical Therapy" and "Professional Association"

Notice the differences. Which results made the most sense to you? Which search engine gave you the results you needed? Was one format more pleasing than another? Which gave the information you wanted in the first few entries, and which ones required that you scroll through several pages first? Which results were the clearest for you? By now, you are probably discovering which search engine will be your favorite.

Why are the searches presenting different sites when you have used the same search words? There are many search engines for the Internet; they each have different policies about which sites to list or search for and which search words to use, and the sponsors of home pages have to think carefully about how they are going to position their site. They also have to determine which search words they want to key into their sites. As you have seen by going to just four search engines, the number of resources seems endless. That is why people have their favorite search engines, depending on how they use the Internet. One of the purposes of this book is to help you get to the really great career sites without having to go through frustrating searches.

An excellent web site that reviews the search engines and which ones are best for various careers, interests, and research is at *http://searchen ginewatch.com*. Another smart site is "The Seven Habits of Highly Effective Surfers" at *http://www.cnet.com/Content/Features/Dlife/Habits/*.

Why Do the Endings of Internet Addresses Differ?

The most common endings of Internet sites are "com," "org," "edu," and "net." "Com" means commerce, so company web pages are going to end in "com." "Org" stands for organization; the Red Cross, United Way, and some professional organizations will have addresses that end in "org." "Gov" stands for government; government agencies will end in "gov." "Edu" stands for education, so any college or school web page address will end in "edu." This makes it easy to try to guess a web page address. For example, *http://www.avid.com* for Avid Technologies, *http://www.redcross.org* for the Red Cross and, *http://www.stanford.edu.* for Stanford University. Try them and see what you find.

What Does It Mean to Log In?

For many sites, you are asked to log in, sign in, or register before using the site; in return you will get a subscriber ID and a password. For example, the *New York Times* at *http://www.nytimes.com/* invites you to do this even though the service is free. You can search the current issue, but if you want to do more extensive searches, you need to register and then log in each time you use the site. The *New York Times* has a link to "privacy provisions" which you should read first.

Likewise, many job posting sites want you to log in before signing up for any personal job search service. Many people feel edgy about this because of privacy concerns. I have given up on privacy ever since I started using a credit card to order things by catalog. So I sign in, trying to use the same user name and password for everything (it is easy to forget them!). Sometimes the username is sbutzel and sometimes sandra butzel and sometimes sandrabutzel. It depends on what the database will allow, but I try to keep it simple. My password is always the same.

CAUTION

If you are signing in for a chat room, it is a different matter. Chat rooms take place in real time, and people usually do **not** use their own names. See "Learn the Net" at *http://www.learnthenet.com/english/html/18webchat.htm* for an excellent discussion of Web chat and what you need to know to protect yourself. Signing in or logging in is also necessary for usegroups, forums, and list services. These are discussed in more detail in Chapter 7.

Let us walk through a couple of sites recommended in the book that ask you to log in. Type in *http://www.careerpath.com* and press return. You will be invited to register for access to all enhanced features of this job posting site. Click Register Here and you will see a very simple form to fill out. It is well worth it.

Now let us walk through a site that is a little more complicated. Go to *http://www.monster.com*. This is currently one of the highest-rated job posting sites on the Net. Click on <u>Search Jobs</u> and you will see two search menus, one for geographical location and one for category. A keyword window is also available.

Scroll the first Search Menu by using the up and down arrows on the right-hand side of the menu until you come to Los Angeles, California. Highlight Los Angeles by clicking one time on the words. In the Category Menu, scroll down to Education and Training; highlight the category by clicking on the words one time. Now click the search button. You will see a list of jobs; click on one of them and read the job description. There will also be an email address listed to which you can send your resume directly and apply for the position.

However, if you want to sign up for all the special features that The Monster Board has to offer such as posting your resume, signing up for help from their personal job search agent called "My Monster," you must log in. Go back one page by pressing the arrow in the top left-hand corner of the page. Click on <u>My Monster</u>; you will see windows for a User Name and a Password, neither of which you have. Scroll down further on the page and you will see Create a New Account. Click the highlighted words and enter your email address. The next thing you will see is a message on your screen saying your user name and password have been sent to you by email. Open up your email account and see what it is. Go back to Monster Board and click again on <u>My Monster</u>. Put in your user name and your password, study the services offered and decide which ones are right for you.

How Do You Print Out and Save Information from Internet Pages?

You can print out any page on the Internet by simply using the same print commands that you use for word processing. To save time printing, I recommend that you turn off color printing and only print in grayscales or black and white. You can save text on Internet pages and print them out later by using standard word processing techniques. Open your word processor program while you have your Internet software working. Highlight parts of text on a web page by clicking and dragging over the desired text, copy it, and paste it into a word processing document. The format may be a little ragged; usually that can be cured by changing the size of the font. You can also cut and paste text from an Internet page into an email document.

What Does "File Not Found" Mean?

Sometimes, you will press the search button and see File Not Found "The requested URL http://www.etc./ etc. was not found on this server." This can mean several things:

1. You may have made one tiny mistake when typing in the URL address. Typing a comma (,) instead of a period (.), typing a period (.) instead of a slash (/), typing a hyphen (-) instead of a tilde (~), missing a letter or any punctuation mark or putting in an extra space will elicit the File Not Found response.
2. It may mean that the site no longer exists, but check very carefully for mistakes.
3. It may also mean that the address has been changed, but may still be on the server. Try the following; start at the end of the address and delete a section marked off by a (/) or (~) or (_) or (.) and press return. Keep doing this. Often you will get back to an address that ends in com, org, or .edu and when you press return, the site will appear. Then carefully search through the site and see if you can find what you were looking for.

What Does "Unable to Locate the Server" Mean?

It could mean that the server no longer exists. It could mean that the server is down at the present time, and sometimes it means that the traffic on the Internet is so heavy that there are glitches. Leave the site and come back to it later, especially if you know it is a valid address.

What Is Email?

The draw of email has recruited more people to the Internet than anything else. Many seniors buy a computer and learn how to use email to keep in touch with their grandchildren. Families with a member in a foreign country learn how to use email because they can talk to their loved one for the price of a local phone call rather than long distance. Email has become a major step in the job search. You will use email to apply for a job and to forward your resume, to hear about jobs from a web posting site, and to communicate with other professionals in forums and through mailing lists.

An email account is provided by your Internet service provider and can be received through your browser such as Netscape, Internet Explorer, and AOL or special email software such as Eudora. For example, my Internet service provider is Mediaone, but I go to Netscape to pick up my email. For example, an email address could be Jones@mediaone. net even though the Jones pick up their email using Netscape. If your Internet service provider is AOL, you will have an AOL address and pick up your mail using AOL as well.

In addition, there are a number of free email sources. There are several good ones, with Yahoo and Hotmail being among the best. Read about them yourself at *http://www.emailaddresses.com/*. Why would you want a free email account? You might not have a computer of your own and need to access your email from the computer at the library, One Stop Career Center, or a friend's house. You can access these free email accounts from **any** computer connected to the Internet. Or, perhaps your family email address may not be appropriate to put on a resume. Or you might want a job posting site to tell you about one kind of job at one email address and information about another job at another address. You may be starting a home-based business and want your business email to have a name on it that reflects your business.

For a tutorial on email for Netscape and Internet Explorer, go to *http:/ /home.voyager.co.nz/email.htm*. This site will show you how to configure email on either browser and all you need to know to send and receive email messages. Another wonderful site answering many questions about email is *http://www.learnthenet.com/english/section/email.html*.

You have now been introduced to searching the Internet by search channels and by refined searches offered by each search engine. To keep track of sites, you have learned how to bookmark and organize bookmarks into folders. You've learned that many steps in using the Internet are the same as basic word processing procedures such as highlighting and copying or deleting. You've also learned the huge part email will play in your job search.

The rest of this book is filled with Internet sites to augment the text. If you feel you need more instruction and practice, go to the Department of Interior's Career Site and take its tutorial at *http://www.doi.gov/octc/ intro.html*. Take your time while reading this book; visit each site, bookmark it, and learn how to navigate the Internet at the same time as you are discovering your Life Work Objective and turning it into a reality.

PART THREE

Finding Your True North: Creating a Personal Mandala

There is a revolution in values taking place among many workers of today who are being affected by changes in the world of work. Some are being dispossessed or disempowered while others are experiencing profound opportunity. Many are feeling betrayed by the workplace, but the truth of the matter is, their own values contributed to keeping that illusion alive. The economic and global forces are such now, that no matter what, all must create a new reality for themselves in relation to earning a livelihood.

In the twenty-first century, many more people will be making work-related, economic and survival choices by going within to discover their "deep gladness." Once that unique form of self-expression is defined, and the "hungry places" in the universe identified, the marketplace will begin to be transformed. An important belief that is influencing the creation of this new reality is the ancient truth: "To thine own Self be true, and it must follow as the night the day, Thou cans't not then be false to any other man." But in order for that to occur in the world at large, we need to realize the fulfillment of another ancient truth, a truth that exists in every culture throughout the world: "Do unto others as you would have others do unto you." The reestablishment of that value, known as the Golden Rule, as a cornerstone of the twenty-first century world of work, may ensure our survival. By fully realizing your potential, you will be putting your spirit to work in ways that are rewarding, fulfilling, and transforming of yourself and the workplace.

The journey of discovery of self and place in the world is ever-changing, ever-renewing, and ever-revitalizing. Whether you choose to stay with the same field to achieve career mastery, change fields, or focus on another sector of life, such as community service, personal growth, or family, the steps in the journey are the same. The journey includes: self-awareness; discernment of emerging and changing wants and needs; prioritizing and decision-making; exploration of opportunities; connection with the new; deepening of meaning; recycling to self-awareness again.

THE CAREER AND LIFE WORK PROCESS FOR MASTERING CHANGE

The two diamond shapes in Figure Pt. 3.1 represent the processes of inner and outer exploration which are best approached consecutively. The inner exploration you will undergo gives definition to that which is unique in you; the outer exploration is your search for ideal opportunities in the marketplace. The diamond shape represents the expanding knowledge that comes from gathering the information and then prioritizing (narrowing) the most essential. Richard Bolles stresses the importance of prioritizing when he says, "No exercise is complete until it has been prioritized." Over the years we have met with many people suffering from information overload; what they needed was help separating the essential from the nonessential in order to create focused objectives and move efficiently into the outer diamond, to explore the world of work.

SELF-ASSESSMENT

The first diamond represents the self-assessment process (Part Three, Chapters 1 through 5) through which you identify the important criteria for creating your personal mandala. This assessment model guides you in answering four key questions to arrive at the core criteria which will define your functioning in a self-actualized state through your work.

Figure Pt. 3.1   Mastering Life Work Transitions

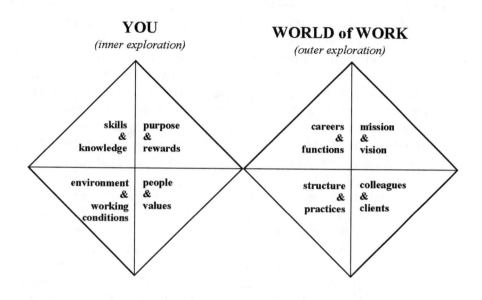

Figure Pt. 3.2   Finding Your True North

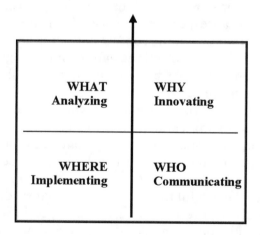

The upper left quadrant emphasizes the assessment of **what** you like to do and do well. The assessment helps you find your language and voice as a means of self-expression. It represents your competencies, areas of interest and expertise, functional skills, and special knowledges which will provide focus into work worth doing.

The lower left quadrant has you gather and record information about **where** you have done and would like to do your best work. This focuses your awareness on the structure, environment, and setting where you have done your best work. Here you can also define lifestyle issues, especially as they relate to earning and thriving in the new millennium. The lower right quadrant helps you focus on **who** you enjoy working and creating with, especially the kinds of people and the characteristics that define your best "people setting." When people experience congruency between their personal values and those of colleagues, or their organization's mission, they will be most satisfied. The upper right quadrant focuses your attention on **why** you do what you do, the rewards, the highest values and aspirations you hope to fulfill. It is in this quadrant that one assesses what is required to feel fulfilled, to experience meaning and purpose, to know that what you are doing indeed makes a difference.

As you learn to function from your core you will be actualizing each of the four areas as you realize that the whole is greater than the sum of the parts. Experiencing self-actualization can be a result of doing what you love, in the perfect environment with the most fascinating people, making a contribution, and feeling fulfilled in your deepest values and rewards. Maslow in his work *Religious Values and Peak Experiences* speaks of those people who are "non-peakers" as being exclusively means oriented, because peak experiences "earn no money, bake no bread, and chop no wood." In the context of finding and creating meaningful work, where the means and the end must be congruent, peak experiences are not only possible, but become more plausible as a result of going through this process.

As you learn to master this process, you will find you can use it again and again to assess any work situation. If you discover one aspect of your work that is out of focus you can begin to strategize what you can do to bring yourself back to center. Often it is helpful to realize what is out of sync; for example, if you are working on a project with people you really dislike, wouldn't it be helpful to know that and address the issues rather than remain upset? As a result, you are able to get on with the project and bring it to completion harmoniously. Later you can review that experience and clarify the lessons to determine new criteria to incorporate into your ever-evolving and more fully refined personal mandala.

This four-part method of questioning and reviewing is at the heart of this process of clarifying and staying centered in your personal mandala, which will result in the creation of several lifework objectives. The process will deepen your spiritual understanding through increased conscious awareness of self in relation to others (your community) and to your work (your purpose). The process can be used to delineate a career path as well as redefine a lifestyle, such as planning for retirement. It can also be used to spiritualize your daily journey as you follow this path of self-actualization. See the Spiritual Autobiography exercise if you wish to undertake this process as a spiritual journey. And finally, as indicated in the Preface, going through this process of career and life work exploration can heal the wounded places in our physical, mental/ emotional, and spiritual lives. David Noer has written a helpful book for people dealing with repeated loss from downsizing in his book *Healing the Wounds* (see *http://www.ccl.org*)

To achieve career mastery the four key questions of **What**, **Where**, **Who**, and **Why** will need to be answered at four different levels:

1. to clarify and define your individual profile;
2. to create objectives and verify your interests,
3. to explore and narrow a specific path or vocation, and
4. to determine that you are uniquely qualified to fulfill this opportunity.

Your goal throughout the process is to maximize the match and the fit between all four quadrants on the inner and outer levels of exploration. Once the internal assessment is solidly completed, you can begin the external exploration which will allow you to identify and select your compromisable criteria. In this way, you increase your individual sense of personal power and choice in the workplace.

EXPLORING THE WORLD OF WORK

The exploration into the world of work begins by seeking the best match between the many facets of your personal mandala and a multitude of employment opportunities. In Part Four you will learn to target and focus a specific employment objective and learn how to research it. While employing the job search strategies and researching the recommended Internet sites you will be gathering new thoughts and insights to validate the information you have gathered about yourself and what you need to feel challenged and stay committed. Your self-awareness will deepen as you gain confidence from making the choices and commitments that each stage of exploration requires. Your intention becomes clearer as you explore opportunities and make connections with others that provide additional clarification. Your commitment to yourself will deepen as you adhere to the process of constantly referring to this inner/outer exploration to define where you are on your journey. If you are spiritually attuned you will come to realize that some deeper truths become evident, thereby making the journey even more mystical and rewarding.

Visiting the upper left quadrant in the second diamond, you will now be concerned with identifying the different career areas and functional areas that best reflect your prioritized skills and knowledge sets. By asking the questions, "**What** are the different career areas and **what** are the functional areas that match my interests?" you begin the external career exploration process. After identifying the appropriate fields or industries, you continue your exploration by exploring the important question: "**What** needs doing in that world?" Remember that this is the key question to finding work that needs doing. And if you are the one to define it, who better to answer the question, demonstrate the necessary skills and knowledge, interests and values that will position you as the primary resource? Using the powerful tool of the Internet you can research all the issues relevant to your focus and gather precise information about the current state of the art in relation to that specific concern.

Information from your individual self-assessment and the results from other career interest inventories will provide you with the criteria you need to identify the environment, structure, and workplace setting, as well as the people and value factors that will best match your profile. In Chapter 5 you will be verifying "**Where** will my work style fit and **Who** are the people I will be working with and serving?" The more information you have about your wants and needs the easier it will be to gather information about various settings. It will also enable you to accept a compromise that is acceptable to and defined by you.

The final area of match that needs to be met is in the area of individual purpose and organizational purpose and mission. "**Why** do organizations exist?" is geared toward helping you assess the mission and value system of the organization to which you are attracted. The following definitions are taken from "Purpose, Mission and Vision," *The New Paradigm in Business*.

Purpose is seen as "the fundamental set of reasons for the organization's existence; purpose is something that is always worked towards, but never fully realized." *Mission* is defined as "a clear, definable and motivational point of focus—an achievable goal, a finish line to work towards." There can be a lot of confusion around mission and purpose. "Because a specific mission can be so compelling, many organizations make the mistake of thinking that their mission **is** their fundamental purpose. The problem becomes: what do you do once you've fulfilled the mission? Without a broader, more creative purpose from which to derive the next mission, there will be a crisis of direction once the mission is accomplished." This issue likewise becomes true for the individual in relation to personal goal setting and overall purpose. The action steps resulting from goal setting become the measurable activities that will enable you to fulfill your purpose.

And finally, *vision* is defined as the "ability to see the potential or necessity of opportunities right in front of you . . . it is intuitive . . . it is knowing 'in your bones' what can or must be done. In other words, vision isn't forecasting the future, it is creating the future by taking action in the present" (*The New Paradigm in Business*, p. 87). As every responsible worker knows, being proactive is key to successfully managing life work transitions and the development of this kind of vision is a key benefit of completing the assessment process that follows.

When you are able to identify where you are on the journey, by referring to the process and models outlined here, you will find yourself self-actualizing through your work. Are the rewards you are receiving from the universe the ones you want or need? If not, why not? What compromises have you chosen to make to actualize some other aspect of your life? Perhaps an illness requires you to refocus your energy, or achieving a goal ahead of the planned time gives you an opportunity to pick up another passion that will help you feel fulfilled. The process of personal journaling as you go through this exploration process will help you become aware of the serendipitous events in your life now, that may provide important clues to your future. Journaling can be done using word processing or done by hand in a beautifully bound blank book. Examples in your daily life you may want to record include writing about the satisfaction felt in knowing beyond a shadow of a doubt you have done your best work. Or, you may choose to write about a changing relationship with a coworker in order to heighten your awareness of your deep connection with another. This level of conscious processing using a personal journal will deepen your sense of connectedness, wonder, and awe as you go through this process.

DISCOVERING YOUR PERSONAL MANDALA

Beginning with Chapter 1 you will be asked to "Tell Your Story." There are several exercises here to begin your self-assessment. The key to each of them is to allow yourself to gain insight into how you would answer the four key questions in a comprehensive and/or historical review of your life. For example, you can analyze each work experience using the simple formula: **What** was I doing? Then evaluate it, Did I like it or not? **Where** was I doing it? What did I like about that or not? **Who** was I doing it with and for? And how did I feel about that? And last, but not least, **Why** was I doing it? What were the expected rewards? What was unexpected? Did I feel fulfilled?

We have also included in Chapter 1 summaries of several major career assessment and interest inventories. We carefully preselected the Internet sites and assessment tools that will provide you with the most accurate, vital, and helpful information for identifying and verifying actual career objectives and functional areas. We have included the Myers Briggs Type Indicator (MBTI), because of its universal appeal to people going through change. The relationship of career areas to type in MBTI language provides an excellent starting point for career exploration. John Holland's Career Game is also recommended to augment our process. We have also referenced several Internet sites that provide an overview to the career development process in general for those who are interested. There are a multitude of sites and plenty of information available if you want additional clarification on any part of our process. But try to remember, "Find it; evaluate it; and act on it." And never forget to prioritize or you'll stay in the information-gathering stage forever.

What Do I Love and Do Best?

In Chapter 2, "Defining Core Competencies," you will begin the systematic analysis of **what** you most enjoy doing. This is the rich upper left quadrant, where your knowledge and the value you add to the workplace is defined. Through the process of identifying skills, knowledges, and adaptive skills directly from your life story, you will become profoundly aware of your unique talents and resources. Using our skills inventory will help you organize your functional skills into multiple skill sets that can be used in a variety of settings. The process of prioritizing and sorting skills increases dramatically your marketability and your self-awareness about the transferability of your multiple skill sets.

A thorough assessment of your skills and knowledges would not be complete without the opportunity to develop a plan for continuous learning. To remain a vital contributor in your chosen area, it is necessary to be self-directed and motivated. The career management competencies included in this chapter provide an inventory of what you already possess and from that you can develop a plan to acquire additional competencies.

Defining and Clarifying Personal Criteria

Chapter 3, "Redefining Your Self: Passions, Preferences, and Purpose," offers many different exercises for getting at the core values you need to have met to self-actualize through your work. The criteria generated from these exercises, as well as the interest inventories on the Internet, offer rich information for further defining yourself. Some of the information will help you to define the ideal kind of working conditions, the environment, even the structure of work as defined by the new employment contract. People who want more security than others may need to honor that value and seek out one single employer who can perhaps meet that need, in spite of the trend toward multiple employment opportunities. Other criteria will be used to identify the characteristics and traits of the kinds of people with whom you wish to associate.

Individuals need first and foremost to experience congruency between their personal value systems and that of the organization or individuals with whom they affiliate. When there is an internal value conflict it must be resolved in order to continue. Knowing your own values will help you to distinguish between internal and external value conflicts. So often, difficulties at work occur because of difficulties getting along with others. Since the new workplace calls for enhanced interpersonal, facilitation, and community technology building skills, we can only hope that when value conflicts arise they will be better managed. Still, when you are cocreating and collaborating with a partner who makes your heart sing, what could be better? Defining your ideal people criteria will help you recognize them when you see them.

In addition to identifying criteria for filling in the **where** and **who** areas of this model, this chapter also helps you get clear on **why** you do what you do. It helps you identify core values that when fulfilled increase your sense of self-esteem. It helps you identify your personal purpose that can give meaning and direction to your entire life or can become the major focus of your life work. For those people who want to make a difference, the fulfillment of this criterion will be most important.

Creating Balance and Wholeness through Goal Setting

The next to final piece of self-assessment (Chapter 4) consists of goal setting and further visualizations around what you need to feel fulfilled and rewarded. This chapter allows you to begin to look at other areas of your life and see what you need to do to increase value in areas such as personal relationships, leisure activities, spiritual practice, health and wellness, and learning. By creating a sense of the whole that is balanced it is easier to focus on those areas that are most out of alignment. There is a wonderful exercise from The Coaches Training Institute that depicts graphically the areas of your life that need attention. You will be able to regulate your energies and achieve what is most important overall, by defining what is "enough" in terms of activity and finances. To develop a career action plan without looking at the rest of your life would be a serious error in our goal for finding fulfillment through work. Not to mention the fact that the important task of managing your career requires a great deal of focus and determination, so you must be vigilant overall in how you spend your time.

Throughout this self-assessment process you will be acquiring increased mastery on the Internet if you visit the supplementary sites we have highlighted. Or you may go directly to our web page at *http://www. lifeworktransitions.com.* to access each exercise in a convenient form for you to use.

Pulling Together Your Profile: A Mandala for Success

As mentioned earlier, the admonishment that "no exercise is complete until it has been prioritized" will now receive your full attention. Each exercise that you completed requires some kind of assessment and delineation of the criteria that are most important to you. In Chapter 5 you will once again review all the information and create a visual profile to summarize it and create a personal mandala. Shifting from the more analytical and linear process of gathering and recording information, we invite you now to move into your creative self and develop a visual representation of all you have discovered. This time you will be prioritizing the information with the intention of realizing your next steps leading toward the fulfillment of your life work goals. You will also be guided

Figure Pt. 3.3   You in the World of Work

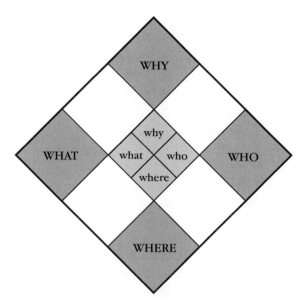

through a detailed process for translating your unique profile into several life work objectives to conduct your search into the world of work.

The process of career and life work mastery offers continual renewal and commitment to that which is highest and most true within ourselves and our genuine desire to make a difference. The journey to discover the truth within is, for the most part, an inner search.

> The longest journey
> is the journey inwards
> of him who has chosen his destiny
> who has started upon his quest
> for the source of his being.
> *Dag Hammerskold*

The journey to finding your right livelihood requires action and reflection, extension of effort, surrender to what is, and mastering the high-tech/high-touch tools included here.

Let the journey begin.

1

Telling Your Story

"To know where you are going, you must know where you
have been."   *David Campbell*

Telling your story is at the heart of this process. It is both time consuming and fulfilling. You will get out of it exactly what you put into it. The
initial selection of the most appropriate exercise for you sets the stage
for the unfolding to follow. By authoring your own story, you begin to acquire the perspective that you have indeed authored your life. Henri
Nouwen, in his book *Reaching Out,* asks the following questions to un-
derscore the value of this approach: "What if the events of our history
are molding us as a sculptor molds his clay, and if it is only in a careful
obedience to these molding hands that we can discover our real vocation
and become mature people? What if our history does not prove to be a
blind impersonal sequence of events over which we have no control, but
rather reveals to us a guiding hand pointing to a personal encounter in
which all our hopes and aspirations will reach their fulfillment?"

You will discover in writing your story, that even in those circumstances under which you felt you had little or no control, you always had
choices of how to respond. By reviewing your past with compassion and
the intention of increasing understanding and personal insight you will
be able to rewrite the script. And finally, you will begin to be in charge of
your own choices as you learn to accept personal responsibility for what
has been.

The key to answering the question "Who am I, at my core?" means
finding the essence of spirit within your life's experiences. The answers
are found through reviewing and exploring work experiences, accom-

plishments, and personal history. By naming our life experience we can give meaning and value to our life choices. Thus, our sense of personal power is enhanced and we can let go of any sense of "victim" mentality, self-pity, or even personal aggrandizement. What remains is a clear strong sense of personal accomplishments, skills, and knowledges learned, and wonderfully rich information about the pleasures and rewards from work that you find meaningful. More specifically, we can often heal the wounds inflicted by dysfunctional workplaces by reviewing the past and telling our stories.

Through any of the self-assessment exercises included in Chapter 1, you will begin the process of uncovering clues to your personal mandala. These exercises provide you with the opportunity to get in touch with positive emotions experienced at better times in your life which will result in higher energy levels and greater self-esteem. By immersing yourself in the process, by selecting an exercise and beginning to tell your story, you will immediately experience an improved sense of well-being. And finally, telling your story using your own language raises your consciousness to better describe yourself. The process of expanding your vocabulary is also crucial to your resume preparation and as preparation for interviewing.

Telling your story often reveals what you might perceive as an insignificant, or seemingly irrelevant, experience that "you just loved" and that may provide clues to discovering what will make you happy in the future. Using our four-part model for analysis ask yourself:

Why did you love the experience?

What were you doing, **who** were you with, what kind of support and energy were exchanged?

What kind of **rewards** were you receiving?

And finally, what else was going on in your life at the time, or after hours?

The exercises that follow will help you get in touch with skills, values, preferences, interests, and directions that will be sorted and prioritized throughout this process.

When a client lights up with a smile while telling her story, we know we are on to something. Other clues that suggest you have hit "gold" may include feeling a burst of energy, or the articulation of such phrases as "I loved that job," "it was my favorite," or "the best thing that ever happened to me." Even people who are in the midst of a very dark phase when undertaking this self-assessment can usually experience some kind of positive awareness. If you have difficulty getting started, think about asking a close friend or loved one to help you by brainstorming activities or experiences where they knew you were really at your personal best. The emphasis throughout this process is to focus on the positive at the exclusion of the negative, so it will be important for you to generate enough positive experiences to continue the self- assessment phase. With over seven different recommended exercises in this chapter you are sure to find one that works for you.

SELECTING THE EXERCISE

The four written exercises are designed to elicit your own form of creative self-expression and reflect your personal circumstances. These exercises have been staples in our counseling for years and their worth has passed the test of time with positive results. You are invited to select one or more that best suits your style. Whichever exercise you select, try to follow the guidelines presented, but use your own imagination. If you think of a way to tell your story that works better for you, by all means go right ahead. This is your story, and it provides valuable clues to your future. Tell it the way it really was; brag a little, brag a lot. Treat yourself to the love and appreciation that may have been lacking from peer and supervisor reviews. No politics here. You are free to tell your story as you experienced it.

TYPES OF EXERCISES

Listed here are the four types of written exercises that can be prepared, with brief definitions, and some pros and cons of why you might prefer one approach over the other. For specific directions for each of the exercises, turn to the end of the chapter or go to our web page *http://www. lifeworktransitions.com.* It is recommended that you complete one of these exercises before going on to the next section.

Life Work Autobiography: Telling Your Story

Writing your life work autobiography provides valuable insight into your life as a whole and your work in particular. As a result, you will better understand the transitions from one job to the next, and the choices you made at different stages in your career. The specifics of each work segment will be analyzed further in subsequent chapters. If you have had a long and enjoyable career, this exercise is best for you.

Accomplishments Inventory

Creating an inventory of accomplishments that were enjoyable and meaningful inside and outside of work can also provide important information. By naming accomplishments from your past and their relative value, you will be able to determine which values still hold meaning for you. This approach will also help you understand experientially why some values are more important to you than others. This exercise is helpful if you have not enjoyed your career thus far, are just starting out, or have a lifetime of volunteer experience you want to carry into the workplace.

An *accomplishment* is anything you did well, enjoyed, and took some action to achieve. Your accomplishments are things you have done at home, in a part-time or full-time job, or in your hobbies or volunteer activities. An accomplishment does *not* mean something you do better than anyone else; it only means something you learned to do which once you could not do, for example, "I achieved the goal of the fundraising drive." We often encourage clients to conduct this inventory from their earliest memories up until their first job, so they can realize the importance and influence of their formative experiences. Or, if you've liked some of your work, but feel it doesn't express all of you, use a combination of these first two exercises.

Drawing Your LifeLine

If you are a visual-spatial person, who doesn't like to write, then the lifeline exercise of drawing your life journey and using visual symbols/metaphors will work for you. It does not mean you have to consider yourself artistic or creative. Often working in a medium with which you are not familiar will allow your creativity to come forth. Another advantage of this exercise is that it gives you the opportunity to see your life as a series of events unfolding in the journey of your life. It offers the added advantage of being able to add details at a later date if you forget them and then ask yourself, "Why did I leave that out the first time? It was so important." For people who don't know where to begin but feel their life as a whole is a story worth telling, this is a good place to begin. It is also considered the first step in preparing to write the spiritual autobiography.

Spiritual Autobiography: Finding Your Voice

If you want to look at your life from a spiritual perspective, then the spiritual autobiography will be the best place for you to begin this process. The purpose of this exercise is to reveal the underlying pattern of your life experiences and help you "uncover the potential within the acorn" as James Hillman said in *The Soul's Code*. This will help you discover your unique perspective and expression. In this exercise you will be looking for meaningful experiences, the turning points, the triumphs and crashes, the "dark night of the soul" experiences where all of your talents and gifts came into being.

For many people undergoing mid-life changes, this exercise will take you on a wonderful journey of discovery and self-awareness. This journey is for the most part an inner search and it calls you to live inside the difficult questions, such as "Why am I here?" and "What is my reason for being?" If you are plagued by these questions, consider the advice of the great poet and mystic Rilke. "Be patient toward all that is unsolved in your heart and try to love the questions themselves." Living inside the questions means living with tension. Many of us may have a vision and a desire to know what we can contribute or how we might make a difference. But in addition to living with the questions, you must also accept the responsibility that for some time, your purpose may be to discover your purpose. How you will fulfill that may be illusive and mysterious. This exercise provides the framework for exploration.

Some of the insights people have as a result of these exercises can yield a great deal of perspective on their current situations. These realizations become evident by examining objectively the previous events of our lives. Such awareness might include the following observations: "I see that every positive experience I had was followed by a real down" or "negative experiences always involved too much contact with people." These natural tendencies or patterns, and we all have them, can be indicators to us—if only we will pay attention to them—of what motivates us and brings out our best. These insights are the building blocks of your new definition.

SELF-ASSESSMENT INSTRUMENTS ON THE INTERNET

There are several assessment instruments on the Internet that will help you understand yourself as the author of your story and provide indicators of your interests. Many career consultants rely heavily on their results. With our emphasis on having you tell your personal story first, the results of these self-assessment instruments will hopefully reinforce your self-definition as they provide vital clues that will connect you to the world of work. They will be useful in verifying your interests and targeting different occupational areas. There is a variation of the Myers-Briggs Type Indicator presented next, and a Brain Dominance Survey, which can be found on our site, *http://www.lifeworktransitions.com*. In Chapter 3 you will find the Career Interest Game to identify interests, and the Birkman Quiz in Chapter 6 to identify vocations.

MYERS-BRIGGS TYPE INDICATOR

One instrument that we feel is of great value is the Myers-Briggs Type Indicator (MBTI). The instrument provides a great deal of insight into your preferred style of working and being. A modified, yet highly reliable version of the instrument itself has been created by David Keirsey, and we encourage you to go to web site *http://keirsey.com/frame.html* for the Keirsey Temperament Sorter home page.

1. Click on Keirsey Temperament Sorter and then take the test. At the end of it, click the button that says score.
2. The next page you see will be your results. The text just below the title says "your temperament is. . . . Your Variant Temperament is . . ." Write them down or print out the page.
3. Then click on the blue and underlined name of your temperament. You will see photos and your temperament described below the photos. Who are you? One of the Guardians, Artisans, Idealists, or Rationals? Print out the page.
4. Then on the left hand frame, click on the four-letter title that depicts your temperament, such as ENTJ, INFP, ESFP, and you will receive a longer explanation of your temperament called "Portrait of a . . . ." Print it out.
5. The last step is to go to a site where you will see occupational clusters for your Keirsey Temperament Sorter. Type http://www.doi.gov/octc/typescar.html in the URL window. This is a difficult page to print out, so you may want to write down the occupational clusters for your four-letter temperament (INFP, ESTJ, ENTP, etc.)

When you have completed these steps you will want to read carefully the description of your type to verify how valid it is for you. Does it speak to you? Does it provide an understanding of yourself that is new or reassuring? What parts do not speak to you? Remember, the results of these instruments vary and if you have questions about them we strongly encourage you to visit a trained professional to help you incorporate this information. If this profile speaks to you, you may want to read Paul and Barbara Barron Tieger's book *Do What You Are*.

This instrument is extremely valid and widely used by many organizations to focus on strengths of contributing team members. The model created by Kathryn Myers and Isabel Briggs Myers draws heavily on the research of Carl Jung, the great in-depth psychologist. The model represents your preferences on four scales. Preferences indicate an ease in style and approach. These characteristics are strong indicators of your preferred working style. Your preferences are indicated on a continuum of opposites. Extroverts (E) tend to focus on the outer world of people and things and are energized by that outer world. They tend to "think out loud" and are more action oriented than the Introverts (I). Introverts prefer to focus on the inner world of thoughts and ideas. They prefer to understand the world before experiencing it, so they often "think first, then act."

The next two scales represent the functions of Sensing (S) and Intuiting (N), and Thinking (T) and Feeling (F) as defined by Jung. These four functions have the most to do with career satisfaction and match our four-part model for assessment. The Sensing (S) and Intuiting (N) functions describe how you prefer to take in information. The Sensing (S) person tends to use the five senses to take in information about the world and sees it in a detailed, practical, sequential manner. Intuiting (N) people tend to overlook the details, and instead look for a pattern, possibilities, or meaning. Intuiting people use their imagination to see what might be, rather than what is. In our model, Sensing (S) people may be most concerned with their environment (the lower left quadrant) and have a preference for maintaining systems and structures. Intuitive people may be more concerned with what could be or what might be, using their imagination to explore why things are the way they are (the upper right quadrant).

The next function has to do with how one makes decisions or uses information. The Thinking (T) person tends to be more analytical, objective, and focused on principles and justice, for example, what is the right thing to do in a situation, that makes sense to them? Feeling (F) people, on the other hand, may be more subjective in their decision-making and focused on values and creating harmony. The Thinking (T) person is often more prone to give precise, immediate feedback, while the Feeling (F) person will be more appreciative and empathic. In our model, the Thinking (T) function is represented by the upper left quadrant, where objectivity, analysis, and doing the right thing are valued. The Feeling

(F) function is represented by awareness of the people with whom we communicate and their values. This decision-making is based on harmony, it does not refer to your feelings about the decision and is represented by the lower right quadrant.

Once you know your functions, you can look at our model again for further insight as to which areas are calling you to further growth and development. Whether this takes place in the area of vocation or in another area of your life, the important thing is to respect the inner urge for growth that is present whenever change is taking place. In this way, you can revisit this model again and again, when change is thrust upon you, to get centered. Likewise, you can use it to focus your energies if you feel out of alignment.

The final scale describes the lifestyle you prefer in relating to the outer world. Those who prefer a Judging (J) attitude tend to be organized and enjoy making decisions. They want to regulate their environment and like to get closure on projects and events. Perceiving (P) persons tend to deal with the outer world in a flexible, spontaneous way. They prefer to gather information, keep their options open, and trust themselves to adapt to the moment. Remember, each of the four MBTI preferences indicate work-related preferences and your overall profile will show strong characteristics related to many different occupations. Understanding your type is important; validating the information about your preferences is essential. Trust the results from this instrument and record the results in your personal mandala.

BRAIN DOMINANCE SURVEY AND CREATIVITY

Another instrument that can be correlated with the MBTI is a Brain Dominance Survey. Many people are familiar with the concept of left and right brain thinking styles. Beverly Moore, a colleague, and president of Choicepoint, a management consulting firm, created a survey that draws heavily on the work of Ned Herrmann (go to our web site at *http://www.lifeworktransitions.com* to complete that survey). In addition to the left and right brain hemispheres, there is a conceptual and experiential component to the model that actually reflects the biological development of the brain and its functioning. This four-part model helps you realize your preferences in the following four areas: Analyzing, Implementing, Collaborating, and Innovating.]

The **Analyzing** quadrant is located in the upper left and represents the analysis of your skills and knowledge—the objective offering you

Figure 1.1   Brain Dominance Model

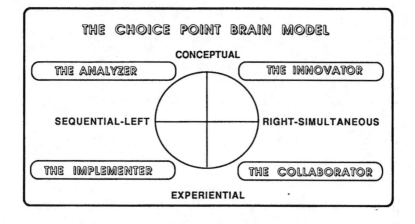

THE CHOICE POINT BRAIN MODEL

CONCEPTUAL

THE ANALYZER   THE INNOVATOR

SEQUENTIAL-LEFT   RIGHT-SIMULTANEOUS

THE IMPLEMENTER   THE COLLABORATOR

EXPERIENTIAL

bring to the world. The lower left quadrant represents the **Implementing** area of providing structure and order to our systems as well as maintaining them. The lower right quadrant speaks (literally) to our **collaborating** mode, how we express our values in ways that ensure our message will be heard. And finally, the upper right quadrant represents the **Intuiting**, or innovating part of our brain, that asks the question "What if we did it this way, this time?" or is open to receiving new inspirations and insights.

Like the functions of the MBTI, most people have preferences—usually two—which reflect their predominant means of processing information. Thus you'll have an Analyzer/Innovator (someone who tends to be conceptual) or an Analyzer/Implementor (someone who is more "left-brained"). Some people seem to have equal access to all four quadrants and they are called "whole-brained." These titles speak to the different tasks required in the creative process as well as in the undertaking of any project. They also mirror the questions posed by the career and life work transition model.

Does one exercise already appeal to you? If so, we strongly encourage you to begin that one now. Otherwise, review the following guidelines of the exercises to determine where to begin. Although one exercise may better help you tell your story, the important point is to begin the telling of it now. The form is less important than the process. Good luck and have fun.

BOX 1.1   WORK AUTOBIOGRAPHY GUIDELINES

To know where we are going we must know where we have been. This exercise is designed to help you recreate your life work history in an orderly, organized manner. The important thing is to be as detailed as possible, as though you were describing your experiences to a child. Autobiographies vary in length from fifteen to forty pages. Start off with a chronological list of all your work experiences according to time segments (some people like to include high school and college as their first "work" segments).

Year	Position	Organization	Location
1967-69	Asst. Production Mgr.	Beacon Press, Inc.	Boston
1969-70	Editing, Design	Freelance	Boston

Use this summary as the framework for your detailed autobiography. Describe exactly what you did and accomplished and try to overcome your natural modesty by bragging a bit. Your evaluation is what counts here. In fact, the activities you enjoyed the most deserve the most attention.

In describing each segment, be sure to respond to the following points.

1. Describe the organization, its size, general purpose, and so on.
2. Outline your responsibilities, personnel supervised, budget concerns, and amounts of money you handled and/or equipment you handled. What exactly did you do?
3. Describe significant achievements, especially those that went particularly well without a great deal of effort on your part. Describe any organizational activities or innovations that made your job easier. Describe any special relations with other people and any personal contributions you made.
4. Describe what was going on after hours—hobbies, activities, organizations, relationships, and so on.

BOX 1.2   ACCOMPLISHMENTS INVENTORY GUIDELINES

1. Take a separate sheet of paper for every five-year period of your life up to and including your present age. On each sheet, make a list of your accomplishments for that period of time. There should be at least three to five accomplishments for every five-year period. Pick those accomplishments that you most enjoyed doing or the ones that were most satisfying to you in some way.

The most useful way to state the accomplishment is by using the "I" statement and an action verb, for example, "I learned how to play the guitar." If you have trouble remembering, just close your eyes and picture yourself actually going through the steps, and answer the question "What was I doing?"

2. Next to each accomplishment you list, state **why** this was satisfying or meaningful to you. You do not need to write a paragraph; one statement will do.

3. After you have listed the accomplishments, choose the five to seven accomplishments that seem to be most meaningful to you. These may come from any five-year period. Your task now is to define your experiences in as much detail as possible. It is important that you mention every action that you took. Just tell it as though you were telling a story to a child, begin at the beginning and go through to the end.

4. Important points to remember:

   a. Describe how the event started and who started it.
   b. Describe any planning or preparation you did for it.
   c. Familiarize yourself with the Action Word sheet in the resume chapter. Discuss every detail of the project using action words.
   d. Describe any interactions you had with people involved in the project.
   e. Describe your personal outcome in terms of accomplishments/ success/good feelings.

BOX 1.3   LIFELINE EXERCISE GUIDELINES

Get a large sheet of easel paper or shelf paper. You will need crayons, magic markers, and pens. For fun, you might want to have stickers, feathers, glitter, and other assorted materials, including pictures cut out of magazines, or pictures of you at various stages of your life.

Begin by drawing a lifeline that best represents your sense of your life. Is it a straight line, or does it have lots of peaks and valleys? Whatever form your lifeline takes will work. Trust your hand as it draws a basic form that will give shape to the following steps in the exercise. You may want to do this first part in pencil so if you need to make changes later on you can.

You will most likely want to include some of the major experiences in your life, such as entering first grade or your first summer job. You will also want to list major events such as marriage, children, jobs, and subsequent career life work events. As you recollect each experience and assess its value, your lifeline will visually begin to reflect the highs and the lows. You can use the crayons to draw pictures or symbols or use words and phrases to identify the value you ascribe to it. When done, you will not only have the wonderful feeling of having created a masterpiece that provides a comprehensive overview of your life, but you will also be able to see and interpret patterns that have occurred throughout time.

BOX 1.4   GUIDELINES FOR YOUR SPIRITUAL AUTOBIOGRAPHY

In order to transform a personal or professional experience into spiritual insight and understanding it is necessary to gain some perspective. The writing of one's spiritual autobiography can cover your entire life, or you can select several significant experiences and write about them in detail.

Use the LifeLine Exercise to identify the events you might wish to write about. Consider events in your life that were formative to your beliefs. As a child, what were some significant "spiritual" experiences? Then think of yourself as an adolescent and remember the first time you might have believed something different from your family. Who were some significant role models for you and why? As a young adult, where did you go for spiritual insight? What kind of peak experiences did you have or what kind of community were you seeking? Create an outline of events from the above that you want to explore from a spiritual perspective.

1. Describe the situation and your role. What went particularly well, with a minimum of effort? What special challenges did you overcome? What special talents did you use?
2. What values were met and which were being challenged or threatened?
3. Describe the people involved and your relation to them. Who was there for you? What relations were deepened as a result of the experience? Which spiritual values were expressed and by whom?
4. Finally, write about the gifts you received as a result of this experience. What were the rewards? Did you overcome a weakness or fear and how has the experience made a difference in your life?

If you choose to continue with this process of assessment at this time, we recommend that you select one exercise, set up your computer or your notebook, and begin to tell your story.

2

Defining Core Competencies

"Our sense of security in this new age will be found in our
toolbox of skills and experiences, in our attitude toward
work, in what we contribute, in what we do that is fantastic,
in what we do that makes us employable, not in passive
dependency on our employer or on a set of unchanging
skills"
Robert Jay Ginn, Jr.

The new employment contract in the contemporary American workplace requires employees to assemble and manage multiple skill sets
that can be arranged in a variety of combinations. The traditional hierarchical workplace providing a lifetime of security has been replaced by a
flattened organization promising change. In order to survive in the new
workplace, employees have to be prepared for employability. Implicit in
this scenario is the assumption that employees continually add to their
skill sets to maintain optimal flexibility in their adaptation to change.
Consequently, identifying your skills—those that you have and those
that you will need—is essential to your future.

The secretary of the United States Department of Labor established a
Secretary's Commission on Achieving Necessary Skills (SCANS) to
identify skills required for the workplace of the future. (The SCANS Report can be found at *http://www.academicinnovations.com/report.html.*)
Other organizations such as the American Society for Training and Development, the National Academy of Sciences, and Stanford University
have also studied this topic. The results of these studies were similar.
SCANS concluded that regardless of job title or position description, employees must be able to demonstrate their skill in managing and using:

1. **Resources**. Workers must be able to identify, organize, plan, and allocate resources such as time, money, materials, and facilities. They must also be able to assess human resources in terms of skills, evaluation, and feedback.
2. **Interpersonal Skills**. Competent employees are those who can work well with team members and can teach new workers; can serve clients directly and persuade coworkers either individually or in groups; can negotiate with others to solve problems or reach decisions; can work comfortably with colleagues from diverse backgrounds, and can responsibly challenge existing procedures and policies.
3. **Information**. Workers need to be able to identify, assimilate, pare, maintain, and interpret quantitative and qualitative records; convert information from one form to another; and convey information, orally and in writing, as the need arises.
4. **Systems**. Workers must understand their own work in the context of the work of those around them; they must understand how parts of systems are connected, anticipate consequences, and monitor and correct their own performance; they must be able to identify trends and anomalies in system performance, integrate multiple displays of data, and link symbols (e.g., displays on a computer screen) with real phenomena (e.g., machine performance).
5. **Technology**. Workers must demonstrate high levels of competence in selecting and using appropriate technology, visualizing operations, using technology to monitor tasks, and maintaining and troubleshooting complex equipment. (As summarized by Boyett and Boyett in *Beyond Workplace 2000*)

How do your skills match up with these rather daunting conclusions? You will know by the end of this chapter. We have provided a skills inventory which will help you determine and express what you can do and what you enjoy doing. The inventory uses words commonly used in the world of work, which will increase your own vocabulary and help you immensely when you write your resume and sell yourself in an interview. When you analyze the results of the skills inventory, you will be able to compare your skills with the five SCANS competencies, choose the skills you enjoy most and want to use in the future, and assess your strengths and weaknesses. The identification of weaknesses gives valuable information and will point you toward the training you need to stay competitive in the workplace.

Many clients think they know what their skills are and are somewhat resistant to the exercises in this chapter. Often we hear, "Well, I know I am a people person." What does that mean? Are you a good speaker in front of a large audience? Are you a very good listener in a one-on-one encounter? Do you want to serve people in a hospital or hospice? Do you like lots of contact with people but not in a personal way? Do you socialize well? Do you like to interview people and then write a story? Do you like to have people around but really work by yourself? Just saying, "I'm a people person," doesn't cut it when you are trying to sell yourself in the marketplace. You need to be able to articulate the specific ways you can work and prefer to work with and for people. We promise you it is valuable to carefully think through your skills inventory and analysis.

You will be using information from "Your Story" written in Chapter 1 to discover and refine the definition of skills you most enjoy or want to acquire. This may seem like a tedious task, and it is tempting to quickly look through the list of skills and check off those you **think** you have. However, if you go through the process outlined in this chapter, you will discover **more** than just the skills you **think** you have. There will be many skills that you haven't thought of in a long time, skills you have taken for granted, or skills you really enjoyed but haven't consciously owned because you used them in nonwork settings. The unexpected insights, the surprises, can play an enormous part in your choices for the future. In addition, the process of "owning" your skills is one of the most powerful exercises for increasing self-confidence and self-esteem.

The process used in this book involves a series of exercises asking you to expand your thoughts as much as possible followed by an exercise guiding you to focus, limit, and prioritize the most essential information. In the first chapter, telling your story encouraged you to expand your thoughts and understanding of yourself. In the process, you connected with feelings, accomplishments, and energy that you may have forgotten or never really owned. Now it is time for you to use all the wisdom and information learned in "Your Story" to define and prioritize your skills.

You can think of your skills in three ways: adaptive skills or traits, special knowledge skills that are learned and specific to an industry or body of knowledge, and functional transferable skills which can be applied in work regardless of the industry or field. Following are exercises that will help you identify your skills in each area.

ADAPTIVE SKILLS

Adaptive skills are the skills we tend to overlook because they seem so obvious. In other words, you have a knack for doing something that comes so easily to you that you don't at first consider it as a valid skill. Or you have a personality trait that is your best attribute at work. These are the things you take for granted but are often among your strongest skills. It is important that you are able to identify and own them.

One of the best ways to get a handle on these is to ask someone close to you, or several people, "What do you see as my greatest strengths or assets? Or if you only had one word to describe me, what would it be?" Another means for identifying adaptive skills is to uncover the common denominator or key character traits that appear several times in "Your Story." Is it your sincerity, steadfastness, determination? Knowing these traits in yourself means knowing what makes your spirit shine. These are your special talents and perhaps your unique contribution when applied to the right setting, people, and circumstances.

Another source for identifying your adaptive skills is your Myers-Briggs profile. Read over your profile again and select words expressing characteristics that best represent you. The Myers-Briggs Temperament Inventory was discussed in Chapter 1. If you haven't taken that assessment instrument, you might do so now. The web site is *http://keirsey. com/frame.html.* There is also an excellent checklist of adaptive skills at Mike Farr's Online Job Search Workshop at *http://www.jist.com/adapt. htm.* The Career Center at the University of Waterloo at *http://www. adm.uwaterloo.ca/infocecs/CRC* gives an exhaustive list of personality traits for your review. Go to this site and click on <u>Self Assessment</u> and then click on <u>Personality & Attitudes</u> and fill out the form.

Listing Adaptive Skills

List the traits and personality characteristics that make you special.

_____

_____

_____

_____

_____

_____

_____

_____

SPECIAL KNOWLEDGE SKILLS

Special knowledge skills are often learned in school or require specialized training. You acquire technical skills in your field by following a specific training program and then developing mastery and/or flexibility through practice, whether it is in acupuncture, marketing, computer science, or advertising. Some of the precepts of special knowledge skills can be transferred, but basically that knowledge is of greater value in its appropriate field.

Listing Special Knowledge Skills

Rank each skill with 1 = never, 3 = would consider if (list the conditions), 5 = would love to use again in the future.

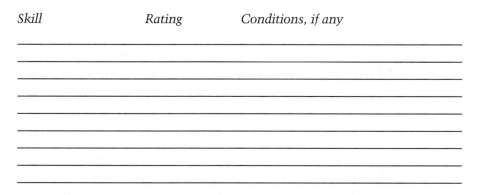

Skill   *Rating*   *Conditions, if any*

Identifying special knowledge skills will help you assess which ones you want to use in your next job and which ones you want to drop. This assessment can also be an asset in the job search; you may need to leverage from your special knowledge skills to engineer a transition to the next job. This might mean delaying short-term gratification for long-term reward, but it works. For example, a medical technologist who is totally burned out wants to sell houses. By agreeing to sell medical products for a while, the technician will accumulate the sales skills needed to "build a bridge of credibility" to the world of sales. With sales experience, it will be far easier to convince an employer to hire you as a real estate agent than it would be if you had no sales experience. You will also be in a far better position to negotiate salary or commission base.

CAREER MANAGEMENT SKILLS

The new employment contract requires a new set of career management skills. Whereas the workplace used to be stable, linear, and hierarchical in nature, now it is fluid and always changing. The new workplace requires preparedness for flexible employment opportunities instead of commitment for long-term job security. This puts a greater responsibility on the individual to think ahead, gain new skill sets, and be able to self-market. The resulting stress requires another set of skills to maintain a balanced life and a healthy lifestyle.

Rank Your Career Management Competencies

Rank the following from 1 to 5, 1 being "not at all" and 5 representing "mastery."

Managing Change = Managing Your Career

_____ 1. Career Assessment: Conduct frequent skill/knowledge assessment; create learning goals to remain current and informed about your inner needs and the outer realities; identify, create, and communicate with multiple networks from diverse areas for self-marketing purposes.

_____ 2. Self-Management: Commit to raising your consciousness, demonstrate initiative and progress through adversity; work independently with increasing awareness of the larger community.

_____ 3. Interpersonal and Facilitation: Demonstrate insight into motivating human behavior; develop and practice team building; manage conflict and practice negotiation and mediation.

_____ 4. Project Management: The ability to manage and acquire information and resources, broker services through partnering and collaboration; anticipate and troubleshoot.

_____ 5. Planning and Decision-Making: The ability to plan and set goals; establish a structure that encourages individual responsibility; review, select, and prioritize criteria.

_____ 6. Leadership: The ability to act as a leader and develop the discipline of building community; be committed to aligning various courses of action that will empower individuals; be willing to cocreate and share the results.

_____ 7. Computer Technology: Knowledge and practice of online resourcing such as Internet and email community accessibility, database management, and retrieval and word processing.

____ 8. Growth and Development: Creation of a plan and identification of resources to realize our goals of continuous learning to become all you can be and realize your potential.

FUNCTIONAL TRANSFERABLE SKILLS

Functional transferable skills are learned and then further developed in the workplace and in volunteer activities. They are the functions performed to accomplish tasks and complete objectives. These include interpersonal skills—the incredibly important skills of getting along with others—the ability to organize a project and implement a plan, the ability to read and apply printed matter. These are skills that transfer with you from one career setting to another.

Skills Inventory Directions

Whichever assessment exercise you chose (Lifework Autobiography, LifeLine, Accomplishments Inventory, or Spiritual Autobiography), choose six accomplishments from it for analysis in the Skills Inventory. A broad range of experiences works best. Obviously work accomplishments are important, but outside-of-work accomplishments might indicate different skills you would like to own. There is value in going through the entire inventory for each accomplishment. As a result you will uncover **more** functional transferable skills and increase the insight and vocabulary gained from this exercise. Your consciousness of self will be increased and enhanced.

Write the six accomplishments in the spaces at the top of the Skills Inventory. Start with the first; then systematically judge whether you used the skills listed in that experience. You don't have to be an expert in a particular skill. If you used the skill you own it, and should put a checkmark in the space next to the skill. Go through the entire report analyzing the first accomplishment. Then go back to the beginning of the Skills Inventory and decide which skills you used in the second accomplishment. Continue the process for the remaining four accomplishments. It is important for you to feel comfortable personalizing this Inventory in any way that would be helpful to you. If you think of more skills to add to a category or if you want to make up your own category and the skills that go with it, feel free to do so. This is your personal information to help you in career choices.

Functional Transferable Skills Inventory

List six accomplishments for analysis using the Skills Inventory.

1. _____
2. _____
3. _____
4. _____
5. _____
6. _____

Verbal Communication	#1	#2	#3	#4	#5	#6
Perform and entertain before groups	—	—	—	—	—	—
Speak well in public appearances	—	—	—	—	—	—
Confront and express opinions without offending	—	—	—	—	—	—
Interview people to obtain information	—	—	—	—	—	—
Handle complaints_in person_on telephone	—	—	—	—	—	—
Present ideas effectively in speeches or lecture	—	—	—	—	—	—
Persuade/influence others to a certain point of view	—	—	—	—	—	—
Sell ideas, products, or services	—	—	—	—	—	—
Debate ideas with others	—	—	—	—	—	—
Participate in group discussions and teams	—	—	—	—	—	—

Nonverbal Communication	#1	#2	#3	#4	#5	#6
Listen carefully and attentively	—	—	—	—	—	—
Convey a positive self image	—	—	—	—	—	—
Use body language that makes others comfortable	—	—	—	—	—	—
Develop rapport easily with groups of people	—	—	—	—	—	—
Establish culture to support learning	—	—	—	—	—	—
Express feelings through body language	—	—	—	—	—	—
Promote concepts through a variety of media	—	—	—	—	—	—
Believe in self-worth	—	—	—	—	—	—
Respond to nonverbal cues	—	—	—	—	—	—
Model behavior or concepts for others	—	—	—	—	—	—

Written Communication	#1	#2	#3	#4	#5	#6
Write technical language, reports, manuals	—	—	—	—	—	—
Write poetry, fiction, plays	—	—	—	—	—	—
Write grant proposals	—	—	—	—	—	—
Prepare and write logically written reports	—	—	—	—	—	—
Write copy for sales and advertising	—	—	—	—	—	—
Edit and proofread written material	—	—	—	—	—	—
Prepare revisions of written material	—	—	—	—	—	—
Utilize all forms of technology for writing	—	—	—	—	—	—
Write case studies and treatment plans	—	—	—	—	—	—
Expertise in grammar and style	—	—	—	—	—	—

Train/Consult	#1	#2	#3	#4	#5	#6
Teach, advise, coach, empower	—	—	—	—	—	—
Conduct needs assessments	—	—	—	—	—	—
Use a variety of media for presentation	—	—	—	—	—	—
Develop educational curriculum and materials	—	—	—	—	—	—
Create and administer evaluation plans	—	—	—	—	—	—
Facilitate a group	—	—	—	—	—	—
Explain difficult ideas, complex topics	—	—	—	—	—	—
Assess learning styles and respond accordingly	—	—	—	—	—	—
Consult and recommend solutions	—	—	—	—	—	—
Write well-organized and documented reports	—	—	—	—	—	—

Analyze	#1	#2	#3	#4	#5	#6
Study data or behavior for meaning and solutions	—	—	—	—	—	—
Analyze quantitative, physical, and scientific data	—	—	—	—	—	—
Write analysis of study and research	—	—	—	—	—	—
Compare and evaluate information	—	—	—	—	—	—
Systematize information and results	—	—	—	—	—	—
Apply curiosity	—	—	—	—	—	—
Investigate clues	—	—	—	—	—	—
Formulate insightful and relevant questions	—	—	—	—	—	—
Use technology for statistical analysis	—	—	—	—	—	—

Research	#1	#2	#3	#4	#5	#6
Identify appropriate information sources	—	—	—	—	—	—
Search written, oral, and technological information	—	—	—	—	—	—
Interview primary sources	—	—	—	—	—	—
Hypothesize and test for results	—	—	—	—	—	—
Compile numerical and statistical data	—	—	—	—	—	—
Classify and sort information into categories	—	—	—	—	—	—
Gather information from a number of sources	—	—	—	—	—	—
Patiently search for hard-to-find information	—	—	—	—	—	—
Utilize electronic search methods	—	—	—	—	—	—

Plan and Organize	#1	#2	#3	#4	#5	#6
Identify and organize tasks or information	—	—	—	—	—	—
Coordinate people, activities and details	—	—	—	—	—	—
Develop a plan and set objectives	—	—	—	—	—	—
Set up and keep time schedules	—	—	—	—	—	—
Anticipate problems and respond with solutions	—	—	—	—	—	—
Develop realistic goals and action to attain them	—	—	—	—	—	—
Arrange correct sequence of information and actions	—	—	—	—	—	—
Create guidelines for implementing an action	—	—	—	—	—	—
Create efficient systems	—	—	—	—	—	—
Follow through—ensure completion of a task	—	—	—	—	—	—

Counsel and Serve	#1	#2	#3	#4	#5	#6
Counsel, advise, consult, guide others	—	—	—	—	—	—
Care for and serve people; rehabilitate, heal	—	—	—	—	—	—
Demonstrate empathy, sensitivity, and patience	—	—	—	—	—	—
Help people make their own decisions	—	—	—	—	—	—

Help others improve health and welfare   __ __ __ __ __ __
Listen empathically and with objectivity   __ __ __ __ __ __
Coach, guide, encourage individual to
    achieve goals   __ __ __ __ __ __
Mediate peace between conflicting parties   __ __ __ __ __ __
Knowledge of self-help theories and
    programs   __ __ __ __ __ __
Facilitate self-awareness in others   __ __ __ __ __ __

Interpersonal Relations	*#1*	*#2*	*#3*	*#4*	*#5*	*#6*
Convey a sense of humor	__	__	__	__	__	__
Anticipate people's needs and reactions	__	__	__	__	__	__
Express feelings appropriately	__	__	__	__	__	__
Process human interactions, understand others	__	__	__	__	__	__
Encourage, empower, advocate for people	__	__	__	__	__	__
Create positive, hospitable environment	__	__	__	__	__	__
Adjust plans for the unexpected	__	__	__	__	__	__
Facilitate conflict management	__	__	__	__	__	__
Communicate well with diverse groups	__	__	__	__	__	__
Listen carefully to communication	__	__	__	__	__	__

Leadership	*#1*	*#2*	*#3*	*#4*	*#5*	*#6*
Envision the future and lead change	__	__	__	__	__	__
Establish policy	__	__	__	__	__	__
Set goals and determine courses of action	__	__	__	__	__	__
Motivate/inspire others to achieve common goals	__	__	__	__	__	__
Create innovative solutions to complex problems	__	__	__	__	__	__
Communicate well with all levels of organization	__	__	__	__	__	__
Develop and mentor talent	__	__	__	__	__	__
Negotiate terms and conditions	__	__	__	__	__	__
Take risks, make hard decisions, be decisive	__	__	__	__	__	__
Encourage the use of technology at all levels	__	__	__	__	__	__

Management	#1	#2	#3	#4	#5	#6
Manage personnel, projects, and time	—	—	—	—	—	—
Foster a sense of ownership in employees	—	—	—	—	—	—
Delegate responsibility and review performance	—	—	—	—	•	—
Increase productivity and efficiency to achieve goals	—	—	—	—	—	—
Develop and facilitate work teams	—	—	—	—	—	—
Provide training for development of staff	—	—	—	—	—	—
Adjust plans/procedures for the unexpected	—	—	—	—	—	—
Facilitate conflict management	—	—	—	—	—	—
Communicate well with diverse groups	—	—	—	—	—	—
Utilize technology to facilitate management	—	—	—	—	—	—

Financial	#1	#2	#3	#4	#5	#6
Calculate, perform mathematical computations	—	—	—	—	—	—
Work with precision with numerical data	—	—	—	—	—	—
Keep accurate and complete financial records	—	—	—	—	—	—
Perform accounting functions and procedures	—	—	—	—	—	—
Compile data and apply statistical analysis	—	—	—	—	—	—
Create computer generated charts for presentation	—	—	—	—	—	—
Use computer software for records and analysis	—	—	—	—	—	—
Forecast, estimate expenses and income	—	—	—	—	—	—
Appraise and analyze costs	—	—	—	—	—	—
Create and justify organizations' budget to others	—	—	—	—	—	—

Administrative	#1	#2	#3	#4	#5	#6
Communicate well with key people in organization	—	—	—	—	—	—
Identify and purchase necessary resource materials	—	—	—	—	—	—
Utilize computer software and equipment	—	—	—	—	—	—
Organize, improve, adapt office systems	—	—	—	—	—	—

Track progress of projects and
    troubleshoot   —   —   —   —   —   —

Achieve goals within budget and time
    schedule   —   —   —   —   —   —

Assign tasks and set standards for
    support staff   —   —   —   —   —   —

Hire and supervise temporary personnel
    as needed   —   —   —   —   —   —

Demonstrate flexibility during crisis   —   —   —   —   —   —

Oversee communication—email and
    telephones   —   —   —   —   —   —

Create and Innovate	#1	#2	#3	#4	#5	#6
Visualize concepts and results	—	—	—	—	—	—
Intuit strategies and solutions	—	—	—	—	—	—
Execute color, shape, and form	—	—	—	—	—	—
Brainstorm and make use of group synergy	—	—	—	—	—	—
Communicate with metaphors	—	—	—	—	—	—
Invent products through experimentation	—	—	—	—	—	—
Express ideas through art form	—	—	—	—	—	—
Remember faces, possess accurate spatial memory	—	—	—	—	—	—
Create images through sketching, sculpture, etc.	—	—	—	—	—	—
Utilize computer software for artistic creations	—	—	—	—	—	—

Construct and Operate	#1	#2	#3	#4	#5	#6
Assemble and install technical equipment	—	—	—	—	—	—
Build a structure, follow proper sequence	—	—	—	—	—	—
Understand blueprints and architectural specs	—	—	—	—	—	—
Repair machines	—	—	—	—	—	—
Analyze and correct plumbing or electrical problems	—	—	—	—	—	—
Use tools or machines	—	—	—	—	—	—
Master athletic skills	—	—	—	—	—	—
Landscape and farm	—	—	—	—	—	—
Drive and operate vehicles	—	—	—	—	—	—
Use scientific or medical equipment	—	—	—	—	—	—

Now that you have finished the Skills Inventory, you will see that some skills, perhaps even whole skills categories, will be either heavily or lightly checked. You will probably think that those skills most heavily checked are the most important for your future. Not necessarily. You may be very good at the skill but not want to do it anymore. There may be a skill lightly checked that reminded you of other experiences when you used that skill and really enjoyed it. Or, when thinking over a lightly checked skill, you may realize that you would prefer to use that skill but haven't had much of an opportunity to do so up to this point in time.

Look over your entire Skills Inventory and summarize your responses in the Summary of Skills Inventory form. (You can print out this form in a 8 1/2 by 11 format on our web site.)

SUMMARY DOCUMENTATION

Summary of Skills Inventory

Write in the skills you most enjoy in the following categories.

Verbal Communication

_____

_____

_____

_____

_____

_____

Nonverbal Communication

_____

_____

_____

_____

_____

Written Communication

_____

_____

_____

Training and Consulting

_____

_____

_____

_____

_____

Analyzing

_____

_____

_____

_____

Research

_____
_____
_____
_____
_____

Plan and Organize

_____
_____
_____
_____
_____

Counsel and Serve

_____
_____
_____
_____
_____

Interpersonal Relations

_____
_____
_____
_____
_____

Leadership

_____
_____
_____
_____
_____

Management

_____
_____
_____
_____
_____

Financial

_____
_____
_____
_____
_____

Administrative

_____
_____
_____
_____
_____

Create and Innovate

_____
_____
_____
_____
_____

Construct and Operate

_____
_____
_____
_____
_____

Most Enjoyed/Best Performed Skill Sets

It will be obvious to you that your skills fall into clusters. These are your **skill sets**; give them a name that fits or use the category titles used in the Inventory. Then choose eight to ten skill sets that you **enjoy most** (regardless of the number of checks beside them) and would like to use in your next career move; write them down in rank order in the space provided. Then make a second list of skill sets that you **perform best,** and write them down in rank order. You will choose from both the "most enjoyed" and "best performed" lists for your portfolio of skills sets.

My Most Enjoyed Skills Sets   *Best Performed Skills Sets*

_____   _____
_____   _____
_____   _____
_____   _____
_____   _____
_____   _____
_____   _____

Training Needs

The next step is to identify any weaknesses or gaps in your skills that you would like to acquire through some extra training. List them now.

Identify Training Needs

_____
_____
_____
_____
_____
_____
_____
_____
_____

SCANS COMPETENCIES

Compare your skills with five competencies from the SCANS report. Are you well prepared for the future in the following areas? Rank them from 1 to 5 with 1 being "not prepared at all" and 5 representing "well prepared."

_____ 1. Ability to identify, organize, plan, and allocate resources such as time, money, materials, and facilities. Must also be able to assess human resources in terms of skills, evaluation, and feedback.

_____ 2. Excellent interpersonal skills with coworkers and clients: teaching, persuading, selling, negotiating, responsibly challenging procedures.

_____ 3. Ability to identify, assimilate, and integrate information; ability to interpret quantitative and qualitative records; ability to convert information of one form to another.

_____ 4. Ability to understand your work in the context of those around you, to understand how parts of the systems are connected, anticipate consequences, identify trends and anomalies in system performance, integrate multiple displays of data, and link symbols.

_____ 5. Demonstrate high levels of competence in selecting and using appropriate technology. Use of technology to monitor tasks; ability to maintain and troubleshoot complex equipment.

If ranking yourself on the SCANS Competencies makes you think of some more gaps in your skills, list them in the space with the other training needs.

Now it is time for you to look at the four skills assessments (Adaptive, Special Knowledge, Career Management, Transferable) and choose the skills you want to to put into your Skill Set Portfolio. We have included a pie-shaped diagram for you to record your final decisions. Notice the wedge labeled "training." You may have already discovered some skills you need to add to your portfolio. Put those in the Training wedge now. If you are not aware of any training needed at the present time, wait until you have researched job options and add them then. Once you have accumulated the skills in the Training wedge, you will want to assess what training should be next. Congratulations, you now have a picture of your Skill Set Portfolio.

Figure 2.1   Skill Set Portfolio

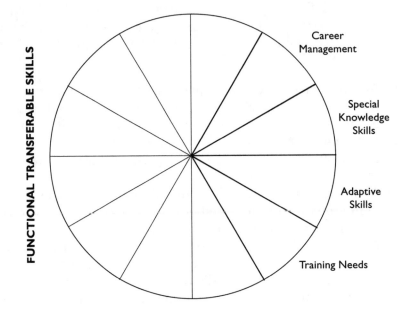

QUESTIONS TO CONSIDER

1. Are the skill sets in your portfolio broad enough? (Need well-balanced portfolio of interpersonal and communication skills, project management skills, and problem-solving skills.)
2. Are there a sufficient number of special knowledge skills to anchor your functional transferable skills?
3. Are there several ways you could group your skill sets to make you employable in more than one position? Try filling out two groupings of skills sets in the circles in Figure 2.2 and see what you discover about your potential.

Figure 2.2   Alternative Groupings of Skills Sets

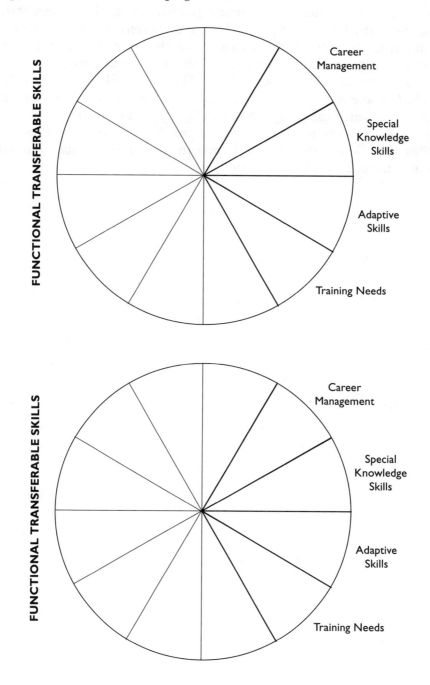

If you would like to look at some other models of skills analysis, there are several on the Internet. The best is provided by Bowling Green State University at *http://www.bgsu.edu/offices/careers/process/competen.html*. Print out the Inventory and perhaps see another way of identifying your skill sets. Another is the University of Waterloo Career Center at *http://www.adm.uwaterloo.ca/infocecs/CRC*. This link will take you to the Center's homepage. Click on Self Assessment; when you get to the the Self Assessment page, click on Skills & Achievements. It will take you to a form that you can print out and then answer the questions. This is a terrific self-assessment site, and I don't think you will be able to resist some of the other topics. Have fun.

CHAPTER

3

Redefining Your Self:
Passions, Preferences, and Purpose

"It is the longing to know our authentic vocation in the
world, to find the work and the way of being that belong to
each of us."
                                        Theodore Rosak

This is the chapter that focuses on discovering the answers to the questions posed in the last three quadrants. It addresses the concerns: Where do I do my best work? Who are the people that I most want to collaborate with and serve? And finally, why do I do what I do and what are the rewards I hope to achieve?

Assessing skills is the practical part of this process, since it provides the vocabulary you will use in introducing and selling yourself in the world of work. Assessing values is the spiritual part of the process and provides the centering template for decision-making and balancing inner psychic energy. Discovering core values and defining one's purpose are keys to finding one's authentic vocation.

Our clients love this part of the process the most and find it most revealing. They discover values they never thought about before, but that seem so obvious once expressed. Once you know your authentic self there is no excuse for not expressing it in your daily life. Going through this process of values clarification puts you in charge of your compromises and that is empowering. When people get in touch with what they need, they are able to assume responsibility for achieving it.

In this chapter you will identify what nourishes you in your work and you will use that criterion to evaluate options in the workplace. When people become aware of what is coming into their life and what is going out, they realize that work has to provide revitalizing energy or else they feel empty. Realizing core values and finding them in the workplace will help make work nourishing psychologically. When these values are realized and combined with skills you love, you will find yourself wanting to go to work in the morning. The feeling of being nourished, fulfilled, and exhilarated intellectually is exciting. Many people who are burned out by the workplace think it is their own fault. They blame themselves for being "out of sync" with the organization's values, especially if they don't know their own values. Once they are invited to claim their values, they can be more objective in evaluating future options.

Arriving at the core of one's personal value system can serve as an infallible radar system to enlighten and deepen professional choices and activities. Identifying what is most precious and unique about your vision is at the heart of the matter. This chapter provides eight exercises for assessing values and preferences and the Career Interest Game on the Web, to help define what motivates, nourishes, and interests you. Knowledge of personal motivators can guide the selection of employment opportunities as much as application of one's skills. Reflecting on values is the first place to turn when an existing employment opportunity is no longer considered viable.

Going through these exercises will give you the confidence in self to either change or renegotiate your work environment. For the authentic person seeking employment, finding ways of matching your values and the values in the workplace is the most challenging part of the job search. Fortunately, the Internet is a great help; you can do more informational interviewing and viewing of cultures on the Internet than you would ever be able to do physically.

IDENTIFYING CORE VALUES AND WORKPLACE PREFERENCES

The focus in this section is to identify the characteristics of the work environment and people that are most supportive and receptive to your unique expression. It also serves the purpose of identifying the kind of authority and autonomy you need to do your best work. Clues to the kind of environment you might best function in come from selecting and prioritizing existing criteria; others come from exercises that ask you to envision what your ideal self would desire and then allowing yourself to explore the possibility of receiving that.

What is it that makes work really important to you? What is it above and beyond its most obvious function of earning a living? If something is of value to us we cherish it all the more, and that will affect our attitude toward it. As a result, even the most mundane acts and routines can be imbued with greater meaning. People who are using their talents in work that is congruent with their values have a sense of mission and fulfillment. These people may be fulfilling their souls' task according to Gary Zukov, in his book *Seat of the Soul*. He says: "When the deepest part of you becomes engaged in what you are doing, when your activities and actions become gratifying and purposeful, when what you do serves both yourself and others, and when you do not tire within but seek the sweet satisfaction of your life and your work . . . then you are doing what you were meant to be doing."

This is no easy task. Unfortunately, there is no one exercise that will neatly tie up a value package for everyone. In fact, there are more exercises in this chapter than any other, and that is not by accident. Each exercise taps your values at a different level giving you more and more information about what is important to you. The variety of exercises are designed to work for everyone—young and old, left and right brain, introverts and extroverts, freelance artists and organizational men and women. We encourage you to do each exercise and determine later its value and worth in the overall definition of you. There is a worksheet for each exercise included at the end of this chapter and on our website, *http://www.lifeworktransitions.com*.

What makes each one of us unique is the sum totality of our individual nuances, beliefs, attitudes, and personal expressions. Your thoughtful and spontaneous response to each one of these exercises will provide you with the information needed to translate your dreams into your life work.

Work Values: Rating Satisfactions from Work

This exercise is essential to our practice. We often use it in the first session to get people started thinking about what is most important to them in their choice of career. After completing the inventory you will want to expand your thinking about some of the items you considered important. If "helping society" ranked high on your list, you can generate new possibilities and personalize the values by brainstorming your responses to the following questions:

- What aspect of society do I wish to see improved?
- Who do I really want to help and how can I be most helpful?

After you have identified the top values (3's and 4's) visualize what that would look like to you. How do you want to have that value expressed in your work life? Or if not in your work life, what other parts of your life should be sure to reflect that value? If other values come to mind now, please feel free to add these to the list of core criteria, to be reviewed at a later date for inclusion in your personal mandala.

Motivating Factors

The next worksheet will help you identify other motivators and rewards. If you experience some redundancy as a result of these exercises it indicates that your values are consistent. In order to get the most out of this next exercise, think of what is most important to you now and prioritize the top five. Sometimes people wonder about the consistency of their values. If you have been in a traumatic work situation you may identify some value as being important because its presence or absence contributed to the difficulties you just experienced. By completing the various exercises here you will have the opportunity to double check and verify how lasting these values are. When you actually create your personal mandala (Chapter 5) you will have another opportunity to review these values and determine what really is most important to you.

Factors in the Workplace

In this exercise you will identify from your own work experience the factors in the workplace that provide motivation. Most people enjoy the opportunity to revisit the past one more time to glean important criteria that contributed to success. You may be able to complete this exercise just by reflecting upon your past, or you may find it helpful to reread what you have written to refresh your memory. Our clients seem to take great pleasure in this exercise, because it serves to bring closure on old, outdated patterns that no longer work.

Preferred People Characteristics, Physical Environment, Structure of Authority, Emotional Climate/Corporate Culture

There are four different categories of workplace factors to be identified. Begin by listing the negative characteristics of the following components of your past work environments. Some of you may have trouble with this approach but, trust us, it is healing to let those negatives surface. Listing the negatives first will help you unload a lot of anger and criticism you may hold toward difficult situations and free you to be creative and open in the next step of the process.

The first area for you to identify is the negative characteristics of the **People** with whom you worked, your colleagues and customers. What fun to be given permission to be outrageous and call them what they really are! For example, when you are considering the people characteristics, visualize the nastiest customer or boss you have experienced, and vent your true feelings.

The **Physical Environment** includes the characteristics of the ideal physical setting and the attributes of the environment. Think about the type of building and office space, the length of commute, the availability of resources and ease with which you can access them.

The next area for you to consider is the **Structure of Authority** demonstrated in each of your work environments. This has to do with identifying your own preferred work style and includes such items as autonomy, the ability to self-direct and plan, and how comfortable you are working under pressure. Is your preferred environment team-oriented or is the lone-wolf given status and preference? Think of the least creative and supportive environment and list those factors first.

The last factor to be considered is the **Emotional Climate/Corporate Culture**. What kinds of emotions were triggered in your last job? What kind of communication existed between employees? Was there an atmosphere of trust? Was professional development encouraged? What was the employee morale? What was the predominant management style? How did things get done? What behaviors were rewarded?

After you have gotten all those negatives off your chest, list the positives of each factor in the workplace. The positives are not always exact opposites, and sometimes the order in which you list things is revealing. After you have created both lists, restate the negatives positively. Now you can prioritize the long list of positive values. This list should include the items most essential in that ideally supportive future work environment. Following is an example for corporate culture.

Negatives	*Positives*
cold, impersonal environment	friendly atmosphere at outset
low morale	mentor as boss
little informal communication	plan my own work
no professional development	collegial atmosphere

Negatives into Positives
Cold, impersonal environment *becomes* friendly atmosphere
Low morale *becomes* all employees feel ownership
Little informal communication *becomes* regularly scheduled social events
No professional development *becomes* training is financially supported

Out of your final list of eight positives for Corporate Culture, select the top three, for example, 1. Collegial atmosphere 2. Training is supported and encouraged 3. Employee ownership is valued.

My Fantasy Work Day

The next exercise, My Fantasy Work Day, may provide additional reinforcement to some of your previous criteria. It can also offer a totally new picture—an "aha" if you will—that produces an awareness of what you are really looking for. Whether the results are specific in the form of the details generated, or total as in a complete new visualization, this exercise usually provides valuable insight. Many of our clients site this as the picture they carry with them of what their ideal job will be at an unconscious level. Note that there is an important step of prioritizing your indispensable (I) criteria that you'll want to include in your personal mandala.

Ideal Job Specifications

This exercise differs from the previous one in that you may find yourself being more practical. Even though you are asked to identify the ideal characteristics of the job, the ideal here means realizable in the not too distant future. This picture may be more concrete and serve as an initial attempt to summarize the information you have gathered thus far. It does not necessarily indicate the actual job you will be doing, but it offers a template that when realized would make you very happy.

After completing this exercise, use the words you have uncovered to describe the ideal job. You will have an opportunity to create a more thorough life work objective in Chapter 5 that summarizes all the information in your personal mandala. At this stage you are still gathering important information about core values and workplace preferences.

DISCOVERING PERSONAL PURPOSE

Discovering meaning or finding purpose in what we do is one of the most spiritual exercises in which we can engage. Some people come by this search naturally and seem to know intuitively how to bring clarity and focus to whatever they do. Others are hoping to realize what is meaningful as a result of going through our process. Irene de Castillejo, a Jungian therapist, speaks in her book *Knowing Woman* of an inner clarity as the conscious awareness of being "on one's thread, knowing what one knows, and having an ability quite simply and without ostentation to stand firm on one's inner truth." She goes on to say, "I like to think of every person's being linked to God from the morning of birth to the night of his death by an invisible thread, a thread which is unique for each one of us, a thread which can never be broken." Defining this thread and understanding your personal purpose can provide guidance and influence to a myriad of professional activities. Your unique presence in the marketplace will be defined by your personal vision, your values and sense of purpose. Your leadership style will be enhanced with a clearly defined personal purpose statement.

Moving beyond the physical and immediately practical values to the metaphysical, the remaining exercises in this chapter will help you focus on defining your purpose and how that can manifest in your life work or your personal life. James Hillman, in *The Soul's Code*, refers to the individual's calling as the acorn image or blueprint in us that is an archetype of who we are and why we are here. What is the one thing you should try to express or accomplish? Defined in general terms, it can be fulfilled through work or nonwork activities. The metaphor of the acorn or the invisible thread can be a core image for you that manifests itself in different ways. Understanding and acting upon your personal purpose can bring rich meaning and fulfillment.

What Needs Doing in Your World by Others?

The first exercise that has us explore purpose is one of our favorites from John Crystal, and it really works at defining what you see as the world's "deep hunger." The question "What needs doing in your world by **others**?" is a key to discovering your unique perspective. The idea behind the exercise is to generate a list of as many problems as you can without feeling like you have to have a solution. Great ideas can lead to wonderful places in and of themselves. Let your imagination soar; it and you are limitless. These ideas show in part what you value. We can choose to support these values in our work, our volunteer experience, or in our personal lives.

The exercise has you first list all those things you would have **others** do to improve our society or the world. This prevents you from ignoring a good idea just because you don't think you would actually know how to proceed. The follow-up is to select one idea that you might be willing to work on and see what you come up with as an approach to this particular problem. How would you tackle it? Are you the planner, manager, or implementor? What needs to happen next? Be as detailed or as profound as you like, or light and sketchy—whatever works for you. This will give you an indication that you may have more knowledge or power than you realize in a particular area. It might provide a clue to some totally new direction.

Ninetieth Birthday Feature Article

The next exercise will encourage you to envision what has not yet shown up in your life and begin to think about including it in your future. In it you'll pretend it is your ninetieth birthday and the local newspaper is doing a feature article on you. In this exercise you are asked to imagine and describe the many personal and professional accomplishments of your lifetime. What have you done over the years? You have already written your life story up until now, so continue the story as only you can. Be sure to include family and volunteer experiences along with work-related successes. What is the tone? Are you fulfilled? Did you work long and hard at something, or meet with overnight success and then move on to something else?

Discovering Your Personal Purpose

Most people find this exercise thought provoking and stimulating. Your response to the questions gives you the opportunity to review aspects of your past in another fashion and to use your vocabulary to create a powerful purpose statement. By completing this exercise, you will have defined for yourself in meaningful soul language your purpose. This is not something necessarily shared, especially in an interview, but knowing it means you can select where and when to disclose it.

After you have completed the exercise you will be able to refer to your *haiku* as a centering exercise when deciding whether to undertake a certain project or client. Each time you use your purpose statement you can reevaluate its meaning and relevance. If you get to the point where you are visiting your purpose on a daily basis to check out the right-liveliness of an endeavor, you will become deeply intimate with it. If it is no longer true or working for you, recreate a new one the next time you visit this work. We are constantly changing and growing and one of the benefits of living on purpose is to be able to take responsibility and be purposeful in our pursuit of right-livelihood.

Purpose is one of several values you may like to incorporate in work. However, not everyone has to have their purpose fulfilled through their work, but their values must be met. One of our clients is a superb flutist who recognized that she was not going to be able to make a living as a professional musician. Her next step was to get an MBA and became a consultant, traveling all over the world. She loved it because of the time it gave her to practice the flute. After marrying, she no longer wanted to be on the road. She was able to rearrange her skills and knowledge in such a way that work would incorporate her changing values. She had an opportunity to be an equity analyst in a nine-to-five job. She chose the firm after researching what kinds of boards were supported by top officers. She chose a firm whose senior executives were on the boards of the Boston Symphony and other arts organizations. With her new time schedule, she was able to perform her work in a setting where the corporate values mirrored her personal values. Likewise, this new nine-to-five job left time for playing in the local symphony orchestra and becoming a mother. She achieved her purpose of pursuing meaningful work that incorporated the balance required to fulfill her new family responsibilities.

INTEREST INVENTORIES

Holland Career Interests Game

Since so much of the work world is organized around vocational categories, fields, and occupational areas, this is a good point for you to turn to the Internet to assess your interests. Interests are a key motivating factor and the occupational codes created by John Holland have stood the test of time. By describing personality traits and characteristics of different preferred kinds of activities, you will be directed to a number of fields, industries, or professions that may prove to be satisfying for you.

1. To complete the Self Assessment for the Career Interests Game go to *http://www.esc.state.nc.us/soicc/planning/c1a.htm*. Print out the instrument. Fill it out and total your scores for each of the six interest themes.
2. Then go to the actual Career Interests Game at *http://www.missouri.edu/~cppcwww/holland.shtml*. Click on your theme with the

highest score and look at the results. Print it out. Then also click on the specific careers that interest you.

3. Go back to the Career Interests Game and click on your interest with the second highest score.

EXERCISES

BOX 3.1   WORK VALUES

The following list describes a wide variety of satisfactions that people obtain from their jobs. Look at the definitions of these various satisfactions and rate the degree of importance that you would assign to each for yourself, using the following scale.

1. = Not important at all   3. = Reasonably important
2. = Not very important   4. = Very important in my choice of career

_____**Help Society**: Do something to contribute to the betterment of the world I live in.

_____**Help Others**: Be involved in helping other people in a direct way, either individually or in small groups.

_____**Public Contact**: Have a lot of day-to-day contact with people.

_____**Work with Others**: Have close working relationships with people as a result of my work activities.

_____**Affiliation**: Be recognized as a member of a particular organization.

_____**Friendships**: Develop close personal relationships with people as a result of my work activities.

_____**Competition**: Engage in activities that pit my abilities against others where there are clear win-and-lose outcomes.

_____**Make Decisions**: Have the power to decide courses of action, policies, and so on.

_____**Work under Pressure**: Work in situations where time pressure is prevalent and/or the quality of my work is judged critically by supervisors, customers, or others.

_____**Power and Authority**: Direct the work activities of others and have the authority to make decisions.

_____**Influence People:** Be in a position to change attitudes or opinions of other people.

_____**Work Alone:** Do projects by myself, without any significant amount of contact with others.

_____**Knowledge:** Engage myself in the pursuit of knowledge, truth, and understanding.

_____**Intellectual Status:** Be regarded as a person of high intellectual prowess or as one who is an acknowledged "expert" in a given field.

_____**Artistic Creativity:** Engage in creative work in any of several art forms.

_____**Creativity (General):** Create new ideas, programs, organizational structures, or anything else not following a format previously developed by others.

_____**Aesthetics:** Be involved in studying or appreciating the beauty of things or ideas.

_____**Supervision:** Have a job in which I am directly responsible for the work done by others.

_____**Change and Variety:** Have work responsibilities that frequently change in their content and setting.

_____**Precision Work:** Work in situations in which there is very little tolerance for error.

_____**Stability:** Have a work routine and job duties that are largely predictable and not likely to change over a long period of time.

_____**Security:** Be assured of keeping my job and a reasonable financial reward.

_____**Fast Pace:** Work in circumstances where there is a high pace of activity, work must be done rapidly.

_____**Recognition:** Be recognized for the quality of my work in some visible or public way.

_____**Excitement:** Experience a high degree of (or frequent) excitement in the course of my work.

_____**Adventure:** Have work duties that involve frequent risk-taking.

_____**Profit, Gain:** Have a strong likelihood of accumulating large amounts of money or other material gain.

_____**Independence:** Be able to determine the nature of my work without significant direction from others; not have to do what others tell me to do.

_____**Moral Fulfillment:** Feel that my work is contributing significantly to a set of moral standards (to be defined by you) that you feel are very important.

_____**Lifestyle:** Find a place to live (town, geographical area) that is conducive to my lifestyle and affords me the opportunity to do the things I enjoy most.

_____**Community:** Live in a town or city where I can be involved in community affairs.

_____**Physical Challenge:** Have a job that makes physical demands that I would find rewarding.

_____**Time Freedom:** Have work responsibilities that I can work at according to my own time schedule; no specific working hours required.

Now choose six of these work values that are the most important to you. Each will be relevant to the career exploration that you do. If you can think of any other intangible work rewards (desired satisfactions) that are not included in the previous list and that are especially important to you, add them to the six values you have chosen.

1. _____   2. _____
3. _____   4. _____
5. _____   6. _____

BOX 3.2   MOTIVATING FACTORS

Check the five items you believe are most important in motivating you to do your best work.

1. Steady, secure employment
2. Respect for me as an individual
3. Good pay
4. Chance for promotion
5. Not having to work too hard
6. Feeling my job is important
7. Attend staff meetings

8. Having a flexible work schedule
9. Lots of free time
10. Having consistency in my job
11. Knowing my supervisor trusts me
12. Working by myself
13. Prestige
14. Growth potential with the company
15. Financial support for lifelong learning program
16. Being able to participate in the decisions that affect me
17. Knowing I will be held responsible for my own performance
18. Freedom to make decisions without approval from supervisor
19. Good physical working conditions
20. Up-to-date technology and resources
21. Chance to turn out quality work
22. Getting along well with others on the job
23. Opportunity to do creative and challenging work
24. Pensions and other fringe benefits
25. Knowing what is going on in the organization
26. Formal and informal companywide communication
27. The organization's interest and concern for social problems (i.e., ecology, pollution, human service areas)
28. Having a written job description of the duties for which I am responsible
29. Being commended by superiors when I do a good job
30. Getting a performance rating, so I know here I stand
31. Having a job with minimal amount of pressure
32. Agreement with organization's objectives
33. Large amount of freedom on the job
34. Opportunity for self-development and improvement
35. Having an efficient and competent superior
36. The organization's willingness to let me spend time working on community activities
37. Being able to problem-solve in my job
38. Having regular staff meetings to discuss policy issues
39. Socializing with other employees during the workday
40. Other_____

BOX 3.3   FACTORS IN THE WORKPLACE

1. People Characteristics
2. Physical Environment
3. Structure of Authority
4. Emotional Climate/Corporate Culture

These are the four different categories of workplace factors to be identified. Begin by listing the negative characteristics from your past work environments. First, identify negative characteristics of the people with whom you worked, your colleagues and customers. Next, identify negative factors in the physical environment such as setting, light, air, style, and location. The next area to consider is the structure of authority demonstrated in work environments. The last factor is the emotional climate/corporate culture. After you have gotten all those negatives off your chest, make a list of positives for each of the four factors in the workplace. After you have created both lists, restate the negatives positively. Now you can prioritize the long list of positive values. Out of your final lists of positives, select the top three for each factor. (See example in the text.)

BOX 3.4   FANTASY WORK DAY

Close your eyes and try to imagine the ideal work day for yourself. Don't be concerned with realities—just let your imagination go. See if you can picture, in full detail, what you would be doing. Then open your eyes and answer the following questions.

You wake up—at what time?
You get dressed—describe clothes.
What kind of preparations do you have to make?
Do you have to work or do you work because you want to?
You are ready to leave for work—at what time?
How do you get there? How far is it?
Do you do anything special on the way to work?
You get to work. Where are you? (city, small town, office park, home, etc.)
Describe the work setting.
What kind of work do you do?
How long have you worked here?

What are your hours?

What do you get paid?

What are your benefits?

What level is the job? (professional, management, technical, training, apprentice)

Do you plan your work or does someone do it for you?

How do you work? (alone, in a group, contact with others)

What do you work with? (people, data, things, nature, a combination)

Describe some of the people who work in your area.

To whom do you report?

What do you like about your job or occupation?

How long do you see yourself remaining at this job?

What is the next move (job step) for you?

What are your highest aspirations in this field or place of employment?

Go back over each section and put an "I" for those you feel are indispensable, an "O" for those that are desirable but optional, and an "F" for those that are basically frills.

BOX 3.5   IDEAL JOB SPECIFICATIONS

To your best ability, at this point in time, describe in detail the ideal job specifications you would like in your next position. Include the functions you would perform, the physical environment and emotional milieu, the working conditions, your preferred people characteristics, and whatever else is needed for you to do your best and be your most productive self. The final step in this exercise is to create a tentative definition of an ideal job. I want to use these skills _____ in this kind of environment _____ which would help me respond to the following values and concerns _____.

BOX 3.6   WHAT NEEDS DOING IN YOUR WORLD BY OTHERS

Make a list of all the important activities you think **others** should do. Include in your list political, social, national, and local concerns. Select one and develop a plan of action.

BOX 3.7 NINETIETH BIRTHDAY EXERCISE

Write a feature story describing your many life accomplishments. Imagine yourself at the age of ninety looking back over a long, rich, personal and professional life.

BOX 3.8 DISCOVERING PERSONAL PURPOSE

On a separate sheet of paper, respond to the following questions thoughtfully and truthfully. You may also print out the entire exercise on our web site.

1. What activities do you enjoy performing? (List why you enjoy them and what is enjoyable about them)
2. What are you good at? (list skills, talents, and special knowledges)
3. Think of a specific situation in which you felt successful. Describe the time, place, activity. Write what you were doing and how you were feeling.
4. Think of a time you did something meaningful that was satisfying to you. Describe the situation (as in 3 above) and why it had meaning.
5. Think of another specific situation in which you felt successful. Describe the time, place, and activity. Describe what you were doing and how you were feeling.
6. List three qualities you are proud of, and describe why.
7. Describe your vision of an ideal world if you could make it happen.

Review the above information and circle fifteen to twenty key words or ideas. Summarize the key words and select the ten to twelve that are most important to you and record them here. At this point it is often helpful to share your answer with a close friend. The images you have recorded and the language used describe what is meaningful to you.

To create a purpose statement, use the words in the list you just created to develop a series of reiterative statements until you find the one that resonates with you.

My purpose is to
My purpose is to
My purpose is to
My purpose is to

Since purpose is often referred to in soul language, some people like to translate their purpose statement into a metaphor or *haiku* that summarizes the essence of the statement. To create a *haiku* you'll want to arrange the wording from your purpose statement to fit the following formula:

First line (five syllables) —/—/—/—/—/
Second line (seven syllables) —/—/—/—/—/—/—/
Third line (five syllables) —/—/—/—/—/
Example: Leading, Creating
                Fulfilling an Abundant
                Universe of Trust

(This exercise is adapted from Dave Morrison and Andre de Zanger and presented at the Creative Problem Solving Institute (CPSI) , State University at Buffalo, NY in 1985.)

CHAPTER

4

Goal Setting:
Creating a Life Worth Living

"In the process of setting goals, we come to know ourselves.
Virtually every cultural tradition holds among its central
principles, 'know thyself.' Knowing ourselves, the capacity
for reflective self awareness, is perhaps our greatest personal
achievement, at least the one that is important to career
success."   *Robert Jay Ginn, Jr.*

In the three previous chapters you have uncovered old experiences and
accomplishments that revived wonderful memories. You have discovered how skillful you are and expressed your skills in words that define
you appropriately for the world of work. You have uncovered what really
motivates you internally and externally. Now we have to consider how
you are going to put all you have learned into action.

But before that, we want you to take a "time-out." You have collected
a lot of information about yourself and are about to embark on a time-
consuming project, researching a new position and marketing yourself
in the workplace. When you commit yourself to a shift or change in your
career, it is renewing, exhilarating, and a period of significant personal
growth. It is also an enormous addition to your life which will take time
and a great deal of physical and emotional energy. If you are already in
"full-time" mode, something has to be modified or you will be exhausted, very stressed, and unable to do a good job search. In general, it
is a good idea to follow the rule, "If you add something to your life, you
should drop something from your life." This is the time to consider life

work balance with a serious look at how the "life" part of you is going to fare with the "work" part of you.

We live in a high-speed society that values working full-time, parenting full-time, participating in professional associations, developing a home, caring for our parents, being a good friend, being significant for a significant other, taking an interest in our community, building a fund for retirement, and now acquiring competency to adjust to a constantly changing workplace. There simply is not time to "do it all" or "have it all."

In addition, some of you may be committing to a career shift or change that is not of your choice. It may have been forced on you because of a reorganization of your company, loss of a job, a change in marital status, illness, family crisis, a geographical move, or an empty nest. All of these losses are great stressors in and of themselves and should not be shoved aside. We recommend that you read William Bridges' book *Transitions* (Bridges' three stages of transition are discussed in Part I), or take some time to read and process Hyatt and Gottlieb's chapter on "The Stages of Loss from Losing Your Job" from *When Smart People Fail.* You will be able to read and print out a hand-out adapted from that chapter on our web site. The point is to avoid getting stuck in one of the stages, and you do that by going through the stages, not avoiding them.

One of the classic books in goal setting is Alan Lakien's *How to Get Control of Your Time and Life.* As the title suggests, time management is an integral part of goal setting, and goal setting helps you get in charge of your life. Goal setting provides an opportunity to project into the future, maintain a better balance in your life, and increases effective use of time. It also grounds you and helps you evaluate your life as a whole so that life work balance can be a reality. It helps you decide what to set aside as you add career development and a job search. There may not be enough time to "have it all" or "do it all" but goal setting can make you more "in charge of it all."

We have had students in goal-setting seminars who have returned year after year. Many have said they achieved their goals even though they hadn't looked at them during the year. The single act of thoughtfully writing their goals helped them keep their priorities in mind and their time devoted to the action needed to achieve them. We can't emphasize too much the act of writing down your goals. Writing down a goal as specifically as possible, and in the form of an "I" statement makes goals concrete: "I plan to own a house in the suburbs." "I want to be vice president of marketing for a high-tech firm in Silicon Valley." "I will get trained in the basics of computer technology." Writing down your goals makes them concrete and preserved in your mind. That is why our clients felt coming to a goal-setting seminar once a year was well worth the effort. So do we, but you can also do it on your own with the help of the exercises in this chapter.

The following goal exercises will walk you through a goal-setting process. Again, we have included exercises that will expand your thoughts and then prioritize them. You will be looking at your life, at this point in time, by general categories with work/career being only one of them in "Goal Setting by Life Category." You will be asked to write your thoughts about work/career, money, lifestyle/possessions, relationships, creative self expression, fun and recreation, personal growth, and health.

The second exercise is a visual representation, a Wheel of Life, with each category from the Goal Setting by Life Category exercise in pie-shaped wedges. The purpose of this exercise is to assess your current level of satisfaction with each area. You may also want to indicate the amount of time you are spending on each area. When completing these exercises, you will have an enhanced consciousness of the areas of your life, their importance to you, and the amount of time you spend on them.

Those exercises are followed by one that will help you prioritize what you have learned, focus on the changes you want to make in your life, and state these changes in the form of goal statements. This exercise, "Goal Setting: Lifetime Goals," was created by Alan Lakien. To help you get to the core of how you want to spend your life, he asks questions related to time periods. "What are your lifetime goals? How would you like to spend the next three years? If you knew now that you would be struck by lightning six months from today, how would you live until then?" Lakien and every other goals expert stresses the importance of writing down your goals. In addition, he feels you can tap into your intuitive side by writing within a limited time period. At the end of the exercise, you are asked to choose your most important goals and prioritize them.

TIPS FOR WRITING YOUR GOALS

When you write your goals there are several points to keep in mind.

1. Write your goals down on paper as specifically as possible. A goal committed to paper becomes a concrete expression of your intentions.

2. State goals in the positive, as something you want, not something you want to leave behind; you can even state it as a goal you have already attained. "I am the vice president of marketing for a high-tech company."
3. Make your goals realistic, challenging but not discouraging. Goal setting is not supposed to put you on a guilt trip or make you depressed.
4. Goals should be measurable so that progress can be noted. Make realistic deadlines so you can anticipate closure.
5. Keep a long-term focus so that you may learn from the setbacks rather than being discouraged.
6. Review your goals regularly; goals are a work in progress and will naturally need modifications.
7. Prioritize your goals, over and over.
8. Celebrate your successes.

The next step in your goal-setting process is to compose action steps that will make your goals a reality and increase balance in your life. Action steps are concrete things that you can do. They prevent you from setting goals that will make you feel helpless. If you can't write action steps for attaining your goal, it isn't a proper goal for you at this time in your life. Writing down action steps for each goal is a necessary grounding activity; you will always know what you are supposed to be working on. Activities from this list can be included in your ongoing weekly list of things to do. You will have things to check off and feel rewarded.

Presumably one of your most important goals is getting a new job, changing careers, trying to figure out what graduate program would be best for you, or exploring the vocational world to identify options for yourself. This book will help you with all the action steps. For example:

Goal: I want to be a pediatrician for a family practice in rural Vermont by the time I am thirty.
Action Steps:

1. Study the industry of health care.
2. Learn everything about being a family practitioner.
3. Talk to a pediatrician in rural family practice.
4. Compare and contrast the various medical school programs.
5. Go to medical school.

6. Check out the economy and opportunities in Vermont and similar rural settings.
7. Find specific job opportunities.
8. Write resume and cover letters.
9. Interview for the job. Negotiate a salary and benefits package.
10. Take the job and prepare for the next.

Within each action step can be a number of other action steps. You will get plenty of help in Part IV of this book. Writing down your goals and action steps at each point in the process will very likely ensure that they will happen. In addition, you will be able to measure your progress, stay focused on the long-range goal and ultimately be celebrating your success.

We recommend that you keep a notebook in which you write your goals in the form of a working draft. Goal statements, if they are any good, are always an ongoing process. They will evolve as you gather more information and as major changes occur in any area of your life and in the lives of people close to you. If one of your goals is not serving you, it is okay to give it up.

Repeating the goal-setting process at least once a year is a good idea; many people use their birthday as a reminder. You may want to set goals once, twice, or three times a year, which is terrific. You may want to have an overall plan for your life and, in addition, set specific goals for yourself each week or each day. The process of goal setting is the same at any level. These intermediary goal-setting activities should not interfere or conflict with your overall lifetime goals. Rather, they will enhance the original list.

When you finish the exercises in this chapter, you will have an overall working plan, focusing on the changes you want to make in your life. This plan will result in easier decision-making and consequently better time management. Reward yourself each time you accomplish an action step. You deserve it! Before you know it, you will have attained your goals.

If you would like to read more about goal setting, there are some excellent sites on the Internet. A wonderful site is from Australia and the goals section is called "If It's to Be, It's Up to Me" at *http://www.smc.qld.edu.au/goals.htm.* "The 7 Steps to Creating Powerful Written Goals" by Gene Donohue cuts right to the chase. He will also also email a "Personal Achievement Quote of the Day!" if you want to subscribe. I enjoy it. You will find his site at *http://www.topachievement.com/.*

BOX 4.1   GOAL SETTING BY LIFE CATEGORY

1. Very quickly write down what you would do to change or improve circumstances immediately in each area of your life.
2. Then write a detailed paragraph about the ideal circumstances for each area. Dare to dream. Explore in fullness your desires.

   Work and Career
   Money
   Creative Self-Expression
   Relationships
   Health
   Personal Growth
   Fun and Recreation
   Lifestyle/Possessions
   Other

(Adapted from *Creative Visualizations* by Shakti Gawain.)

Figure 4.1   Wheel of Life (Adapted from *The Coaches Training Institute.*)
The eight sections in the wheel of life represent balance. Visualize the center
of the wheel as 0 and the outer edge as 10, and rank your level of satisfaction
with each area by drawing a line to create a new outer edge. The new perim-
eter of the circle represents balance. How bumpy would the ride be if this
were a real wheel? Draw a second line to indicate how much effort you devote
to this now. Then create an action plan to increase your satisfaction in those
areas most important to you right now.

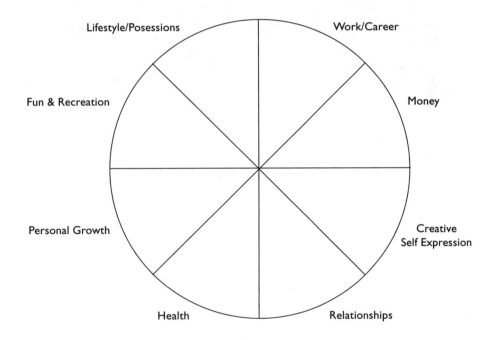

BOX 4.2   GOAL SETTING: LIFETIME GOALS

Give yourself two minutes to answer the first question. Your immediate response is valuable. Then take another two minutes to make any revisions necessary to make the statements feel right to you. Go through the same process for questions #2 and #3. Then prioritize your listings in #4.

1. What are your lifetime goals?
2. What are your 3- to 5-year goals?
3. What do you want to accomplish in the next six months?
4. Go through your goals statements for the first three questions and develop a priority listing. What is most important to you?

(Adapted from *How to Get Control of Your Time and Life* by Alan Lakein.)

CHAPTER

5

Pulling Together Your Profile:
A Mandala for Success

"There is one elementary truth, the ignorance of which kills countless ideas and splendid plans: that the moment one definitely commits oneself, then Providence moves too. All sorts of things occur to help one that would have never otherwise occurred. I have learned a deep respect for one of Goethe's couplets:

'Whatever you can do or dream, you can, begin it.
Boldness has genius, power and magic in it.'"

W. H. Murray

The focus of this book, thus far, has been on finding and redefining "right livelihood" as a vehicle for self-realization, fulfillment, and economic independence. The culmination of the process of self-assessment is to create a new definition of yourself and this chapter provides you with the opportunity to reflect again, reprioritize your core criteria, and create a visual profile that is truthful and accurate. What does this new definition of you look and feel like? Now is the time to find out.

We have chosen the multifaceted mandala with four quadrants at the core for you to fill in your criteria. Mandala is a Sanskrit word meaning center, or circle. It conveys the notion that any center is tied to its circumference and any circumference is always determined by its center. Together they represent wholeness. (See Figure 5.1 at the end of this chapter.) In the upper left quadrant you will record the information about **what** you like to do and do well. It will hold your functional/transferable skills and your multiple skill sets, your special knowledge areas and your career management competencies. The lower left quadrant will contain all the information you have gathered about the structure, the environment, and the setting **where** you will do your best work. In the lower right quadrant you will record the information describing the kinds of people, their characteristics and values that best define **who** you enjoy working with. And finally, in the upper right quadrant you will record your insights about **why** you do what you do, the rewards and aspirations that will give purpose and create a sense of fulfillment.

Your one-page personal profile defines the conditions that will nurture you in work, make you eager to get to work each morning, and feel exhilarated intellectually and mentally at the end of the day. Most people spend more waking hours in their job than in any activity. If you work in an environment that only takes from you, an environment that requires you to give in ways untrue to your sense of self, you will be exhausted. Many people have very well-paying jobs with lots of security that leave them lifeless, uninspired, and tense at the end of the day. However, if you commit to the criteria in your profile while choosing your work, the opposite will occur. You will perform your responsibilities, **and** you will also be receiving a great deal personally from your job, colleagues, and setting. You will feel enriched rather than empty, have the energy to perform well, and also have a life after work.

You may use the mandala design provided at the end of this chapter or you may create your own. We have had clients return their profiles on one page of paper in outline form, in a ten-page poem, as a quilt, as web pages, as interactive multimedia games, and as paintings. Whatever works for you is just fine, and we encourage it, but a summary on one page in addition to the work of art is very useful. This one-page profile will be a definition of who you are in terms of your skills, strengths, values, and goals. The mandala will provide the criteria by which you will judge and choose work opportunities and puts you in charge of key compromises inevitable in any job search. The mandala will provide you with the blueprint of what you need to feel fulfilled and continue the journey for this life work transition.

WHAT DO I LIKE TO DO? (UPPER LEFT QUADRANT)

Turn to Chapter 2 and review your final list of your **Functional/Transferable Skills** sets (refer to Figure 2.1). How do they look? Do they present you accurately? Are they a true, honest, and sincere expression of what you do best? It is permissible to alter or change your skills list now based on insights from this process. For example, review the Fantasy Work Day Exercise in Box 3.4 and look at any indispensable (I) criteria you identified that reflects your interest in what you do, what you work with, and so on. Should this information be incorporated? This kind of flexibility exists now and throughout the remainder of this process. What about the **Special Knowledge** areas? (Refer to Figure 2.1.) List those areas of expertise that you bring to the table. Test yourself by asking, "Is this the kind of knowledge and expertise I want to further develop and hone through my life work?" List these now. You should also list out the **Career Management Competencies** that will bring added value to the workplace. While you are reviewing this list, be sure to select a Training Goal from the list of skills to be developed from Figure 2.1 and place at the bottom of your mandala in the appropriate place.

Congratulations, you have just created a current and comprehensive profile of your skills, knowledges and abilities that you can rearrange into multiple portfolios to bring to the workplace.

WHERE WILL I DO MY BEST WORK? (LOWER LEFT QUADRANT)

Now let us turn our attention to listing the criteria that will define the ideal work setting, and the kind of structure and support you need to do your best work. In the lower left quadrant you will record the information that will describe your preferences about working conditions and workplace values. Turn to Chapter 3 to review and select the criteria that will describe your preferences in the categories listed. Use these categories as guidelines for completing this quadrant of your mandala and use your imagination to envision the ideal setting. Many times clients ask us to be more specific about what information goes where in this final mandala. But let us say, once again, that it is not easy to tie up a values package. We invite you to return to the simple question of **where** will I do my best work and get grounded while sorting through your information. Be sure to refer to your MBTI results to fill in additional criteria that seem important to you at this point.

- **Emotional Climate:** Describe here your preferred style of leadership in relation to such issues as autonomy, authority, personal and professional ethics, the morale of the place, and so on. Refer to Chapter 3 and the results of your MBTI.

- **Work Environment:** Describe here the factors that contribute to a harmonious, supportive work environment, such as a flexible schedule, the pace of work, etc. Refer to Chapter 3.
- **Structure of Authority:** List here the information that describes how you like to work in relation to others, your criteria that will define the right amount of structure, control, deadlines, and access to resources. Refer to Chapter 3 and the results of your MBTI profile.
- **Physical Environment:** Describe here the length of commute, the location and description of the physical setting, your preferences about travel, hours, and so on.

By defining all the characteristics in the these areas you will have the criteria you need to recognize and assess the ideal corporate culture when you see it. Since this area is so difficult to define, it is especially important that you be clear about the information so you can be flexible and open in how you interpret it and make decisions. In Chapter 9, "Winning the Interview" we discuss how to gather information about the culture of the organization.

WHO DO I ENJOY WORKING WITH AND/OR SERVING?
(LOWER RIGHT QUADRANT)

In the lower right quadrant we want you to review and record the criteria that best describe you, because your personality factors are an important part of this quadrant. To complete the category **Personal Style**, look at your Adaptive Skills in Figure 2.1 and review the traits from your MBTI profile. List your best traits in this quadrant so they will be recognized and validated by others. Then look at Chapter 3 for the criteria you used to describe colleagues and clients and your relation to them and record them as your **Preferred People Characteristics.** Refer to Chapter 3 to select the **Values** that must be reflected in your ideal setting.

WHY DO I DO IT? (UPPER RIGHT QUADRANT)

And finally, this rich upper right quadrant must be filled with a myriad of information about what inspires and rewards you. Think of these factors that will provide meaningful **rewards** in terms of **intangibles**—the values and motivators such as recognition, sense of accomplishment, being able to influence others, intellectual status—and the **tangibles**, such as salary, profit and gain, and the chance to turn out quality work.

Refer to Chapter 3 and the results of your MBTI. Do you have certain ethics or beliefs that must be incorporated as a **Mission/Purpose** in your work? Review the exercises in Chapter 3 and record your personal purpose statement from Box 3.8. Do you want to work for an organization that serves a mission that is dear to your heart? Refer to Chapter 3 and record what is important to you. Look at and record the results of What Needs Doing in Your World.

This brings to a conclusion the creation of your personal mandala with the physical, emotional, and spiritual criteria that will help you determine your optimal work opportunity. To reassure yourself of the usefulness of your mandala, compare the criteria with a job or accomplishment you loved and with one that was not a good experience. For the position you loved, you will see that a high percentage of your criteria were fulfilled. For the job you didn't like, you will see that a lower percentage of your criteria were met, and you will be tempted to ask yourself, "Why did I take that job?" If you follow the process in this book and commit to the criteria in your personal profile, you will never ask that question again because you will be aware and in charge.

From now on, you will test each position you consider with/against the criteria in your personal profile. It will keep you on course with your values and goals. Positions rarely yield 100 percent satisfaction; after all, life is a series of compromises. For example, you may give up location for a position offering growth or you may take a job with tuition reimbursement even though the skills required in your job are not in your most enjoyed skills list. However, most importantly, you will know exactly why you have compromised and will never ask yourself, "Why did I take that job?" The best jobs for you will be the ones that closely match your personal profile.

ADDITIONAL INFORMATION

This one-page summary would not be complete without a review and recording of your goals. We have already asked you to record **Training Needs** that will ensure that you are prepared for your next step. Now identify an **Immediate Goal** from Box 4.2 that will keep you focused on what needs to happen in the immediate future to ensure the fulfillment of your life work objective. As we mentioned in the Chapter 4, it is important to identify your immediate priorities in order to focus your attention to proceed. What are your short-range, immediate six- month goals?

Refer to Box 4.2 to identify a **Long-Range Goal** that may provide additional focus and direction for determining your life work objective. Is there some area of your life you need to have in balance before you can begin the next phase of your job search? If so, refer to the Wheel of Life in Figure 4.1 and list an area as a **Personal Priority.** You will want to keep this area in focus as you begin the all-important job search exploration process in Part IV.

And finally, this profile would not be complete without a picture of your **Interest Areas.** List five areas of major interest that you identified in Chapter 3 from the Career Interest Game, as well as the vocational areas that interest you from your MBTI/Keirsey profile.

CREATING A LIFE WORK OBJECTIVE

Now that you have all the criteria of your personal profile on one page, we are going to ask you to distill this information further and write your Life Work Objective (LWO). This functional and organizational definition will be qualified by people, place, and purpose. It will answer the following heart-centering questions:

What do you most want to do?
Where will you be best supported physically, emotionally, and
     spiritually?
Who do you want to work for and with?
Why do you want to work?

Here are some examples of life work objectives.

I want to use my *advising and counseling* skills to *help people with health related issues in my own business* where my colleagues are *other independents*, my work space is *at home in a newly renovated guest room* and my values for *family, autonomy, and helping society* will be honored.

I want to use my *accounting and interpersonal skills* to *help clients with financial planning* in a *small consulting firm* where my colleagues would include *a lawyer and a financial analyst*, my work space would *be cheerful and organized*, and where my values of *working with others, profit gain, and recognition* would be fulfilled.

I want to use my *organizational and planning* skills to *efficiently manage employees and the production of new computer appli-*

cations in a *fast-paced high-tech* company, where my colleagues are *smart, laid back, and lots of fun,* my work space *is centrally located so that I can always know what is going on,* and my values of *profit gain, knowledge, and leadership* will be fulfilled.

Using the criteria from your personal profile, please fill in the blanks for two life work objectives. Let your personal profile guide you; consider the data you have accumulated and reviewed as an internal blueprint of what you need to satisfy you. We recommend writing two statements, one that represents your dream but may be a little ambitious at this point and, an alternative that would be "good enough" but not necessarily perfect. We recommend you consider Plan A as a passion or mission that poses a real stretch in the world of work, while Plan B represents very satisfying work that allows attending to the passion in other ways. The two statements could also represent seemingly opposite directions. Both alternatives can and should be explored.

1. I want to use my _____skills to_____in a _____company/organization where my colleagues are _____, my work space is _____, and my values of _____ will be fulfilled.
2. I want to use my _____skills to_____in a _____company/organization where my colleagues are _____, my work space is_____, and my values of _____ will be fulfilled.

Please feel free to amend the suggested sentence in any way that works for you. Some clients like to write paragraphs rather than one sentence. If you are already at the point where you can create a life work objective that is very specific with a job title and the names of a couple of companies you would consider, do so. The point is to begin a draft objective that will give you direction in your exploration of work and your subsequent job search. With additional information you will gather in the next phase, you will be writing and rewriting your objective with more focus and additional specifics. It is an ongoing process until your life work objective is realized.

Your inner reflection has lead you to the point where you can trust your intuition to proceed. Relax and affirm the rightness of your choices. Perhaps seek input from interested others. But basically, trust yourself and this process enough to make the decision to move on to the next phase of exploration as we approach the world of work.

Figure 5.1   My Personal Mandala

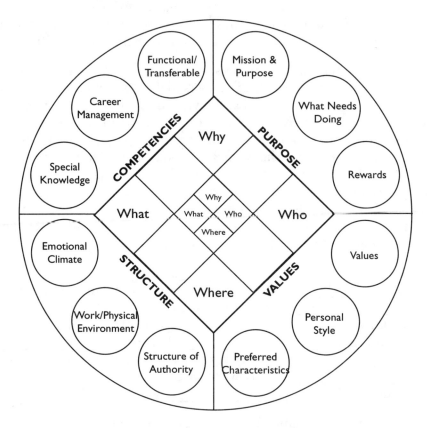

Additional Information

MBTI Type:

MBTI Careers:

Brain Dominance Profile:

Holland Interest Areas:

Goals – Immediate:

Goals – Long Range:

Goals – Training:

Personal Priority:

IV

PART FOUR

Putting Your Spirit to Work in the Marketplace: Making the Connection

It is easy to feel overwhelmed by the marketplace or by doomsday predictions if one is unclear about work and purpose. The marketplace is getting bigger and more unwieldy while the global village is shrinking, and the expanding virtual community is providing more opportunities or access than ever before. But it won't matter if you don't know what you are looking for; you may only be more overwhelmed. If you haven't a clue as to what you're supposed to be doing, or what is worth doing, or what needs doing, then the opportunities literally exist in a vacuum.

But with our definition of work—as meeting unmet societal needs—you will discover that within every idea you can possibly conceive there is a universe of work. Thus, as you proceeded through the self-assessment process, defining your unique skills, talents, interests, and values, you also identified a myriad of needs, ideas, possibilities, and concerns. Whether your interest is in demographics, saving the planet, communicating effectively with others, designing the perfect teapot, or helping the elderly, each idea is the opening to a new world of work. The more precisely you define your interests, the more efficiently you can target a new galaxy of work opportunities. With your personal mandala completed, the opportunity to find "true north" is expanded enormously.

The new age and its expanded use of technology holds the promise of powerful paradigm shifts in how the marketplace is viewed and constructed. The marketplace offers new examples of creative career opportunities in the expanding market for artists using technology to design web pages and to create exciting visual statements to market products and services. Likewise, the fields of health care, education, and library research have expanded as technology offers new possibilities for finding or creating meaningful work. Societal and cultural issues about how our organizations are run and how the inhabitants of planet earth are fed, clothed, and housed are being impacted by the technological revolution. The Y2K challenge offers endless opportunities for important community-based work to be performed. Paradigms shift when beliefs change. Every day a new technological breakthrough changes the fabric of our world. When enough individuals share a vision of what "could be" (which is the result of asking the question "What matters to me?") and are willing to take personal responsibility for being on purpose, then serendipitous connections and breakthroughs for meaningful activity can occur.

Learning to use the Internet efficiently by visiting the preselected sites included in this book will give you the confidence to explore your fields of interest and discover the places where your "deep gladness" can be met and you can be most effective. Through the **high-touch techniques** of informational interviewing and networking you will be able to gather information to make thoughtful and conscious decisions. Through the **high-tech tools** introduced, you will master the Internet search as you visit the suggested sites for every step of the job search process.

First targeting the broadest possible range of opportunities, you will then narrow and refine your life work objective as you gather more specific information about the world of work. With our systematic process you can master the use of the Internet, learn the latest, most reliable research tools, while developing the ability to proactively explore any area of interest. First, you will explore the **lay of the land** using networking sessions; then you will **verify your in-**

terests with informational interviews; and finally shift gears into **getting the job**. Using the forums found at your professional association sites, and meeting with people in your field of interest will validate much of the printed information you discover. These individuals may help you identify specific openings in the "hidden job market," but they will also hopefully become colleagues and part of your ongoing personal/professional network.

Let us refer once again to our four-part model as we make the bridge from the inner exploration (resulting in your personal mandala) to the outer exploration of the world of work. Chapter 6, "Exploring the Wide World of Work through the Internet," presents an action plan for you to begin your external exploration. Through a systematic nine-step approach you will gather the information you need to match the four quadrants in your personal mandala. By visiting the specific steps in Chapter 6 for research purposes in general, and then specifically for job search purposes in Chapter 7, you will be exploring your targeted world of work.

The first area you will try to match is careers and functions with your description of **what** you like to do. Then you will want to explore how the structure and environment of different functions and vocational areas match your preferred working conditions and environment defining **where** you will do your best work. Next you will review and match the characteristics of the people and the values you hope to have met through networking and informational interviewing. **Who** are the people that enliven this field? Would you like spending time with them? And finally you will attempt to find a match between what you will find meaningful and rewarding by exploring the vision and mission of the company or the profession you have identified. You will have found the "right fit" with an opportunity when your reasons for doing **why** you do what you do will be fulfilled. You will know when you are at "true north" when most of the aspects of the new opportunity match your profile.

As you explore the marketplace you will learn everything you need to know about your chosen area of interest. As you begin to exchange ideas, you establish an energy field. As your interest deepens, you will find yourself getting more excited. As the field begins to respond to you and your energy, especially if there is a positive connection, you will begin to generate more energy. Soon you will find yourself being replenished by it. The exploration, when it becomes real enough, results in the actual exchange of money in terms of a paid opportunity or whatever else one has defined as valuable.

The fulfillment of one's life work grows out of this developmental exchange of ideas, energy, and intention. Intention will take you there. Purpose and interests define the marketplace. Energy is the journey. As the global village gets smaller through the Internet, you can specialize your market even further, thereby increasing the chances of finding the "perfect opportunity." Defining and pursuing what you truly love provides ongoing, deepening self-awareness and actualization. The possibilities for personal growth and transformation are endless, as you will see. As you enter the marketplace you are called to reveal your true self. Can you ask questions about meaning and purpose? Can your personal values be met and rewards achieved? Are you interested and challenged by the industry issues? Do you like the people you've met? Is truth spoken here? As you self-actualize through your individual journey, you will find yourself spiritualizing the marketplace.

The remaining chapters in this section will lead you through the process of validating your interests as they appear on your one-page summary. You will learn how to put yourself on paper and write a resume that will effectively introduce you to the marketplace. You will learn how to search the Internet for potential occupations that reflect your unique skills and interests. You will learn the essentials of interviewing for information and for the job. You'll remain in charge of the exchange of information, from negotiation, to turning down offers that aren't correct for you and beginning the new job with the right approach and attitude. Good luck on your journey. It provides a wonderful new opportunity to present yourself to the world of work and address the issues you are uniquely qualified to meet.

6

Exploring the Wide World of Work through the Internet

"For every idea, there is a universe of work."

Sandra Butzel

In Chapter 5 you completed a life work objective. Many clients have said to us, "This statement really sums up who I am, but how is it going to get me a job?" In this chapter we will help you refine your life work objective in a way that combines the rich internal personal information with the language of the real world of work.

Often clients come through our doors knowing what they want personally but tell us that they do not know enough about "what's out there" to put together a coherent strategy for a job search. Others come to us stuck, and say they haven't a clue about where to look or what to consider. There are many ways you can find out "what's out there," which we will be happy to share, and the Internet will be your best friend.

The content of this chapter is exploratory in nature. Please visit the web sites, hot linked on our Web page, *http://www.life worktransitions. com*, as you read the text and follow the directions for navigating the site to important information. This kind of guided practice will steadily increase your confidence and comfort level in using the Internet. It will also familiarize you with sites that you will be using in more detail when you shift gears and transition from exploring the world of work to actually applying for the perfect job and selling yourself to an employer.

We want you to begin the process by having some fun becoming savvy about the wide world of work (www). At this point, don't narrow yourself to a particularly focused or specific area; keep an open mind to the endless possibilities of the world of work. Read the business section of your newspaper and discover what is exciting and changing in your business community. You will find out about the latest merger, employment forecasts for your area, who are the new CEOs and the names of the up and coming companies. Flip through *Business Week*; it is the *Time* magazine of business magazines with lots of pictures and headlines, or check it out online at *http://www.businessweek.com/*. Take a look at *Ad Week* at *http://www.adweek.com/*; its articles and job postings give you a feel for where the action is, and it now has an online Classifieds Search. List the objects you use each day (i.e., computer, toaster, car, office equipment, newspaper, stock report) and think of the companies that manufacture or service them; go to their Web pages; more often than not, there are job openings posted. Study job trends and the labor market through the links at *http://www.bls.gov/news.release/ecopro.toc.htm*. Go to *Money Magazine* to see the "Fifty Hottest Jobs in America" at *http://www.carmelmiddle.org/olclass/math/jobs.html*. Browse the list of occupational titles in the Occupational Outlook Handbook at *http://stats.bls.gov/ocohome.htm*. Think of any idea that interests you and then ponder the concept, "For every idea, there is a universe of work." Play this game with your friends, and you will come up with all sorts of ideas.

For example, we had one client who had strong generalist skills and only one interest that revealed any kind of passion—horses. We took her to the computer and Internet and plugged in the word "equestrian" in one of the search engines. Thousands of possibilities came up: horse riding schools, horse breeding farms, horse riding clothes and equipment—the manufacturers, retailers, and catalog trade, journals and magazines about horses, art collections around horses, gaming, horse riding vacations, the whole business and culture of horse racing, and on and on. All of the ideas require people with a variety of skill sets in paid jobs to make them happen. Our client went from a blank state of mind to a list to research that could have been overwhelming if she had not had her personal profile/mandala to help her sort out the best possibilities for her within the equestrian industry. Believe it or not, there is even a job and resume posting site for people who want to work with or around horses, *http://www.equimax.com*. If we could come up with so many employment possibilities connected with horses, think of what you could do with marketing, health care, software, or environmental safety.

BOX 6.1   CAUTION: WHAT IF YOU NEED A JOB ASAP?

It is important for you to realize that this is not the time for you to be applying for jobs unless you are desperate and cannot go without income. In that case, make good use of the temporary agencies, including the speciality ones that now exist for almost every expertise: executive temps, accountemps, temporary physicians, temporary architects, temporary graphic artists. Check out *http://www.dbm.com/jobguide/misc.html#temp* at The Riley Guide for a listing of general temp agencies. Click on <u>Temporary Services Firms from Yahoo</u> for a list of specialized temporary agencies. Working in temporary assignments may also give you an opportunity to explore an interest.

If there is a specific company you would like to pursue, call its human resources department and ask which temporary agency it uses. Then sign up with that agency and specify that you would be interested in positions in that company. Sometimes it is a good idea to take a lateral move as a "holding" job, something that won't require a lot of energy in terms of a steep learning curve, but will provide the income you need, and still allow you to continue your exploration and search for a position that will be fulfilling in every way. You may want to go forward to the Job Search chapter (Chapter 7) for further strategies to use at this time.

NINE STEPS FOR IDENTIFYING OPTIONS USING THE INTERNET

Although it is great fun surfing the Internet and brainstorming with friends to find out what's out there, there are also systematic approaches to answering the question. We have outlined such an approach in nine steps. You can start your research with any of the nine steps, but we recommend proceeding through the following steps in the order listed. They take you from the general to the specific aspects of the world of work.

1. Your Personal Profile and Objective Statements.

Look at your one-page personal profile and your life work objective statements. What are the clues? What directions do you see in terms of what you want to do and where? Your goal is to discover and **define where your interests, skills, and values intersect with the world of work.**

2. Industries.

e.g., Health, Education, Manufacturing, Finance/Banking, Agriculture, Recreation and Leisure, Hospitality, Government, Information Technology, Toys, Cars, Academic Areas, Self-Improvement, Entertainment

First, cast a wide net to explore industries. There is one huge directory of companies grouped by industry at Yahoo *http://dir.yahoo.com/ Business_and_Economy/Companies/* that will expose you to the whole world of work. Print out this page and study it carefully. Choose five areas or industries that interest you; then verify that these industries have a glowing economic future through several "trends" sites. One that will connect you to a galaxy of information is *http://galaxy.tradewave.com/ galaxy/Business-and-Commerce.html*, and another great "how-to guide" for industry information sites on the Internet is *http://home.sprintmail. com/~debflanagan/industry.html*.

3. Information from Assessment and Internet Tests.

Review your MBTI/Keirsey results from Chapter 1 and the Career Interests Game in Chapter 3. If you haven't taken them, do so now. The Keirsey Temperament Sorter can be taken at *http://keirsey.com/frame. html*, and you will find your corresponding occupational profiles at *http://www.doi.gov/octc/typescar.html*. Holland's Career Interests Game is at *http://www.missouri.edu/~cppcwww/holland.shtml*. Which of the suggested occupations of the Interests Game overlap with those suggested by the Keirsey Temperament Sorter? Which ones seem interesting to you? Check them against the criteria in your personal profile. How do they measure up? Are your ideas becoming clearer? Do you see any patterns emerging? Clues should be building and indicating a direction for you.

At this point, you may have chosen a career field that you feel certain is right for you or you may have several possibilities that you are considering. And there will be a few of you who are just not sure, and would love to hear about more possibilities.

4. Definitions of Career Fields or Vocations.

e.g., Accounting, Counseling, Public Relations, Teaching, Construction, Engineering, Consulting, Administration, Sales, Marketing, Communication, Graphics, Advertising, Human Resources

In order to increase your exposure to a variety of vocations or test the ones that interest you, proceed to *http://www.uhs.berkeley.edu/career*

library/links/career.cfm, Berkeley's Career Exploration Library. You will see a rather short list of industries or categories; don't let that fool you. Click on the one that interests you most, and you will discover possibilities that never occurred to you. One of my clients was searching for an occupation that would be out-of-doors and allow him to live in a warm climate. Under the Agriculture category, we found information about "A Career in Golf Course Management." It had an education and an informational icon beside it; we printed out the information, and he left my office thrilled. Use the "go back" arrow at the top left-hand side of your browser and visit other career areas at this site.

Three other career overview sites are worth a visit. Yahoo's Career Fields directory is located at *http://www.yahoo.com/Business_and_Economy/ Employment/Jobs/Career_Fields/*. A really upbeat and smart site is *http:// jobsmart.org/tools/career/spec-car.htm*. Click on <u>Media</u> and then <u>Motion Picture Information</u>. If you love movies, dream on. A standard reference guide is the *Occupational Outlook Handbook*. For years it has been the definitive source for both vocational interests and job title information. It can be found in text at your library or at *http://stats.bls.gov/ocohome. htm* on the Net. Click on the <u>Occupational Clusters</u> or try the <u>index</u>. You will visit the *Occupational Outlook Handbook* several times during your research. You should be getting a sense that every career exploration site has a slightly different orientation and look, but all work very well together as a cross reference.

5. Specific Job Titles.

e.g., Director of Public Relations, Advertising Executive, Product Manager, Accountant, Hospital Administrator, Labor Lawyer, Financial Analyst, Computer Programmer, Web Page Manager

The next step is to research the job titles within your vocational interest so that you can begin to understand the required skills and training. For those of you who enjoy taking tests on the Internet, a terrific instrument is the Birkman Quiz hosted by the Princeton Review site. *http:// www.review.com/birkman/*. This short quiz with twenty-four questions gives you results telling you about your interests and style. Interests describe the type of activities you are drawn to, and style describes strengths that you could bring to a work environment when you are at your best. The quiz also links you to appropriate job titles on Princeton Review's Career Search database at *http://www.review.com/career*. Click on <u>Search</u> under Seek and Ye Shall Find. With each job title, you will get a fabulous description of the job, It's Daily Life, Paying Your Dues, Something to Fall Back On, the Past and the Future, and What to Expect From Your Life.

You can type in any job title in the Career Search window, and you will get the results that most closely match your search words. For example, if you type in "financial analyst," you will find that title exactly, click on it and you will be given a job and career description. But if we try the title "psychiatric social worker," the closest thing in the database is "speech therapist." This database is not all inclusive, but if it has what you are looking for, you will get all the pertinent information you need.

For a less conventional way of learning about job titles, look them up in newspapers. CareerPath *http://www.careerpath.com/* enables you to search several newspapers at one time. Click on the <u>Find a Job</u> button and then the <u>From the Newspaper</u> button. Highlight a field such as advertising and type in Account Executive in the keyword window. Scroll on down the page, and you will find seventy-five newspapers from every big city in the United States. Check the ones that interest you, click the <u>Search</u> button, and you will be pleased with the list that appears. Read a few of the ads, and you will know all about the qualifications necessary for an Account Manager.

You can also look at job postings for particular job titles on any of the major job and resume posting sites on the net, such as *http://www. usnews.com/usnews/nycu/work/wo4find.htm*. An even better idea would be to visit field-specific job posting sites. Go to The Riley Guide, *http://www.rileyguide.com*, and click on <u>Work Opportunities</u>. Look at the selections in <u>Resources for Specific Industries and Occupations</u>. Try clicking on <u>Agriculture-Forestry and Animal Sciences</u>, and you will be very surprised by what an extensive field this is and how many field-specific job posting sites exist on the Internet. There is even a site for weed science called, what else?, WeedJobs! This site is approved by the Weed Science Society of America. The same is true for all the areas. Have fun.

Once again, refine your life work objective so that it responds to the information you are gathering.

6. Professional Associations.

e.g., American Historical Association, Institute of Management Consultants, Association for Multimedia Communications, Association of School Business Officials International

How will you know if you like the people in a particular industry and vocational area? A good way to find out is to look up professional associations related to it at Associations on the Internet at *http://www.ipl.org/ref/AON/* or Yahoo's Professional Organizations Directory *http://www.yahoo.com/Business_and_Economy/Organizations/Professional*. Professional Association home pages provide all kinds of information such as background of the organization, mission and purpose statements, upcoming meetings, newsletters or journals, and very often job postings. Attending a meeting of a professional association will give you a good idea of the kind of people in this vocation and whether or not you would like to work with and for them.

7. Professional Journals or Magazines.

e.g., AdWeek, Journal of Higher Education, Business Week, Modern Hospital, American Scientist, Computer Reseller News

We live in an information-based society necessitating a never-ending learning curve. Professional journals and magazines are a great source for employees trying to stay on top of what's new in their fields. Many of these journals have full text sites on the Internet. My favorite site is *http://www.ecola.com/*, which provides an enormous listing of online newpapers and magazines/journals by topic. I was able to find everything from the *New England Journal of Medicine* to *Fire and Rescue*. Browse for a while. See if you enjoy the required reading of professions that interest you.

8. Educational Requirements and Continuing Education.

e.g., MA in Educator, Executive Development Programs, AA Physical Therapy Assistant, Sales Training Programs, PhD in the Sciences

Besides the required reading for a profession, there may be a required degree or continuing education courses. Research the education required for the job that interests you, which is given at all the vocational interest sites mentioned earlier. Look up educational programs, both undergraduate and graduate, that train for the vocation you are considering. You can also go to *http://www.altavista.com* and type, "What academic institutions offer programs in (whatever interests you)?," in the search window. Almost every college and university is on the Internet, and you can usually guess the address. For example, *http://www.harvard.edu* is Harvard and *http://www.umd.edu* is the University of Maryland. Study the program and course list carefully. Would you like to take the classes? If your immediate reaction is no, pay attention to that. Trust yourself; if none of the information seems interesting, consider other vocational areas. If the training program feels good and fits with the guidance provided by your personal profile, you are definitely on the right track. Go to an open house and meet some of the other people in the same place you are.

9. Specific Companies or Organizations.

e.g., Lotus, AOL, Beth Israel Hospital, AT&T, BankBoston, Fidelity, Gillette, Newtonville Copy Shop, Bloomingdales, Time-Warner, Disney, Harvard

Your life work objective should now contain everything but the specific place you would like to be working. This could be an organization, company, franchise, consulting firm, or your own business. The best sources for researching your targets is to look up the organization's web page. Use your favorite search engine, type in the name of a company in quotes in the Search window, and look for results. You can also go to JobSmart's company information page at *http://jobsmart.org/hidden/coinfo.htm* or Hoover's huge company database at *http://www.hoovers.com*. For a tutorial that will take you through the process of company research step by step, go to *http://home.sprintmail.com/~debflanagan/index.html*.

You now know all of our secrets. We have just outlined how to learn about the world of work. After all this exploration, you should feel very well informed and like a veteran on the Internet. However, if you ever feel lost on the Internet, remember that you can always fall back on the Riley Guide at *http://www.rileyguide.com*. When you get to the site, click on Help with Everything and you will see a text outline of the entire Guide. Even better, click on Quick Index. Whenever I am stumped, I go to the Riley Guide and wonder why I spent so much time searching when Margaret Riley makes is so easy for all of us.

7

The Job Search:
Using the Internet to Set Yourself Up
for Success

"You can't count on getting today's jobs with yesterday's
search techniques."   *Joyce Lain Kennedy*

In this chapter, we will be addressing the job search within a model
proven to protect you from rejection and set you up for success. Using
all the Internet skills you have accumulated so far and some new ones
introduced in this chapter, you will be able to turn your life work objective into reality.

THE THREE-STAGE JOB SEARCH PROCESS

Think of this model in three stages. The first stage is **Getting the Lay of
the Land,** gathering all the information you can acquire through research in the library, the Internet, and contacts made through professional associations, alumni, and friends. The type of interviewing used
at this stage is **networking**. The second stage is a conscious effort on
your part to make sure you have chosen the right position, **Verifying and
Validating Your Interest.** This means talking to someone at a collegial
level, a person doing something close to the type of position you are considering. Interviewing at this stage is more formal and is known as an
informational interview. The third stage is when you shift gears and
sell yourself to key decision makers—**Finding, Applying, and Getting**

the Job. At this stage you implement a strategy for identifying job openings and prepare for the important **job interview**.

This model recognizes that researching for information and connecting with people are inextricably intertwined. As a result, we will be discussing networking and informational interviewing in the context of the three-stage model. For teaching purposes, we have chosen a sample life work objective to use as a case study to illustrate how to use the Internet in each step to success. The steps work with any life work objective. The only difference would be substituting the relevant data (industry, vocational area, job title, professional organization, etc.) from your life work objective instead of those from the sample life work objective.

THE STEPS TO SUCCESS FOR GETTING
THE LAY OF THE LAND

In this stage you will be employing many of the research techniques and Internet sites we discussed in the last chapter, but this time you will be approaching a specific target rather than browsing for information and ideas. Gathering all the information you need for your job search is not rocket science or magic; it can be accomplished by using tried and true research methods in a systematic, logical way. We will be going from the general to the specific, the big picture to the details, in a series of research steps that utilize the power and connectivity of the Internet. This systematic approach will make you comfortable with your choices and prepare you for conversation with professionals in your vocational area.

Turn on your computer and go to our Web site *http://www.lifework transitions.com* so that you can easily go to the recommended Web sites as you read the text.

1. The first step is to look at your **personal profile** and remind yourself of your true north. Then review your life work objective for the specifics in the world of work. Our case study life work objective is:

> I want to be a human resources manager for a health maintenance organization with a good reputation for service and located near my home. I want to use my functional transferable skills in counseling and management as well as special knowledge human resources skills. This kind of position would satisfy my values of service to others and preventive health care.

2. Review the overall **trends of your chosen industry** (e.g., health care). The industry in our sample life work objective is health care, so the first thing to do is check out the trends and forecasts for that industry. In the last chapter we mentioned several web sites for looking at the broad picture, and in this chapter we are going to another excellent site, *http:// www.Hoovers.com,* to look for Hoover's snapshot of the health care industry. This page is a little tricky to navigate. When you get to Hoover's home page, look for Hoover's Features and click <u>Industry Zone</u>. On the next page, look for Industry Sectors and click <u>Health Care Products and Services</u>, and the <u>Go</u> button. On the next page, click <u>Health Care Services</u>. A very good snapshot of health care services will appear with valuable links within the article, a chart showing the National Health Services expenditures, Inside Track links, and links to News and Features. You will have all the information you need to determine whether or not the trends for health care are promising. If you want more information, try Fuld & Company at *http://www.fuld.com/i3/index.html* and Dow Jones Business Directory at *http://businessdirectory.dowjones. com/* and search for Health Care.

3. Study the outlook for your chosen **vocational area**. (e.g., human resources). The next step in getting the lay of the land is to learn about the vocational area of human resources. We mentioned several sites for vocational exploration in the last chapter. In this chapter, we are going to introduce you to America's Career InfoNet, a complete one-stop career center, at *http://www.acinet.org/acinet/occ_sea1.htm.* On your computer screen, you will see a menu search and a keyword search. Type "Human Resources" into the keyword search window; it will come up in another menu; choose a state and click the <u>Search</u> button. You will see an Occupation Report with human resources wages for your state and for the United States. Trends are also shown for the number of jobs in 1994 and the number expected in 2005.

In the left-hand column or frame there are a number of choices for more information. Click <u>Industry Trends</u>, then <u>Hospitals Public and Private</u>, then the <u>Search</u> button and you will have human resources figures for the health care industry. Click on <u>Detailed Trends</u> and you will have an opportunity to compare the salaries and number of jobs for human resources with another field. Click on <u>Detailed Wages</u>, and you will be able to add a city and get another detailed chart comparing wages. You can also take a look at <u>What it Takes</u> in the left-hand column to discover knowledges, activities, education/training, and web resources for the career field of human resources. This one site, America's Career Info-Net, will give you an enormous amount of information and is a site you will want to use in the future.

4. Job descriptions within your vocational area (e.g., manager in human resources). Although you have knowledge of the trends and forecasts for human resources, you need to know more about the types of jobs within the field. We are going to a site, not listed in Chapter 6, by the Canadian government called Job Futures at *http://www.hrdc-drhc.gc. ca/JobFutures/*. Click <u>English</u>, then <u>Occupational Outlooks</u>, then <u>Alphabetical Index</u>, then <u>H</u>; scroll down to Human Resources where you will have three choices: managers, professionals, specialists. Print out all three, and you will have an excellent definition of the careers/job titles within human resources as well as their outlook and educational requirements. Other sites with occupational definitions are Princeton Review's Career Search at *http://www.review.com/career/*, Berkeley's Career Exploration Library *http://www.uhs.berkeley.edu/careerlibrary/ links/occup.cfm*, and the *Occupational Outlook Handbook* at *http:// stats.bls.gov/oco home.htm*.

5. Identify **professional associations** and **professional journals** related to your vocational area or career field (e.g., human resource professional associations and human resource journals). Keep detailed records of all contacts, potential contacts, and pertinent information that may be of help to you at a later stage of your job search.

Armed with facts and information about human resources, it is time to meet the people in the field and start networking. Professional associations are an excellent avenue, and there are several directories on the Internet. Our first stop will be The Internet Public Library's site *http:// www.ipl.org/ref/AON/* called Associations Online. This search is a little tricky but will be a good learning experience for you. When you type "Human Resources" into the search window, none of the results are appropriate. But if you type in "Personnel," you will have a number of appropriate responses with one of them being the Society for Human Resource Management (SHRM) at *http://www.shrm.org/hrtalk/*. Click on it and you will arrive at an award-winning site with a wide range of free information about human resources, including information about its flagship publication, *HR Magazine*. Read some of the articles. Did you enjoy them? This is the kind of material you will be reading throughout your whole career. To find even more professional journals, go to the Scholarly Societies Project at *http://www.lib.uwaterloo.ca/society/overview.html*.

The SHRM site also includes a list of **local chapters** with contact data. Click on <u>Local</u> <u>Chapters</u>, and find the one in your area. Make contact by phone or email and plan to attend a meeting. Find out if you really like the people you will be working with and for. Collect business cards and get acquainted. You will use these contacts later.

SHRM also has a **forum** called HR Talk. This is an online feature allowing you to share conversation and interests with SHRM members through email. You will be sitting in on conversations with professionals and get a chance to find out if you would enjoy being a colleague. When you first join a forum group, it is best to just read for a while (called *lurking*) before you post any questions. There will also be rules with each forum specifying the type of entry that is welcome. Be sure to read the "Frequently Asked Questions" (FAQs) before you sign up. In SHRM's forum, as in many of the forums sponsored by professional groups, you must join SHRM before being allowed to participate in the forum discussion. This can be a worthwhile investment, but you may want to try HR forums on some of the public sites first.

Mailing lists are similar to forums; they also require you to join before being included and the communication is through email. Check out two excellent mailing list services: The Liszt at *http://www.Liszt.com* and Kovacs List at *http://www.n2h2.com/KOVACS/*. Both offer a well organized and varied selection of lists. Lists are excellent for networking and many clients find them more helpful than newsgroups. In Liszt, for example, there are categories to choose from. Select <u>Business</u> and then <u>Human Resources.</u> There are eleven lists to consider. In addition, you can go to Infoseek and type in "human resources"+chat or "human resources"+newsgroup (be sure to type in the quotation marks), and you will find even more free opportunities to "hear" people in HR talk.

6. Learn the **educational requirements** of your vocational area (e.g., human resources) and research various educational programs. Attend an open house and/or make an appointment with a program director. Again, add information from people to your growing knowledge of the field.

Another way to meet and talk to people in human resources, or any vocational area, is to follow up on the educational requirements. Go to the web site of a college or university near you and research the concentration areas available in its curriculum. If business and human resources is part of its program, contact the admissions or program director and ask for a catalog and/or for an appointment and a schedule of open houses. The open houses provide excellent opportunities for meeting other people interested in human resources. You'll also be able to ask for names of former students, now in the field, who would serve as references for the program. Not only will you find out if the program adequately prepared them for work, but you will be identifying potential colleagues in your future career. Don't forget to contact professors; they are an excellent source of information and can lead to additional contacts, namely their former students.

7. The last step in getting the lay of the land is to **research specific companies** or specific organizations mentioned in your life work objective (e.g., health maintenance organizations).

There are many ways to find information about companies, traditional and not so traditional. The key to success is to think creatively. For example, using any search engine, type in state + "health maintenance organizations." When I tried that, I found the New England Association of Health Maintenance Organizations with all the HMOs listed and links to most of them.

Look up HMOs in your phone book, then type the name of each HMO in the search window of any search engine, for example, Tufts Health Plan. You will find the web site and information about the organization, its history, what it is proud of, and job listings. Excite *http://www.excite.com*, Dogpile *http://www.dogpile.com*, and Yahoo *http://www.yahoo.com* are search engines recognized for the ability to find names of companies on the Internet.

To find out the details and inside story about a company, go to "A Tutorial in Company Research" at *http://home.sprintmail.com/~deb flanagan/index.html* that will walk you through many of the best known sources for research. Deb Flanagan tells you **exactly** what to do, step-by-step, by means of instructions in a left-hand column.

Think backwards; go to several health specific job posting sites and look up profiles of the employers. You can do this by going to The Riley Guide at *http://www.rileyguide.com*. Click Work Opportunities and then look under the heading "Resources for Information for Specific Areas," and click on Health Care or Business. If you choose business, click on Human Resources next. You will see a list of industry-specific job posting sites which will often give you profiles of the employers using that site. For more ideas and web sites for company research, read the information in Step 9 in Chapter 6.

You may also want to check out Bolles research at *http://www.jobhuntersbible.com* and The Riley Guide's "Tell Me About This Employer" at *http://www.dbm.com/jobguide/employer.html*.

Networking

Networking is the appropriate type of interview during the getting the lay of the land phase of the job search. Loosely defined, networking is the process of gaining and sharing information, advice, and support. It can take place anywhere people come together, such as a neighborhood health club, church or synagogue, alumni group, news group, forum, professional organization, or other special interest group. It can also be more focused by creating a contact list, in which you identify everyone you know related to your interest and anyone you know who might know someone else related to your vocational interest. Then diligently contact each person.

How you network depends upon your own personality and style. Some of you will feel perfectly comfortable walking into a room full of strangers and entering into conversation. The same people will not flinch over calling up strangers for information. Not all of us are blessed with such an outgoing nature, and that is okay. If your style is more reflective, you can go to an association meeting and just listen, maybe pick up some information to read, and observe what is going on. At the next meeting, you might feel more like speaking with people. Likewise, instead of picking up the phone right away, you may prefer to write a note first and follow up with a phone call. Know your style, act upon it, and accept yourself. No guilt trips!

The benefits of networking: You will learn more about your potential area of work interest and the people in it. For some of you it can be fun. You will have some sense of control about the job search process because you are taking positive actions rather than waiting for something to come your way. You are making something happen for yourself. Most important, it offers you the opportunity to practice presenting and defining yourself and asking appropriate questions. Doing so is excellent practice for the more important interviews that will follow.

There is a thin line between **networking** and **informational interviewing**. However, in our model, we see networking as appropriate for getting the lay of the land, and informational interviewing as appropriate for verifying your interest. Networking is more casual than informational interviewing. During networking, you are exploring, building layers of information you will use later when you are hosting informational interviews and when selling yourself during a job interview. While networking, if a contact wants to tell you about a job opening or give you the name of a key decision maker, note the information for your records, thank the person for the information, but **hold on**. Too often job seekers talk to important decision makers before becoming thoroughly prepared; this is a big mistake and sabotages your efforts with possibly the most important contact you have made.

Keep a systematic record of your networking contacts, including their names, where you met them, how to reach them, and any pertinent information you might need at a later date. Get into the habit of asking for business cards. If a networking conversation turns into a rather formal occasion, be sure to write a thank you note. When you are in your new job, write a note to all your contacts and let them know the outcome of your search. They will really appreciate your note and in the process will become your colleagues.

And speaking of **systematic records**, it is a good idea to keep some paper records of your job search. While writing this book, I would have been overwhelmed if I hadn't printed out many of the sites on the Internet and put them in folders. The Internet is so vast and exciting that good old paper folders can be very comforting and grounding. So when you find the site of a company that you really want to remember, bookmark it, but don't feel guilty about printing it out and putting it in a folder entitled "Interesting Companies."

When you feel you have a foundation of information including an understanding of your job description, the education required, the normal salary range, the long-range opportunities, an appropriate professional association, the name of journals usually read by people in your field, labor trends and forecasts for your global area of interest, and background information on specific companies or organizations within your area interest, you are ready to move on to the second stage of your job search.

THE STEPS TO SUCCESS IN VERIFYING YOUR INTEREST

1. Utilize all available resources and networking contacts to identify people in your vocation in a position similar to the one you are targeting (e.g., manager of human resources). It is important to talk to someone actually doing what you think you would like to do in order to verify your interest in more detail, up close and personal. Find out if their ex-

perience has been as you thought it would be. You may already have a list of people from your networking to call for a more serious interview. If you haven't compiled your own list, here are some resources you can use to identify people who are currently in positions at or about the level you hope to enter.

Go back to the detailed records you kept while networking. The records will reveal people in the industry, people with knowledge of people in the industry, names you have seen in articles or journals, and names of speakers at association meetings or conferences. You will come up with several ideas of people who could help you find, or introduce you to, someone doing the same thing you want to do. Call them now.

Contact your college or graduate school career services office, a gold mine for contacts that many older job hunters forget. Once a graduate, always a graduate! Conduct a search on its database for names of alumni who are currently working in your vocational area. Talk to professors who teach courses relating to the position or company that interests you, and ask them for names of students currently in the field.

2. Make **appointments** for informational interviews and prepare for the questions you want to ask. Call or write these contacts and ask if they could introduce you to someone in a similar position to the one you are targeting. Follow through and arrange an interview at the other person's convenience for a specified length of time, no more than twenty or thirty minutes. This is an **informational interview** and implies that you have done your homework and will not waste the time of the person gracious enough to see you. Be prepared to present your interests and give some idea of the research you have done before the appointment. Explain that you have learned everything that you could about this position but want to verify that interest by talking to someone already doing that job. Stick to your agenda and be mindful of the time, never exceeding the agreed-on twenty or thirty minutes. Some useful questions are:

1. What has been your experience in this position; what do you do in a typical day?
2. How is the company or department organized? (An organizational chart really helps.)
3. What was the position you had before this one? Are there other entry points?
4. How long do you anticipate being in this position? What is the career path?

5. Where do you see the field in the next few years?
6. What training was most helpful?
7. What advice would you give someone starting out?
8. What professional association is most helpful for networking and professional growth?
9. What professional magazine or journal do you feel is a must?
10. Could you refer me to others in the field who might be helpful?

An excellent and in-depth Internet source for informational interviewing is an "Informational Interview Tutorial," at *http://www.quintcareers. com/informational_interviewing.html.* You will see an outline of subjects covered in the tutorial; scroll down to the bottom and click on the arrow to begin the tutorial. Print it out as you go along if the information seems helpful. If you don't want to go through the entire tutorial, you can click on any subject in the outline and go directly to it. In the middle of the outline is a title "The Interview and the Questions to Ask." It is huge, but worth printing out so that you can pick and choose questions that relate to your particular interview.

The key to the effective use of an informational interview is your own self-confidence and enthusiasm. Think of the other person and create a climate of appreciation, warmth, and trust. Having done your homework, you will be perceived by the other person as genuine and someone who wishes to listen and learn. Most people are willing to help at that level and will share what they know.

It is appropriate, in fact a must, to write a thank you note expressing your genuine appreciation for the time spent with you. You might highlight what information was most helpful or ask a question that occurred to you since the interview. It is perfectly all right to include a resume with your thank you note, adding that the person should feel free to share it if an appropriate opportunity exists.

3. Continue **networking**. Stay active and be seen by professionals in your newly chosen field. Do not stop networking. Continue attending all appropriate association and networking meetings or events. Cruise job fairs for contacts, business cards, and any new information that would be helpful. Make sure you are seen and heard in the marketplace. If you remain interested and enthusiastic about your targeted vocational area and position after several interviews, you are ready for the next stage of the process, applying for the job.

THE STEPS TO SUCCESS FOR APPLYING FOR THE JOB

1. Look at **job postings from a variety of sources**: contacts within the field, job postings found through professional associations, company or organization home pages, college or graduate school career service offices, Top Ten Job Posting Sites cited here in our text, niche/industry specific job posting sites, newspapers, and job posting sites for your state.

Look over your record of **contacts** and determine which ones would be appropriate to approach at this time. This can be done either through a phone call or a note or both. Your agenda now is clearly at a different level; you are not just verifying your interest, you are applying for a job. State that explicitly. Tell them that you would appreciate any help they could give you regarding open or opening positions or names of people that could help you discover and uncover positions.

Review positions posted in **newspapers**. Your paper may have a web site and its classifieds will be accessible through a search menu. Or you can go to CareerPath listed in Box 7.1 and search many newspapers at the same time at *http://www.careerpath.com.*

Read the job postings in **professional journals and professional organizations** in your vocational area. This is an excellent and efficient source because you are targeting your job search by considering listings only in your field (niche or industry-specific postings). You can access these postings either in print, in person, or over the Internet. Internet sites for professional associations include *http://www.ipl.org/ref/AON/* and *http://www.yahoo.com/Business_and_Economy/Organizations/ Professional*; Internet sites for professional journals and magazines include *http://www.ecola.com/*, electronic journals at *http://www. libraries. rutgers.edu/rulib/socsci/busi/busejour.htm*, and scholarly societies projects at *http://www.lib.uwaterloo.ca/society/.*

Go to the **home pages of all the companies** you have targeted or are considering. The fastest way to find them is to type the name of the company in the search window of any search engine. If you don't find it on the first try, go to one of the other search engines. You can also call up the company and ask for its Web address or use one of the many company search possibilities on the Net. Employment opportunities are listed on most company home pages. Additional company research internet sites are Your Town's Business Journal at *http://www.amcity. com/* and Yahoo's Company Research at *http://dir.yahoo.com/Business_ and_Economy/Companies/.*

Contact college or graduate school **career services offices**. They always have lists of positions that have come into their office. Ask for a password to enter JobTrack, *http://www.jobtrack.com*, a very reputable job posting site on the Net which requires a password from your alma mater before you can enter.

Attend **job fairs,** both **real and virtual**. The advantage of a job fair is that it is a one-stop shop. Employers love job fairs, and that is why segments of certain industries are holding virtual job fairs on the Internet. You send in one resume, and many, perhaps hundreds, of companies will receive it. You can type in "Job Fair" or "Virtual Job Fair" (be sure to type in the quotation marks) in any search engine's search window, and you will get a huge listing. If you want to find the job fairs in your city, type "Job Fair"+Your City. Career Mosaic *http://www.careermosaic. com* is a good source for job fairs, so you may want to go there first.

Browse the huge and well-known **job posting sites** on the Internet. There are thousands of other general and niche job posting sites so that if you only surf, the experience can be absolutely overwhelming. In addition, almost every search engine has its own career channel with its own job posting service. And most job posting sites, even those in journals and professional associations, have supporting career resources. There is a danger of information overload. However, do not despair, because we have given you information to help you narrow the list of job search and resume posting sites to a "Top Ten." This list will give you a more targeted search and help you manage your time on the Internet.

There are three excellent sources you can use to review and target job posting sites for yourself. One source is Richard Bolles site *http://www. jobhuntersbible.com*. On his homepage, there are links to <u>jobs</u> and also to <u>counseling</u> as well as several others that you might want to browse at another time. The <u>jobs</u> link takes you to an essay by Bolles and then to job <u>listing sites</u>. We differ with Bolles' rather negative assessment of the Internet, but we admire the depth, scope, and up-to-date information about web sites helpful to career and job seekers. After clicking on <u>job listing sites</u>, you will see a list of reviewed job and resume posting sites. Some of them have parachutes by them, and those are Bolles recommended sites. You cannot go wrong with these sites. You can also click <u>counseling</u> on his homepage, click <u>job hunting</u> and you will find a variety of rich resources to enhance your search.

The second is "Weddles Web Guide" on the *National Business Employment Weekly* web site at *http://www.nbew.com/weddle/index.htm*. The site tells you: who developed the site and when; important data about the listings; what other resources are offered; and the nature of resumes posted on the site.

The third excellent review of job and resume posting sites is a book titled *Careerxroads* and its web site *http://www.careerxroads.com*. Gerry Crispin and Mark Mehler reviewed over 1,000 posting sites, chose the top 500 for 1998, and categorized them by 47 industry and specialty niches. Of the 500, 37 are called "The Best of the Best." All entries are cross-referenced by Career Management, College, Diversity, Industry and Specialty, Jobs, Links, Location, All States, Publications, Push Capability, and Resumes.

If you own the book, you can register with the authors through the email address on their site and get regular email updates. This is a worthwhile investment in your future because it will help you target your job search and therefore save you time.

The sites in Box 7.1 are the best and offer you help in every area of job search. In order to use job posting and resume posting sites, you will need an electronic resume suitable for faxing or pasting into an email document. This is discussed in detail in the next chapter.

BOX 7.1   TOP TEN JOB POSTING SITES

As mentioned before, the Internet is a moving target, so these sites may change. Be sure to check our web site *http://www.lifeworktransitions.com* for the latest. Also, check The Riley Guide at *http://www.dbm.com/jobguide/more.html#guides* for changes and additions.

Name of Site	Internet Address
Monster Board	http://www.monster.com
Career Builder	http://careerbuilder.com
Career Path	http://www.careerpath.com
America's JobBank	http://www.ajb.dni.us/
Job Options	http://www.joboptions.com
Headhunter.Net	http://www.headhunter.net/
Career Mosaic	http://www.careermosaic.com/
Career Web	http://www.careerweb.com/
HotJobs.com	http://www.hotjobs.com
NationJob Network	http://www.nationjob.com/

**BOX 7.2   A SAMPLE OF INDUSTRY-SPECIFIC
JOB POSTING SITES**

Nonprofits	Community Career Center	http://www.nonprofitjobs.org/
Human Resources	Society for HR Mgmt	http://www.shrm.org/jobs/
Social Work	NASW Jobs Online	http://www.naswdc.org/
Medicine	DocJob	http://www.docjob.com/
Accounting	AccountingNet	http://www.accountingnet.com/
Software Engineer	Jobs.Internet.Com	http://jobs.internet.com/
Education	Chronicle of Higher Ed	http://chronicle.com/jobs/
Park Service	Nat'l Pk Service Careers	http://www.nps.gov/pub_aff/jobs.htm
Advertising	Adweek Online	http://www.adweek.com
Telecommuting	Telecommuting Jobs	http://www.tjobs.com/

Box 7.2 contains a listing of some industry-specific job posting sites. More niche or industry-specific job posting sites can be found at *http://www.dbm.com/jobguide/jobs.html.*

To locate **job posting sites for your area of the country**, go to *http://www.dbm.com/jobguide/local.html* where you will be able to see resources in your state.

2. The second step in Applying for the Job is to put your **resume** (Chapter 8) **on the Internet** and sign up with personal agents.

3. The third step is **managing your time** on the Net. One of the dangers of the Net is the temptation to surf for hours without accomplishing much. Set goals for your Internet searches just as you do for the other parts of your life. Also take advantage of services that will assist you on the Net while you are doing something else. Two services that we will be discussing are signing up for personal search agents and using JaveLink.

The first of these services is the "Personal Search Agent" on many job posting sites. Most of the sites on our list have the capability of providing you with this service. You sign up, specify the kind of job you are looking for, and the service will put each new job posting that matches your specifications into an email message. Some services actually "push" the message to your own email at home. Others require you to go to their site, sign in, and then access an email message with all the new postings.

There is also a service called JaveLink, *http://www.javelink.com*, that will go to all your selected personal agent sites, gather the information there, and then "push" all the messages to your email at home. JaveLink will also monitor professional associations that you specify and collect information about upcoming meetings or conferences. You can program JaveLink to keep track of anything on the Net for you. JaveLink can save you time and also remove the temptation to surf the Net for hours.

Another time saver is a job posting site that searches several of the Top Ten Sites **at once**. It is called "Westech Career Index," *http://www. careerindex.com/*. It takes a little time to search all the sites even with a very fast computer. So you may want to check only three job posting sites at a time if you are feeling impatient.

4. **The Rule of Three.** When you discover a job that suits you, we recommend that you find two more jobs just like it in different organizations. Always have at least three applications in the works. This "rule of three" protects you from the devastating results of rejection. If you apply for only one position at a time, you will give it all your energy, become very invested, and probably wait for a long time before you find out the results. If you are not chosen, you will be very disappointed, have nothing to fall back on, and won't feel like applying for other positions until you have recovered from the hurt of rejection. However, if you have applied to three positions and aren't chosen for one of them, you still have two more in the works, and the rejection is not nearly as hurtful. You will have the energy to apply for another similar position, keeping three applications active at all times, without a long delay.

By getting the lay of the land and verifying your interest with colleagues, you will be preparing yourself for the most important interview, the one in which you can demonstrate your knowledge of the company or organization, its mission, goals, competitors and how you can best make a contribution. The art of interviewing and how to prepare are discussed at length in Chapter 9.

The Resume and Cover Letter:
The Perfect Introduction

"Your resume is a skillfully designed advertisement, or marketing piece . . . that reflects who you are and showcases your
qualifications. It should make you feel proud."

Kit Harrington Hayes

Resumes are often a major stumbling block to action for career shifts
and development. Some people feel they must have a resume before
even beginning the process. Not true. Others resist writing a resume because they unconsciously fear that they will have to use it if they have
prepared it. Others feel resumes must include everything they have ever
done and cannot bring themselves to eliminate anything. Writing a resume seems to bring about writer's block even for professional writers.
Resistance and anxiety surrounding the idea of a resume exist for a very
good reason. After all, writing a resume means putting your identity on
paper, and this can be daunting for even the most secure person because
our culture considers one's work and career one of the most important
components of one's internal and external identity.

In this chapter, we will recommend some new ways of thinking about
a resume as well as some very practical suggestions and guidelines that
will help you overcome your resistance and actually help you increase
your sense of self-esteem. You will be able to put the best features of your
work history and preparation on paper and feel really good about it.
Most of our clients end up looking at their resume and saying, "I like
this person."

Try to think of your resume as an introduction and use the same common sense and good manners you would use in introducing yourself in everyday life. For example, if you went to your son's nursery school to meet his teacher for the first time, you would say, "Hello, I am David Ogilby, Johnny's daddy." You wouldn't say, "Hello, I'm Mr. Ogilby, I have a Harvard education and work as a financial analyst for Goldman Sachs." You would be street wise and appropriate, giving the teacher information that related to the purpose of your visit. The information would help her **connect** with you and facilitate the beginning of a meaningful conversation. A good resume should do the same thing.

Too often, people write resumes that are absolutely accurate but in which fifty percent of the information is irrelevant. We have engineers wanting to make a career change to teaching, who then write very technical resumes in language that only an engineer could understand. That won't work! They have to figure out what makes them interested in teaching, and what there is in their life and work experience or education that suggests that they might be good teachers. They may have to do some volunteer teaching, attend some educational conferences, or take a few teaching classes in order to prepare a resume that will introduce themselves appropriately to the educational community. The extra work or education undertaken is the "bridge of credibility" needed to be taken seriously in a new field.

Another illustration is the specialist in marketing research who wants to shift into management but writes a detailed resume listing every technical functional mastery. Why? That kind of an introduction will land him/her in a staff position employing a functional expertise. If management is the objective, you should write about your management experience and accomplishments, and then list your marketing research and technical abilities in a skills section or as relevant background, not as the focus of the resume.

What if you have a brand new graduate degree in a field completely different from the one you worked in previously? One of our clients was a medical technician who went back to school for an MBA and loved graduate school. He had no business experience except for his projects and internship in school. Following the rule that you introduce yourself appropriately, we wrote a resume that opened with his newly acquired MBA featured prominently, with a section that followed called "relevant experience." Under that heading we illustrated his business skills and critical thinking skills with short descriptions of his graduate school projects, internships, and consulting projects. The "relevant experience" section was followed by one called, "detailed work history," which included a reverse chronological listing of his places of work and titles without going into the details of his scientific knowledge and laboratory skills.

What if you want to stay in the same industry but want to move to a company with more growth potential? You know you have the right experience, but how do you introduce yourself as a leader instead of just a master of the facts and a good soldier? It may be that you have had a history of promotions, or that you started out at a very entry level and have made the spectacular rise to management in a very short time, or that you have a passion for this field and feel you can make a unique contribution. In any of these scenarios, you can write a resume that introduces yourself that way, and it will separate you from the rest of the pack with the same experience in the same industry.

By writing a resume that introduces you appropriately, you are writing a personal marketing document that is savvy and to the point, targeted. Your resume and cover letter are two opportunities to make a significant impression and should not be taken lightly. Your goal is to make the employer think, "I should meet this person." If written well, you may get your foot in the door even though your career path or training hasn't been in a traditional straight line of development.

There are many sources on the Internet to guide you in preparing a resume and you can easily access them from our web site, *http://www. lifeworktransitions.com*. Our favorite is The 10 Minute Resume at *http://www.10minuteresume.com/* where you can compose a resume that will be saved for you in text, html, and print formats. Others are *http://eresumes.com/* and *http://www.damngood.com/jobseekers/tips. html*. We have also included guidelines in this chapter to help you assemble your resume, as well as sample resumes as illustrations. It is important to remember that there is no **one** right way to write a resume. There are **many** right ways. The key is, does the resume introduce you appropriately and in a way that piques the interest of the reader?

FREQUENTLY ASKED QUESTIONS (FAQS) ABOUT RESUMES

1. Should education be placed at the beginning or end of the resume?

It depends. If your education is relatively new and definitely targeted for your objective, then put it at the beginning. If your education is particularly prestigious or if you graduated with honors, put it at the beginning.

If your education is old and doesn't relate to your objective, it can go at the end of the resume. In almost all cases, the employer wants to know your level of education and will look for it first whether it is at the beginning or end of your resume. A college degree doesn't entitle you to anything, but it often opens doors and can prevent your resume from being screened out on the first cut. Sometimes, putting your degree at the beginning of your resume saves the employer time.

2. Do I have to have a lot of white space on my resume?

For a while there was so much written about one-page resumes and white space that clients were appearing with resumes so brief that you couldn't get a clue about the person behind the resume. A real hazard of the briefly worded one-page resume is that it sounds like a job description rather than a description of **your** accomplishments and how well **you** carried out the job. Layout, neat appearance, and readability are important, but if the descriptions of your accomplishments are so brief that they are impersonal and say nothing about how **you** did the job, the most beautiful, artful, white-space resume will go in the trash.

3. Does my resume have to be limited to one page?

If you feel you can introduce yourself perfectly well on one page, do so. If the company you are responding to requests a one-page resume, do so. However, if you are engineering a transition for yourself, and have enough compelling accomplishments to fill one page, write it that way and then put your detailed work history, publications, community service, and so forth on the second page. We have included a resume that illustrates this.

We also encourage a second page as an addendum, a helpful but not necessary addition to the first page. For example, you may have solid work experience that you can adequately describe on one page. Yet within that experience you have a number of repeated specialties that you would like to share as an addition to the experience on the first page. For example, training, creative productions, workshop presentations, speeches, clients, community service, or impressive continuing education programs can be listed on a second page as a supplement to your resume. This technique helps clients with a generalist background illustrate a special expertise or set of experiences that will help their introduction. We often have clients create several addenda pages to have ready in case the opportunity calls for it. This works particularly well for consultants and the portfolio person.

Academic and medical curriculum vitae or resumes are almost always more than one page, and it is expected in those professions. Electronic resumes prepared for scanning or email do not need to be limited to one page. The technology only looks for keywords, not the length of your resume.

4. How do I handle gaps in my experience or several short-term jobs?

First of all, honesty is the best policy. You are who you are, and you do not have to apologize for anything. Your effort in the present is what is important, and you must believe that and be able to articulate it effectively. That being said, there are several ways to write a good case for your experience. If you are changing careers, generally the gap includes retraining, and you can simply say that. You can even write the name of your school as the company, use the word "student" as your title and bullet the highlights of your course work as the "job" experience. If you have several jobs between 1990 and 1999 but in the same area, you can make a heading of that **type of experience** and lump the dates (1990–1999) and then list the work experience under that heading. For example:

Teaching, Greater Boston Area, 1990–1993
Substitute Teacher in the Newton, Needham, Brookline, and Wellesley school districts

- Substitute taught high school students in English, history, and art
- Managed classrooms of 20 to 30 students
- Quickly assimilated teaching plans and adjusted teaching style and technique to match students' cognitive styles and expectations

Several short-term employment engagements are not so unusual anymore; in the age of mergers and acquisitions, many very high-level employees have resumes with several jobs that lasted one year or less.

5. Should I only list paid experience?

No. Very often the experience that will introduce you best for the position you want is either volunteer experience or unpaid work you have done as a student or intern. By all means, include them in your resume. It is not necessary to separate paid from unpaid experience with headings. In fact it is much better to include it as either relevant experience or in the correct order in a reverse chronological section.

6. What are keywords?

With the advance of the Internet and special electronic software that allows resumes to be scanned into databases, keywords in resumes have become very important. They are part of the "electronic applicant tracking" system being used more and more each day. Keywords do NOT represent a new idea. If you look at five newspaper ads for advertising jobs, you will notice that several words will be in each ad; those are the keywords for that position. The keywords can be level of education, skills, experience, education, professional affiliations, software, or words that describe functions and traits. For example, if you were applying for an advertising job, you would want to include nouns such as director of advertising, direct mail, strategic planning, market niche, MBA, and Association of Women in Advertising in your resume. Those keywords would ensure that your resume would be retrieved from a database for advertising positions.

When writing resumes with our clients, we have found that writing the resume as we always have usually includes the necessary keywords. However, it is always a good idea to check and be sure. In addition to looking at ads in the newspaper, you can search resumes on the Internet by putting keywords in the search windows of newsgroups like *http://www.dejanews.com*. Some job posting sites also allow you to view resumes. It has become quite accepted and even expected to put a section on your resume called "keyword summary." In this section you can summarize the keywords in the text of the resume and add others that are appropriate for and truly represent your knowledge and experience. You can also list traits that describe yourself.

7. What is an electronic resume?

There are two kinds of electronic resumes: one that can be sent and received over the Internet and one that can be scanned by an electronic device for a database. Electronic resumes are no different than regular resumes except for appearance. An electronic resume is a vanilla (as in plain) resume. It has no lines, no lettering in bold or italics, no fancy fonts, no columns, no bullets, and all margins left-hand flush. The techniques available to distinguish layout or types of information include space and capital letters. There are hard-copy resumes and their electronic counterparts illustrated later in this chapter. There are also wonderful guidelines for electronic resumes listed throughout this chapter.

BOX 8.1   TIPS FOR MAXIMIZING ELECTRONIC RESUME SCANNABILITY

(Taken from "Preparing the Ideal Scannable Resume" *http://www.resumix.com/resume/resume_tips.html*. This site no longer exists.)

- Use white or light-colored 8 1/2 x 11 paper, printed on one side only.
- Provide a laser printed original if possible; avoid dot matrix print outs.
- Do not fold or staple.
- Use standard typefaces such as Helvetica, Futura, Optima, Universe, Times New Roman, Palatino, New Century Schoolbook, and Courier.
- Use a font size of 10 to 14 points (avoid Times 10 point).
- Don't condense spacing between letters.
- Use boldface and/or all capital letters for section headings as long as the letters don't touch each other.
- Avoid fancy treatments such as italics, underline, shadows, and reverse (white letters on a black background).
- Avoid vertical and horizontal lines, graphics, and boxes.
- Avoid two-column format or resumes that look like newspapers or newsletters.
- Place your name first and at the top of the page on its own line. Your name should also be the first text on pages two and three.
- Use standard address format below your name.
- List each phone number on it's own line.

BOX 8.2   GUIDELINES FOR COMPOSING RESUMES FOR EMAIL

(From Rebecca Smith's "eResumes & Resources" *http://www.eresumes.com/tut_asciiresume.html*)

1. Set margins in your word processing document to 6.5 inches (6 inches to be sure); this will accommodate most email formats.
2. Compose a resume from scratch or paste in a resume from another document.
3. Select all the text and choose a standard typeface, 12 point. Courier is often recommended.
4. Save your resume as text only

5. Open new document with a text editor such as Notepad for Windows and Appletext or Simple Text for Macintosh, and review your resume.
6. Replace all unsupported characters with text equivalents (e.g., replace bullets (if they look like question marks) with asterisks or hyphens). Make sure that no line is more than 65 characters.
7. Copy and paste the text of the resume into the body of a test email message and send it to yourself. How does it look? Make any corrections.
8. Compose a very short cover letter in text only (as described above) and insert it above the resume in the email message. Do not send it separately.

If you do not want to bother with any of the instructions in Boxes 8.1 or 8.2, go to "The 10 Minute Resume" *http://www.10minute resume.com*. Instead of 10 minutes, it will take you about 30 minutes. You first choose the professional area, functional or chronological resume, and headings you want. Then you type your resume in easy-to-use online forms. You can paste in a resume you have already composed or type it in on the spot. At each step there are prompts and tips to help you with wording appropriate for your professional area. The result is a resume formatted for print and digital transmission. The three printed styles are basic, framed, and contemporary. The digital formats are html, text-ASCII, and email formats. (You can also make your resume into a web page.) Your resume will be kept for you at that site, and you can easily modify it any time you wish. Your email format resume is waiting for you to send to any destination. You can either save your html and text versions on your own computer or access them from 10 Minute Resume whenever you need them. We highly recommend this site. The finished product is beautiful, and it will simplify your life and save valuable time.

8. Should I put my resume on the Internet?

Yes, but very carefully. Check out the privacy provisions. Do you have control over where the resume is sent? Can you edit your resume at any time? Really know the site you are choosing. Research them in *Career xroads* at *http://www.careerxroads.com* or Weddle's Web Guide at *http://www.nbew.com/weddle/index.htm*. Many sites have personal agents who will gather job postings that match the kinds of positions you are seeking and save them for you in email. Some agents are excellent; others send all kinds of positions that have no resemblance to the jobs you listed. If the latter happens to you, remove your registration from that site. You have the most control over your resume when you respond to a posted position by email directly to a targeted company, professional association, or journal. We strongly recommend that you put your resume right into an email document rather than as an attached file. This assures that your resume will be accessible by the receiving party. Always precede your resume with a note or cover letter in the email document.

"Should You or Shouldn't You? Evaluating Resume Banks" is a site on the Internet at *http://jobsmart.org/internet/reseval.htm* that goes over four important areas: evaluating resume banks, questions you might try to answer before you subscribe, confidentiality, and making the decision—should you or shouldn't you? Print out this site and use it as a set of criteria to judge which, if any, resume posting sites are right for you.

9. Should I have an industry-specific resume?

In most cases, it is the content and readability that matters most. One very good way to review resumes in your industry is to go to the Internet and look up newsgroups relating to your field through *http://www. dejanews.com*. You will be able to see actual resumes posted by people in your field and can assess whether your resume is on the right track.

10. What is the difference between chronological, functional, and accomplishments resumes, and what are the advantages of each?

A **chronological resume** takes your education and experience and arranges it in a reverse chronological order emphasizing names of companies, titles, and accomplishments. The advantages are that it highlights continuity of work experience and is easy to follow. It is best used when your career objective is clear and the job target is directly in line with your work history or the name of the last employer is well known. It is also the style most preferred by employers.

A **functional resume** goes beyond simply outlining education and experience. It enables you to focus on your "transferable skills," those aptitudes or talents that you can apply in any number of situations. This format allows you to draw from all life experiences, not just work experiences. It is best used when changing directions in your career. In addition to the functional format, you must list your work experience.

An **accomplishments resume** allows you to write a compelling case for yourself. It can be general and summarize what you feel are the most important accomplishments in your work life. Or it can be targeted to the position you want, highlighting the accomplishments from your past work experience that are relevant. You will still need to list your work experience in an appropriate way.

The **hybrid resume** is the kind of resume most of you will write. It will combine the best of all three traditional types to really introduce you in the best way possible. Both the accomplishments and hybrid resumes work particularly well for clients trying to make a transition from one field to another. For even more clarification about format, read, "Which is the Right Format For Me?" at JobSmart *http://jobsmart.org/ tools/resume/res-what.htm.*

11. Do I have to have an objective?

We really recommend an objective because it states **what you want,** sends a clear message to the reader, and helps you stay focused while you are writing your resume. With a clear focus, you are more likely to choose accomplishments that will introduce you appropriately for what you want. But back to the question, the answer is, "No." Many clients write the resume with an objective to keep them focused, but then take it off the resume before it is printed and address the objective in their cover letter. This is particularly true if the client does not have computer capability at home to tailor the objective in response to various job opportunities. See Yana Parker's "24 Questions About Resumes." This a charming and informative site at *http://www.damngood.com/jobseekers/tips.html.*

START WRITING YOUR RESUME

Eventually, you will write your **contact data** (name, address, phone, and email), an **objective** (what you want), a **summary of qualifications** (why the employer should interview you), your **education** (the ticket that qualifies you), **experience** (the proof), **community service** (indication of life/work balance), **professional affiliations** (initiative for professional development), and **keywords** (words that will make your resume retrievable in an electronic database.)

We recommend that you start by writing the **experience** section first. It is important to make a **long list resume** by listing all your work experience, significant volunteer experience, and any other experience that would illustrate your talents and skills. You have already done a lot of this work in your self-assessment and skills assessment exercises. Don't hesitate to look back at those exercises. Start with your most recent experience. Write down the name of the company or organization, the town and state, the dates you worked there and your title. Then use the action word list (at the end of this chapter) and write down everything you did as an accomplishment statement. Don't leave anything out, and don't take anything for granted. Own your accomplishments, and your self-esteem will soar. Then go on to the next experience and the next until you are finished and have a long list resume. You now have a document with all the data you will need for any kind of resume you decide to write.

If you have an objective, a target you are aiming for, you will keep that in mind in the next steps of your resume composition. If you don't have an objective, you can still write a resume that clearly describes where you are at this point in time and highlights your accomplishments. You may want to use this kind of resume while you are networking and doing initial research. Then when you know what you want to do, you will rewrite your resume using the language of your industry or field and editing your experience more carefully so that your resume introduces you to your best advantage. When you get your new job, you will write another resume including your new position so that you will be prepared for the next opportunity.

If you decide to write a **reverse chronological resume**, you will need to decide what you are going to include. You may decide to use only the most important recent jobs and lump together some of your entry-level experiences or even leave them off your resume. Within a particular job, you will want to group similar functional areas together such as budget/ finance accomplishments, personnel related accomplishments, planning, and so on. Then you can either list them in descending order of importance or in a chronological order that tells a story of how you did that job. Do not include things you do not want to do unless you feel that by revealing that knowledge you will be perceived as a more valuable candidate. We recommend that the first bullet be an overview of the position describing size and scope of responsibilities. What if the employer only reads the first bullet? Will it give them a fair idea of what you accomplished and the context in which it took place?

If you decide to write a **functional resume**, you will want to review your long list resume and look for patterns and groupings of functional areas such as management, finance, training, marketing, product development. Determine the functional area titles appropriate for you and list the relevant accomplishments under them. Make the statements more than just a phrase or skill cluster. The statement should be an accomplishment with enough information in it that a reader will be able to figure out where the experience came from when they look at your detailed work history section. Look at the examples in this chapter to help you understand how to do this.

If you are writing an **accomplishments resume** for a transition you must have an objective, because this is by nature a targeted resume. For example, if you have had many generalist management positions but are now applying for (transitioning to) a marketing position, you might start the experience section of your resume with a heading, "Relevant Marketing Experience." Then you would extract marketing accomplishments from each of your jobs. Below that you would have a heading called "Detailed Work Experience" under which you would list your work experience in reverse chronological order with title and any information that would build your case for the position in mind. I use this hybrid form of resume often because it allows for the most flexibility and creativity and, most important gets the attention of the reader for the specific purpose. It also provides the reverse chronological format that many employers prefer.

Now address the summary of qualifications section. By now you know yourself very well. You know qualities and attributes about yourself and the recognition you receive from your colleagues; you know what you are best at; you also know what you would like to accomplish. This is information "qualitative" in nature that isn't appropriate in the body of the resume. Here is where the **qualifications** section plays such an important part in your resume; you can put in qualitative information. It should be a mini autobiography or mini marketing statement from your point of view that captures your essence. It tells the employer in shorthand **why** he should interview and hire you. If written well enough, the reader shouldn't have to read any further. Here is a list of words that will help you get going with your mini marketing statement. Feel free to use your own words as well.

Number of years of experience in	Education-trained in, or
Strengths in	trained at, level in
Consistent history of	Expertise in

Recognized by peers and	Special ability to
and colleagues for	Chosen for
Awards for	Skills in
Traits	Interested in
Dedicated to	Reputation for

We like to end the qualification statement with something special, an exclamation point, on the theory that when readers scan a document, they often see the first and last of things. So if you have a trait or passion that really sums you up, put it last in the qualification statement. Look at the sample resumes to see examples of a variety of qualification statements. We usually write these in a run-on paragraph with ideas separated by semicolons.

The education section of your resume should be short and to the point. Don't waste a lot of space or lines on education. The reader is looking for your degree. So list your education in reverse chronological order and try to keep each education entry to one line. Of course, this is not always possible, but the point is to avoid taking up unnecessary space in the education section. You can bold any part of the education statement, but it is not necessary. Notice that the degree is listed first; that is what most interests the employer.

M.A., Communications, Boston University, Boston, MA, 1996
B.A., English, *summa cum laude*, Colgate University, Hamilton, NY, 1992

There are other appropriate headings on a resume that are optional: community service, publications, professional affiliations. Again, any information you put on your resume should be relevant to the focus of your introduction. If you have recent community service that illustrates either service or leadership within your community, it would add value to your introduction. Do not put college activities if you have been out of college for more than five years. If you are a published author, by all means include a list of your publications. Professional affiliation is important; if you do not belong to a professional association, it is a good idea to join one either in your current profession or the one you hope to enter.

The keyword summary may be placed at the end of the resume or at the top of the resume after education or qualifications. I personally like it at the bottom. The scanner or database robot won't know the difference, and they are the ones interested in this section. I view it as a clean-up section to make sure your resume gets picked up in any relevant database search. Keywords are nouns relevant to your field, traits, education, professional associations, or software expertise. They are the words the employer wants in a resume of anyone interviewed.

LAYOUT

We prefer a fairly conservative layout, as you will see in the examples at the end of this chapter. We also have a theory to back up our layout. As you can see we set off the objective, qualifications, and education sections in a way that makes them look like a section of their own. This is done on purpose. That section should be so well written that the reader only has to read that part of your resume. It tells what you want, why you are qualified, and shows that you have the necessary credentials for the job. The experience section of the resume is proof of the upper section, and can be read in detail by the readers if they are interested in you. However, "getting them interested in you" is what is key, and the upper section of this suggested layout should make it easier for the readers to get a "quick take" on what you are all about.

For clients in creative careers such as fashion, advertising, graphic design, architecture, interior design and others, a beautiful layout is particularly appropriate. Use your own good judgment and creativity. Follow your style and you won't go wrong. The layout as well as the content of your resume will be representing you. Make sure you really like what you have produced; it is very important that you feel comfortable with your resume as you are sitting across from the person reading it.

We recommend another difference in the layout from the vast majority of resumes resources, and that is in the placement of the dates of employment. We tuck them at the end of the place of employment line rather than featured prominently in a left-hand column. We feel that the resume should elicit interest and discussion about you, not your dates of employment. Too often the reader's eye is drawn to that very prominent left-hand column, and their first concern might be a missing year or a short term of employment instead of the quality of that work experience. We also recommend that you do not include months, just list the year.

Examples:

Filenes, Boston, MA, 1996 to present
Avid Technology Corporation, Tewksbury, MA, 1992–1996

REFERENCES

Most often clients put "References Furnished Upon Request" at the bottom of their resume and wait to be asked for references by the employer. When asked, you should have at least three references with name, address, and telephone numbers. A new reference page format was recently introduced to us by one of our clients, and we want to share it. It listed the references with the usual information and then a couple of sentences explaining the work relationship between the references and the client. This is a very effective format and essentially coaches the reader in how to ask questions that will most benefit you.

It is crucial that you also coach your references. Be sure to ask them if they would be willing to be a reference. Then send them a letter accompanied by your new resume. Explain what kinds of positions you are seeking and bring the reference up to date with any information about yourself that would be helpful. Call your references when you have reason to believe they will be called. Tell them about the company and position in question, how your interviewing process has gone, and how they could be most helpful to you. There may be a particular skill set you would like them to emphasize or your management style. Good communication is often the key to your success.

COVER LETTERS AND THANK YOU LETTERS

Now that you have a resume, you need to think about a cover letter. For some of our clients the cover letter is the "last straw." They have worked so hard on self-assessment, figured out what they want to do, taken courses and shadowed people to verify their interests, and written the perfect resume revealing their professional identity on paper. They have also tracked down job opportunities through the Internet, networking, and using traditional media. Now, on top of all that, a cover letter is expected. This is where a trusted career counselor comes in handy to keep up your morale. And for you, we hope this essay on cover letters puts you at ease and takes some of the burden off your shoulders.

The Golden Rule

The best cover letter is one that is **sent**, not one in several drafts sitting on your desk. Even if your letter is only three sentences long, send it. You may be a fabulous candidate but the employer will never know it if you only contemplate applying and never get around to doing it. And it may be that only the resume will be forwarded to the decision maker, and you will have nothing to lose. The risk is worth it.

Of course, you can do a lot for yourself by writing a thoughtful cover letter, and it does not have to be a literary masterpiece. There are many books written on this subject (see the Bibliography) and some excellent Internet sites. A favorite of ours is "200 Letters for Job Hunters" at *http://www.careerlab.com/letters/*. However, you won't go wrong if you follow these simple guidelines that have saved our clients many sleepless nights and hours of procrastination.

The Three Paragraph Letter

1. The first paragraph is the **connection**:

> "John Jones suggested I contact you regarding . . ."
> "This letter is in response to the ad for the position_____in_____"
> "Your company has come to my attention through my research . . ."
> "I found your name searching the data base from our alumnae career
>   services office . . ."

End the paragraph with a transition sentence saying that you feel qualified for the position and are very interested in being considered or that you are interested in a certain type of information.

2. The second paragraph is the **hook**, something interesting and relevant that will make the reader remember you and want to meet you. Obviously, it must be related to the position and company you are addressing or the field of the person from whom you are requesting information. We often recommend vignettes about your experience. Stories are easier to remember than a whole paragraph of repeating the ad or your resume. After an introductory sentence illustrating that you have done your homework about the company or organization and that your experience is appropriate or that the position and company meet the profile you have been seeking, you might choose one of the following leads and expand on it:

> "Some of my most challenging assignments have been . . ."
> "What I have enjoyed most about my career has been . . ."
> "My biggest successes to date have been . . ."
> "The key reasons I would be an asset to your organization are . . ."

These leads, or others you think of yourself, allow you to write fresh, interesting, real-life material that expresses your experience in a different context than that provided in your resume. The result is that you have a better chance of your letter being remembered.

You can even bullet a short list of phrases after one of these openings. It makes it easy for the reader to scan and you don't have to worry about expressing yourself perfectly. Be sure that what you write is relevant to the needs expressed in the job posting. Don't get off the track.

A popular way of handling the second paragraph, the hook, is to list two side-by-side columns: one with the requirements mentioned in a job posting and the second illustrating how you meet those requirements point by point. If that is the easiest way for you to get the letter written, then choose that method. Remember, **sending** the cover letter is what matters.

3. The third paragraph is the **close**, as in closing the sale. You tell the reader that you want and expect or anticipate an interview. Start with a transition sentence expressing interest and confidence and then say,

> "I would like to make an appointment at your earliest convenience to discuss how my career goals and skills match with the position of_____**or any others that would be appropriate**. (The last phrase leaves the letter appropriately open ended for other opportunities.) Enclosed is a copy of my resume for your review."
>
> Sincerely,
> Interested Candidate

Some other pointers to keep in mind when writing cover letters are:

- Be genuine, sincere
- Personalize the information on your resume; let your personality shine through
- Be direct, to the point, and appropriately brief
- Everyone enjoys recognition; so anything you can say showing that you have researched the company will be well received. The Internet site of the company may give company background and recent press releases. Be sure to read them in your preparation.
- You are not limited to three paragraphs. If you are comfortable writing and feel you can weave in some really interesting things about yourself by writing a more lengthy letter, it is fine.

- If you are applying for a writing position or one that requires a lot of writing, you will want to pay a great deal of attention to your cover letter because it will serve as a writing sample.

A resume should always be accompanied by a cover letter, even a resume sent in an email document. However, email correspondence can be shorter. Be sure to follow the directions exactly for responding to a job posting on the Internet. You are often asked to put the number of the position as the first item on your response. Remember, your resume will be part of a database and may be called up by that number. If you haven't followed directions, you will not be included.

Thank You Letters

They are expected and offer another opportunity for you to clarify and sell yourself. We recommend that they be typed in a business format, but many people write hand-written notes on personal stationery. Use your good judgment based on the corporate culture of the person to whom you are writing. If you do not want to be further considered for the position, it is appropriate to say this in your thank you note. It will be appreciated and shows you have respect for the person's time.

There Is No Excuse

Again, we direct you to a truly wonderful award-winning web site called "200 Letters for Job Hunters" with twenty-one kinds of letters to choose from. For each type of letter, there are tips and also sample letters. For example, there are thank you letters for twenty-six topics. Topics cover informational interviews, after job interview, job search help interview, referrals, and many more. If you really have writer's block, go to this site, find the right letter, plug in your information, and **send** it. I recommend the "write a great letter" link on this page. It gives you many tips including "28 Common Letter Writing Mistakes," You will find this gold mine at *http://www.careerlab.com/letters/.*

SIX SAMPLE RESUMES

We are including six sample resumes that reinforce our point that the resume must be a good introduction for the position you are seeking. Most of them are hybrid formats combining chronological, functional, and accomplishments styles. These are true case studies with names and personal facts changed to respect their privacy.

The **first resume** illustrates the story told at the beginning of this chapter of a medical technologist with a brand new MBA trying to make a career change to business development. He wrote a resume leveraging his "bridge of credibility," namely an MBA, consulting projects, and internship during that period of time. His resume is also shown in an electronic (vanilla) format.

Print Format

Richard Mark Jordon
28 Rosemary Street, Apartment F-8
Stoneham, Massachusetts 02180-1532
jordon@aol.com
508-334-6028

OBJECTIVE: Position in business development

QUALIFICATIONS: Proven business skills at graduate level with ten years medical scientific research experience; expertise in business analyses ranging from financial and econometric to capacity utilization, stake holder and corporate culture analyses; ability to work industriously in leadership and supportive roles; genuine affinity for people and communication.

EDUCATION: **M.B.A.**, Management – 3.85 GPA, Babson College, Waltham, MA, 1996
B.S., Laboratory Science, Boston University, 1990

RELEVANT BUSINESS EXPERIENCE:
Acquired through graduate school projects and internships, 1994–1996

Bold & Company, Inc., Business Analyst/Competitive Intelligence
Analyzed competitive intelligence for pharmaceutical clients. Interviewed over 100 individuals at competitors, suppliers, regulatory sources, and other

industry participants. Accurately predicted launch dates, identified competitor strategies, and determined various marketing elements.

Coupons, Inc., a not for profit project for Boston's homeless, Marketing Strategist

Collaborated with Citizen Advisory Board to revise vendors' support and interest. Developed and experimented with market strategies. Expanded community and business participation on three tacks.

Beth Israel Hospital Out-Patient Services, Customer Service Consultant

Analyzed complaint data, hospital culture, and linguistic sensitivity. Built and implemented a viable, informative survey to document and measure customer satisfaction. Developed a working database for survey results using Lotus Approach v.3.0.

Speedy Printer Service Shop, Customer Service Consultant

Analyzed a service shop with annual gross of $400,000.00. Examined: service package and quality, process and capacity, business cycles, customer loyalty, employee pride. Identified specific problem areas and recommended corrective measures which increased productivity, efficiency, and profit.

3M Analysis-Team Project in Business School

Analyzed financial, marketing, operations, corporate, and business strategies. Recommended organization should regain focus on two main Single Business Units, spinning off the third. Assumed roles of team player, coach, advocate, director, and presentation editor.

WORK EXPERIENCE:

Lowe Clinic Medical Center, Burlington, MA, 1991–1993

Medical Technologist (ASCP)

Performed immunological tests; interpreted data; revamped preventive maintenance program.

Work-Study Positions, 1982–1986

Karo Hospital, Stockholm, Sweden – Coagulation studies

Veterans Administration Medical Center, Boston, MA – HIV research

New England Medical Center, Boston, MA – Clinical serology

COMMUNITY SERVICE EXPERIENCE:

Maynard Fire Department, Maynard, MA, 1982–1986

Commanded Fire Alarm Office. Coordinated efforts with fire and police departments from various communities. Performed fire-fighting and emergency medical procedures under crisis conditions.

SUMMARY OF KEYWORDS:

Research, Business Analyst, M.B.A., Competitive Intelligence, Regulations, marketing, market strategies, analysis, customer service, survey, database, Lotus, business cycle, quality control, business strategies, team player, operations, finance

Electronic Format

Richard Mark Jordon
28 Rosemary Street, Apartment F-8
Stoneham, Massachusetts 02180-1532
jordon@aol.com
508-334-6028

OBJECTIVE:
Position in business development /sales

QUALIFICATIONS :
Proven business skills at graduate level with ten years medical scientific research experience; expertise in business analyses ranging from financial and econometric to capacity utilization, stake holder, and corporate culture analyses; ability to work industriously in leadership and supportive roles; genuine affinity for people and communication.

EDUCATION
M.B.A., Management – 3.85 GPA, Babson College, Wellesley, MA, 1996
B.S., Laboratory Science, Boston University, 1990

RELEVANT BUSINESS EXPERIENCE:
Acquired through projects and internships during business school. 1994–1996

Bold & Company, Inc.,
Business Analyst/Competitive Intelligence
Analyzed competitive intelligence for pharmaceutical clients. Interviewed over 100 individuals at competitors, suppliers, regulatory sources, and other industry participants. Accurately predicted launch dates, identified competitor strategies, and determined various marketing elements.

Coupons, Inc., a not for profit project for Boston's homeless
Marketing Strategist
Collaborated with Citizen Advisory Board to revise vendors' support and interest. Developed and experimented with market strategies. Expanded community and business participation on three tacks.

Beth Israel Hospital Out-Patient Services
Customer Service Consultant
Analyzed complaint data, hospital culture, and linguistic sensitivity. Built and implemented a viable, informative survey to document and measure customer satisfaction. Developed a working database for survey results using Lotus Approach v.3.0.

Speedy Printer Service Shop
Customer Service Consultant
Analyzed a service shop with annual gross of $400,000.00. Examined: service
package and quality, process and capacity, business cycles, customer loyalty,
employee pride. Identified specific problem areas and recommended corrective
measures which increased productivity, efficiency, and profit.

3M Analysis-Team Project in Business School
Analyzed financial, marketing, operations, corporate, and business strategies.
Recommended organization should regain focus on two main Single Business
Units, spinning off the third. Assumed roles of team player, coach, advocate,
director and presentation editor.

WORK EXPERIENCE:
Lowe Clinic Medical Center, Burlington, MA, 1991–1993
Medical Technologist (ASCP)
Performed immunological tests, interpreted data; revamped preventive
maintenance program.

Work-Study Positions, 1982–1986:
Karo Hospital, Stockholm, Sweden – Coagulation studies
Veterans Administration Medical Center, Boston, MA – HIV research
Massachusetts General Hospital, Boston, MA – Clinical serology

COMMUNITY SERVICE EXPERIENCE:
Maynard Fire Department, Maynard, MA, 1982–1986
Commanded Fire Alarm Office. Coordinated efforts with fire and police
departments from various communities. Performed fire-fighting and emergency
medical procedures under crisis conditions.

SUMMARY OF KEYWORDS:
Research, Business Analyst, M.B.A., Competitive Intelligence, Regulations,
marketing, market strategies, analysis, customer service, survey, database, Lotus,
business cycle, quality control, business strategies, team player, operations,
finance

The **second resume** introduces a woman who moved to New England
from the Midwest where she was very well known as a music educator at
all levels. In addition, she was well known in music circles and had done
community outreach for her symphony orchestra. When she moved, she
left her identity behind and had to start over. From her vast experience,
she targeted early childhood music education and introduced herself in
the following manner. The first page tells of her compelling accomplishments in early childhood music education, and the second page lists her
detailed work history.

Ruth Buckley
150 Boylston Street
Brookline, MA 02146
rbuckley@mediaone.net
617-480-9912

OBJECTIVE: A position improving the quality of music experiences for young children through classroom programs, parent education, and teacher training.

QUALIFICATIONS: Twenty years experience as a teacher of music at the college, middle school, elementary, and preschool levels. Five years producing and implementing demonstration programs introducing orchestral instruments in preschool settings. Recognized for expertise in educating the nonmusician teacher and student. Devoted to promoting arts in education.

EDUCATION: M.A., Music Ed., Case Western Reserve University, Cleveland, OH
B.A., Music Ed, and Psychology, Brooklyn College, New York, NY

Professional Accomplishments Relating to Early Childhood Music Education
- Analyzed existing course structure and wrote new curriculum for two required Music in Early Childhood courses at Cooksley Community College. Elevated course from passive observation to a learning activity–based experience with actual preschool children. Taught student teachers to respond to the children's behavior and thus follow as well as lead them through the music experience.
- Directed the preschool programs for the Cincinnati Music School Settlement. Created programs to introduce young children to the sight and sound of orchestral instruments. Developed, narrated, and supervised participatory programs with faculty from the Settlement in half-hour programs brought to 600 children in 12 preschool centers throughout the city.
- Served as an educational consultant to the Junior Women's Committee to develop the Cincinnati Orchestra's "Key Concerts" for young children. Initiated preconcert interface and hands-on music activities between children, musicians, and instruments. Reviewed and critiqued concert narrations.
- Initiated and presented MUSED programs for preschool children in Cincinnati Early Childhood Centers which incorporated music, drama, and movement programming for large preschool audiences. The presentation incorporated a variety of musical styles, participatory activities, and a brief presentation of the opera "Magic Flute."
- Presented "A Time for Music," a day-long workshop, for teachers of the Spanish American Day Care Center. Taught teachers how to use and feel comfortable initiating live music activities in their daily teaching. Developed

awareness of musical concepts with the nonmusician preschool teacher and encouraged goal of children's greater musical awareness.
- Served as Keynote Speaker for an annual meeting of the Cincinnati Association for the Education of Young Children as well as speaker before several parent groups.
- Wrote 50-page outline for a Music in Early Childhood Education text which placed music education activities in a developmental and conceptual framework.

EMPLOYMENT:
Revere Early Learning Center, Revere, MA, 1998
Project Director – Early Childhood Music Curriculum

Consultant, Greater Boston Area, 1996 to present
- Teacher training through interaction with children and teachers in conference, workshop, and classroom settings

Freewater State College, Freewater, MA, 1993–1995
Assistant Professor
- Teacher of Music at Burnell, a teacher training K–6 Campus Laboratory School. Created a model music classroom. Provided multicultural music program for school's major "Olympics" event. Fifty songs, rhythms, games, and dances were prepared with 14 classes representing 17 countries.

Wellesley Public Schools, Wellesley, MA, school year of 1993 to 1995
Substitute Music Education Teacher for kindergarten, sixth, seventh, and eighth grades

Kirk Middle School, East Cincinnati, Ohio, 1986–1992
Teacher of Music, grades 7–8
- Researched existing music curricula, initiated seventh grade choir, served on Advisory Team for school reorganization plan. Participated in TESA (Teacher Expectations and Student Achievement). Trained other teachers.

Smith & Essex Elementary School, Akron, Ohio, 1985–1986
Teacher of Music, grades K–6

Cincinnati Area Arts Council, Cincinnati, Ohio, 1985–1984
Coordinator of "CETA (Comprehensive Employment and Training Act) and the Arts"
- Assisted in development, implementation, and administration of a federally funded program utilizing arts to impact 850 disadvantaged youth and 70 unemployed community artists.

Cooksley Community College, Cooksley, Ohio, 1977–1985
Lecturer in Music
- Prepared teachers for certification in early childhood

Cincinnati Music School Settlement, Cincinnati, Ohio, 1975–1977
Director of Preschool Instrumental Demonstration Programs

PROFESSIONAL ORGANIZATIONS:
Music Educators National Conference
Massachusetts Music Education Association
Society for Research in Music Education

SUMMARY OF KEYWORDS:
music education, early childhood, curriculum development, student achievement, classroom activities, orchestra, pre-school, MUSED, Society for Research in Music Education, multicultural, M.A. in Music Education, B.A., Music Education, teacher training

The **third resume** introduces a woman with an MBA and a long, distinguished career in financial services. However, her passion was wine and everything about it. We strategized that she could leverage her financial skills to a position in a major winery or a consulting firm for wineries and then move into the areas of the industry other than financial. We introduced her as a connoisseur and student of wine and wrote her experience emphasizing functional transferable skills instead of her special knowledge skills.

Marjorie Slocum
985 Winston Street
Boston, MA 10128
marslo@tiac.net
617-834-5516

OBJECTIVE: Management position in wine industry leveraging expertise in finance and extensive knowledge of wine

QUALIFICATIONS: Ten years active interest in wine substantiated by extensive training, travel, and retail experience. Fifteen years experience in financial services, strengths in analysis, research, accounting, evaluation, and problem solving; ability to involve and coordinate staff and managers in group decision process.

EDUCATION: M.B.A., Accounting and Finance, Boston University, Boston, MA
B.A., French, Middlebury College, Middlebury, VT
Certificate in Business French from Paris Chamber of Commerce
Twenty-six educational wine seminars and courses classes

RELEVANT EXPERIENCE:
- Developed expertise and in-depth knowledge of wine regions and wine varietals worldwide; focused on wine pairings, tasting skills, wine production and marketing
- Studied the economics of wine industry and have understanding of business sectors.
- Acquired extensive library detailing history of wine making, wines of famous regions, wine and cooking.
- Advised upscale clientele on purchase of wines appropriate for their needs. Established contacts with wine bureaus for special promotions.
- Toured and studied Champagne, Burgundy, and Saussignac regions in France; Napa Valley-Mendocino-Lake County and Alexander Valley in California; Westpot Rivers and Sakonnet in Massachusetts.

WORK EXPERIENCE:
Mutual Funds of America, Boston, MA, 1989 to present
Vice President and Financial Controller
- Managed a staff of six and all functions relating to regulatory reporting for external entities, such as shareholders and bank regulators, and the internal reporting for a division of Chase's global investment services
- Managed the organization changes and systems conversions resulting from business mergers
- Advised senior management, after interpreting financial results, on issues of expense containment, revenue opportunities, competitive information, and industry trends and forecasts
- Guided two financial analysts in client profitability studies, pricing of RFPs and any proposals for new business, annual budget preparation, and monthly management reports
- Supervised three staff accountants covering accounts payable, accounts receivable, and the general ledger for expense base of $50m
- Provided cash management by monitoring cash flow and daily investments

Assistant Vice President Manager, Budgeting and Financial Control
- Managed department and advised Vice President on results of financial analysis
- Analyzed budgeting/reporting system and managed wide-range changes so that reporting categories went from four to forty cost centers resulting in improved level detail for client and department analysis
- Collaborated with finance group in New York to create a new organizational structure, allocation methodology, and divisional financial reporting
- Monitored all internal financial functions including accurate recording of general ledger, accounts receivable and accounts payable, accounting cycle closing, contractual billing, cash flow, and collections to ensure proper operations

Assistant Controller
- Developed five-year plan for software division being sold to AT&T and the retained mutual fund servicing business and plans for expansion

- Prepared annual budget based on analysis of current and projected revenues and expenses
- Organized and improved general accounting systems
- Assumed cash management and line of credit drawdown responsibilities

Savings and Loan Association, Boston, MA, 1972–1978 and 1980–1989
Assistant Controller/Budget and Cost Manager
- Converted all accounting records to a computerized system
- Compiled monthly reports of investment activity for the Board of Directors
- Developed annual financial and operations budget

Serendipity, Wellesley, MA, 1978–1980
Manager
- Sold antiques and maintained bookkeeping records
- Contacted import brokers regarding overseas shipments

O.J. Morton Company, New York, NY, 1969–1972
Senior Marketing Research Analyst
- Supervised marketing analysis unit handling 20 major accounts
- Analyzed data from field representatives and advertising agencies
- Prepared monthly reports for clients concerning product performance and nationally and regionally

PROFESSIONAL ASSOCIATIONS:
American Institute of Wine and Food
Women for Wine Sense

SUMMARY OF KEYWORDS:
wine, varietals, wine regions,tastings, American Institute of Wine and Foods, accounting, accounts payable, account receivable, cost control, financial analysis, budget preparation, forecasts, financial services, consulting, contractual billing, director, supervisor, M.B.A., French, marketing analyst

The **fourth resume** introduces a client who wanted to make a major shift in the business community from a real estate developer to an equity analyst. Despite his pedigreed education and success, this is not an easy thing to do. However, with the following introduction, he did it. This is a combination accomplishments—functional resume with reverse chronological work history on the second page. He chose not to have qualifications or keyword sections because he was approaching prospective employers personally and liked the resume just as it stands here. There is always room for **personalizing** a resume and its format.

Matthew Morse
563 Sierra Terrace
Belmont, MA 02154
morse@hotmail.com
617-775-9210

OBJECTIVE: A position as an equity analyst

EDUCATION: M.B.A., Andrew Scholar, Wharton, University of
Pennsylvania, 1984
B.A., *summa cum laude*, University of Chicago, 1979

RELATED PROFESSIONAL ACCOMPLISHMENTS:
Investing
- Managed investments since 1970. Representative major successful purchases:
  Fortune 500 Company, 1979, up over 38,000%
  Conservative Bank, 1994, up over 700%
  Computer Chip, December 1997, up over 159%
  ABC, March 1998, up over 58%
- Developed systematic, sector rotation approach to real estate securities investing that beat the average REIT market return by 12% per year over the last decade.
- Achieved an above market return on equity investments since 1982.

Market Forecasting
- In 1982, forecast decade-long slump in real oil prices. Projected that conservation investments in autos and housing would lead to slower than expected demand growth.
- In 1986, forecast the glut of rental housing. This projection led the nation's third largest rental housing developer to exit the construction and development business prior to the market down turn.
- Modelled price elasticity for a major consumer good product enabling its marketer to increase profits by 20%.

Industry Analysis
- Created innovative pricing strategy that enabled an emerging medical diagnostics company to gain a dominant competitive position.
- Developed investment and market selection approach for the nation's largest gasoline marketer. Implementation increased its market value by over $1 billion.
- Identified a profitable U.S. acquisitions strategy for an African mining company.
- Advised leading hand tool producer on how to beat Asian competitors. This work resulted in a doubling of profits and awards from a major customer.

Sales
- Penetrated 30 of the 100 largest customers with an industry-specific credit scoring database in under five years. Achieved over 100% annual growth for three successive years.
- Assisted in the sale of $1 million in consulting services.
- Beat Dow Jones and Trans Union in a competition to build a nationwide marketing and demographic data base.

WORK HISTORY:
Analysis, Inc., Belmont, MA, 1992 to 1998
President
- Founded a start-up offering demographic, market, and credit scoring information to real estate owners and managers. Designed an analytic model that helped apartment managers close 3–5% more rental applicants. Built the management and sales team.
- Grew the business from a concept to the second largest information provider serving the rental housing industry. Recruited resellers and obtained endorsement from industry associations. Doubled revenues in each of three successive years. Penetrated most major apartment REITs.

Fortune Development Corporation, Atlanta, Georgia, 1989–1992
Senior Vice President
- Negotiated the profitable sale of Fortune's $500 million construction and development business prior to the market down turn. Managed construction staff and joint venture operations.
- Sold over 50 parcels of land and land options. Supervised the completion of a nursing home and the leasing of an office building.
Vice President
- Advised the CEO to exit the construction and development business in the face of deteriorating market conditions. Reorganized the property management company to focus on speeding the pace of leasing and increasing rental rates. Supervised the marketing and training staff. Managed the annual business plan.

Northwestern Consulting Group, Boston, MA, 1984–1989
Case Leader
- Directed teams that developed and implemented major changes and strategies for Fortune 500 clients. Client engagements focused on asset allocation, market selection, pricing, advertising, manufacturing strategy, and market forecasting.
- Industries served: consumer products, medical devices, hand tools, mining, gasoline refining, and marketing and chemicals.
- Achieved success with clients through effectively interviewing industry leaders and corporate executives, performing analyses of industry trends, developing innovative strategies to achieve competitive advantage and bringing client teams to consensus on recommendations.

The **fifth resume** introduces Sarah, who had accumulated a very successful history with a national upscale retail chain. She loved sales and knew she was very good at it. However, she was tired of the retail hours and also wanted to make more money. She chose a tried and true reverse chronological format emphasizing her corporate experience and recognition. Her goal was to leave retail sales and move into pharmaceutical sales, and she did it.

Sarah Hoyt
101 Washington Avenue #7
Boston, MA 02134
shoyt@yahoo.com
617-625-7845

OBJECTIVE: Outside sales position

QUALIFICATIONS: Six years experience in sales and management positions in high-volume retail; recognized by corporate management for meeting and exceeding sales goals and customer satisfaction standards; consistent history of promotions and recognition; expertise in recognizing and reaching target market; fascinated with big picture and implementing the details necessary for success; self-motivated, goal oriented, determined.

EDUCATION: B.A., Psychology, University of Miami, Florida, 1994

EXPERIENCE:
Banana Republic, Florida and Massachusetts, 1993 to present
The Banana Republic, Corporate Experience
 • Chosen by corporate to manage the opening of six stores in various states; all openings were highly successful with Kansas City having highest opening day in Banana Republic History
 • Trained sales staff in visual merchandising standards, sales techniques, service standards and product knowledge
 • Scheduled staff of 50 around shipment days to receive trucks, process merchandise, set up stock room, and visually merchandise the store
 • Created and designed the image of Banana Republic; trained staff nationally resulting in a Banana Republic "look" emulated by many similar retail stores
Banana Republic, Store Management
Assistant Manager, Chestnut Hill, MA
Assistant Manager, Fort Lauderdale, FLA
 • Managed staff of 80 and all visual merchandising for a store of 15,000 square feet with a volume of $6m in Chestnut Hill; staff of 20, 2,000 square feet, and volume of $2m in Florida

- Awarded **"Catch the Spirit,"** a regional award for excellence in customer service, a result of instilling corporate philosophy in all staff of exceeding customers expectations
- Designed training programs and materials to train staff in customer service standards, visual standards, product knowledge, and sales techniques
- Recruited, screened, hired, supervised, and evaluated staff; established a record of high retention, satisfaction, and productivity; motivated staff to achieve and exceed sales goals, in

Disney Store, Fort Lauderdale, 1991–1993
Sales Associate – promoted to keyholder position
- Took part in highly recognized Disney Training Program known for its excellence in customer service, theft prevention, sales approaches, visual marketing, and business generation techniques
- Sold products with price points ranging from $2.00 to $2,500.00 to a wide variety of clientele
- Assessed customer needs, recommended appropriate products encouraging upsales and add ons, all of which resulted in multiple and repeat sales

Gap, Mississippi and Florida, summers of 1990 and 1991
Sales Associate

PROFESSIONAL ASSOCIATIONS:
Sales and Marketing Executive of Boston

KEYWORD SUMMARY:
sales, quota, customer service, upsales, B.A., motivated, goal oriented, determined, manager, target market, training, Sales and Marketing Executives of Boston

The **sixth resume** introduces a client who was the manager of a rock band with a number of his college friends and loved it. However, many of the band members had come to the conclusion that they were not going to make it "big time" and wanted to enter the more traditional world. Colin loved sociology and the academic life and wanted to return for graduate work. We wrote a hybrid resume using traditional reverse chronological style to write about his band experience and his day job to pay the bills. Then we wrote a paragraph about each experience from the view of a sociologist. What do you think of this introduction? It is very different but works.

Colin O'Connor
89 Cooper Street, Apt. 8
Watertown, MA 02172
ocon@erols.com
617-818-2579

OBJECTIVE: A research position in social science to complement
                     graduate studies in sociology

QUALIFICATIONS: Twelve years work experience in a variety of environments;
                     strengths in organization and management; recognized by
                     peers and colleagues for hard work, persistence, and keen
                     social insight.

EDUCATION: B.A., *cum laude,* Sociology, University of Michigan,
                     Boston, 1995
                     Relevant courses: Research Methods, Social Theory,
                     Sociology of Work, Social Stratification, Medical Sociology

EXPERIENCE:

Crawler (Rock Band), Medford, MA, 1995–1998
Manager and Bass Player

- Managed and played rock band which played many shows, received
  considerable press and airplay, released a record nationally and two tapes
  locally
- Booked shows in Greater Boston Area and New York and took charge of all
  business transactions
- Organized and implements all facets of recordings from working with
  musicians to booking site and following through on post production
- Won the "Demo Derby" sponsored by *Boston Phoenix* and had a record
  released on a California label
- Reviewed favorably by music critics in a number of national and local
  publications

Extensively researched the medium of rock with particular attention paid to music
theory, rhythm, organicity, subject matter, and live performance. By means of
participation, observed and contrasted the subculture of local bands. Assigned
particular significance to correlations between the subculture and the society at
large (stratification, the notion of an open system, the importance of secondary
functions, etc.). Became well versed in the politics of group dynamics within the
context of a creative endeavor.

Landon's Liquors, Revere, MA, 1995 to present
Receiver/Warehouse Manager

- Received and stored stock for a ten million dollar liquor business
- Gained overall knowledge of fine wine and assisted customers in selection
- Delivered orders to individual customers, restaurants, and wholesalers

Studied social, political, and economic forces underlying the wine and liquor retail industry. Observed the subcultures of retail employees, wine enthusiasts, and wholesale distributors. Paid particular attention to the division of labor, role allocation, and conflict theory as these concepts proved to be especially relevant in this owner occupied business.

Various Positions in Service Industries in the Boston Area, 1987–1995

ACTION WORDS

accelerated
accomplished
achieved
acquired
activated
adapted
adjusted
administered
advised
allocated
analyzed
annotated
anticipate
applied
appraised
arranged
articulated
assembled
assessed
assigned
attained
authored
balanced
briefed
budgeted
built
calculated
carried out
cataloged
categorized
chaired
changed
channeled
charted
clarified
coached
coded
collaborated
collated
collected
committed
communicated
compared
competed
compiled
completed
composed
computed

conducted
confronted
consolidated
constructed
contacted
continued
contracted
conveyed
convened
coordinated
corresponded
counseled
created
critiqued
decided
defined
delegated
delivered
demonstrated
derived
designed
detected
determined
developed
devised
diagnosed
directed
discovered
dispensed
displayed
distributed
drafted
dramatized
drew up
earned
edited
educated
effected
elicited
employed
encouraged
endured
enlisted
entertained
established
estimated
evaluated
examined

executed
exercised
exhibited
expanded
expedited
experimented
explained
explored
facilitated
financed
focused
forecasted
formulated
fostered
functioned
generated
governed
grouped
guided
handled
helped
identified
illustrated
implemented
increased
influenced
informed
initiated
inquired
inspected
installed
instilled
instituted
instructed
insured
interpreted
intervened
interviewed
introduced
invented
inventoried
investigated
judged
lectured
led
licensed
listened
located

managed
marketed
mastered
measured
mediated
modeled
modified
monitored
motivated
named
negotiated
observed
obtained
operated
ordered
organized
originated
outlined
oversaw
participated
perceived
performed
persuaded
planned
predicted
prepared
prescribed
presented
presided
processed
produced
programmed
promoted
provided
publicized
published
purchased
questioned
rated
recommended
recorded
recruited
reduced
regulated
reinforced
rendered
repaired
reported

reproduced
researched
resolved
responded
restored
retained
retrieved
reviewed
revised
rewrote
routed
rescheduled
searched
selected
served
serviced
shared
showed
simplified
sold
solicited
solved
sought
specified
spoke
staged
stimulated
structured
studied
succeeded
suggested
summarized
supervised
supported
surveyed
synthesized
systematized
targeted
taught
tested
trained
translated
tutored
updated
utilized
verified
visualized
wrote

CHAPTER

9

Winning the Interview

"It's never what you say, but how. You make it sound
sincere"
Maria Mannes

The interview is the culmination of everything you have learned in Part I
and Part III in this book. It is an extension from inner self-exploration to
the outer world, the defining moment connecting you and the world of
work. With clarity of purpose plus the important knowledge relating to
your life work objective, you are equipped to engage in a two-way dialogue with an employer. Your knowledge, personality, and purpose will
shine through. If you are hired, your relationship will follow the one
modeled in your interview, mutual respect and two-way communication.

Good interviews always consist of a dialogue with each of you having
an agenda. The interviewer wants to learn about you. What are your talents, abilities, and skills? How do you present yourself? How well do you
communicate? What motivates you? In short, what contribution can
you make to the company? Will you fit in? What are you going to cost?

You, the interviewee, want to learn about the job opportunity, what
needs doing, and about the cultural environment. You will want to ask
about the position itself; what are the duties and responsibilities? You
will want to know about the working conditions, the physical and emotional factors that make up the corporate culture. And you will want to
know about opportunities for developing and advancing as well as the
tangible and intangible rewards.

The key to having a successful interview is preparation, preparation,
and preparation. We don't worry about out clients when they arrive at
the interview stage because of all the preparation they have done in their

BOX 9.1   CAUTION — DO NOT INTERVIEW IF YOU ARE IN CRISIS

Clients often come to our offices in a state of crisis. Losing a job unexpectedly, or after years of poor treatment, or needing to make major changes in work because of a family crisis can be some of the most stressful situations you will face in life. Our advice is to do nothing for a while! If you interview in this state of mind, your anxiety will radiate, and you will not make the best impression or the best decisions. Take some time off. Absorb the loss. Do some initial research and actively take care of yourself. Doing so will shorten your period of crisis dramatically. Instead of frantically looking for a job, carefully set up social support for yourself. Perhaps you should visit with a career counselor who is experienced in counseling people through these stressful times. Go slowly. If you feel you have to "do something," select activities that do not require that you sell yourself. Use your time and resources wisely. The attitude to take is that you are exploring (when you are good and ready to do so.)

One of the dreaded questions in these periods is, "What do you do?" Take a big breath, because this is your moment of power. If you answer negatively, that will determine the course of the conversation. However, if you say, "I'm exploring a number of opportunities, one of which is _____. Do you know of anyone who has done that?" Then the conversation will be positive. And many times, the person will say, "Good for you; I wish I had done that instead of rushing into the job I have now."

personal assessment exercises, research and interviews to verify their life work objective, and the soul searching and analysis that went into writing a resume. However, we also believe that interviews should not be taken for granted and recommend several strategies for additional preparation.

PREPARATION

The **first twenty seconds** of the interview are as important as you have heard they are. First of all, get in the proper mindset. This is an opportunity not a test; it is one interview not the only interview. You must walk into the interview and be yourself; you are who you are and have no apologies. Make sure the interviewer gets a sense that you are a real person, not a totally rehearsed robot, and genuinely interested. Keep eye contact, shake hands confidently, and watch for cues from the interviewer about where and when to sit.

Be sure you wear comfortable clothes. We tell our clients not to wear something new, but something conservative that you like and trust, something that will not wrinkle and that will not cross your mind if you want to cross your legs. Decline a beverage if it is offered to you; there is nothing more embarrassing than spilling a drink. Bring either a briefcase or nice leather folder with extra copies of your resume and paper in case you need to take notes. It is perfectly all right to have a cheat sheet with facts about the company in your folder along with a list of questions you want to be sure to ask. You should have your resume memorized but just in case your mind goes blank, have a copy in front of you so that you can easily respond to questions directly related to your resume.

We know from experience that one of the best ways to prepare for questions that might come up in an interview is for you to get into the head of the interviewer. We are assuming that you have researched the company and its needs, its competitors, the customer, and trends for the industry (see Chapters 6 and 7 if you haven't). You are also familiar with the qualifications listed for the position in the job posting because you have met with people having a similar job. **What would YOU want to ask a candidate applying for this position?** Write down the questions and then answer them in a straightforward manner accompanied by an example of how you have applied the concept or skills in another situation. The example, illustration, or story is easy for the interviewer to remember and may be what separates you from the other candidates. If you have any trouble answering your own questions, you may want to gain some additional information before the interview. The questions you have written are probably far more difficult than the questions you will be asked in the interview, but you will be prepared.

We also recommend *Knock 'em Dead* by Martin Yate as an excellent book to get you in the right frame of mind for the interview. He identifies many questions often asked in interviews and explains the thinking process you should go through in answering them. Read or browse through the book quickly, absorbing the strategy for answering the questions but not memorizing any of the answers. It is a good idea to pick out a few questions that stand out as either right on target or problematic for you and practice your answers in writing and out loud. Martin

Yate has put "Ten Questions You Must be Prepared For" and "Five Stress Questions and How to Keep Cool" on the Career City web site, and it is well worth your time to read them and the thinking process for answering the questions at *http://www.careercity.com/content/interview/index. asp.* This site also provides information covering many interviewing issues from dress to body language.

Yate also defines "twenty admired key personal traits" that he feels are sought by all successful companies. The traits fall within the following categories: **Personal**: drive, communication skills, chemistry, energy, determination, confidence; **Professional:** reliability, honesty/integrity, pride, dedication, analytical skills, listening skills; **Achievement**: money saved, time saved, money earned; and **Business**: efficiency, economy, procedures, profit. Being able to articulate these traits as they apply to you will increase your repertoire for answering questions. You can fall back on this information if you are asked a substantive question that you cannot answer. Demonstrate that you appreciate the importance of the topic and have the traits necessary to overcome your deficit.

Another web site on interviewing worth your while is from Rice University's Career Center called "Elements of a Successful Interview." Print it out, and you will have an excellent check list to go over before your interview which will remind you of many practical do's and don'ts. The address is *http://riceinfo.rice.edu/projects/careers/channels/six/Interview/text/The.interview.html*.

FREQUENTLY ASKED QUESTIONS (FAQS)

In addition to the questions you may have composed, you must be prepared for the following questions, which in our experience, are the most frequently asked questions. A more lengthy list of questions you may be asked as well as questions you should ask are included at the end of this chapter. We have given you some suggestions on how to think about your answers, and some explanations of what the questions mean to the employer. Be sure to plan how you can ask questions of the interviewer and what these questions might be; remember to keep the interview a dialogue. You shouldn't be the one to do all the talking.

1. What are your strengths?
The answer to this should be within a framework relevant to the company and job. Again, get inside the head of the interviewer. What are the

essential strengths demanded by the mission and goals of the company? In your answers, include the ability to understand the overall goals/ mission of the company, the competencies you own and have used that are similar to those required for the position, and your personality traits that fit the job and corporate culture. Plan an ending to your answer; don't be tempted to ramble. Give the interviewer a chance to ask a follow-up question to one of the good points you have made.

2. What are your weaknesses?

If you are asked the question with this phrasing, you can handle it fairly easily. The straight-up question allows you to speak of a weakness you had in the past that you have corrected through your initiative and training. Do not let this question get you talking about your personal life, no matter how nice and understanding the interviewer may appear to be. If you do, you will lose your focus and valuable time.

Be aware of "weakness" questions asked in a more oblique fashion, such as have you ever been criticized, what problems did you have on your last job, what is difficult for you, where do you want to improve, what bothers you in this profession? Often these questions provide you with a great opportunity to share something positive about yourself that hasn't been asked. Try to keep that attitude, take your time, and you will turn a negative into something good for yourself.

There are also questions that you dread that could easily fall under the "weakness" category. These might be, why have you changed jobs so many times, why did you leave your last job, were you ever fired or asked to resign, what were you doing during the five-year gap on your resume, do you have a college degree, why haven't you listed your last supervisor as a reference? In response to a "dreaded" question, we often coach our clients to say, "I am glad you brought that up because. . . ." Just saying those words out loud will empower you and take your interviewer by surprise, giving you the advantage. Your answers to your "dreaded" questions should definitely be rehearsed. Say them out loud in the shower or at a red light until the words flow so easily that no visceral feelings of stress are kicked off.

3. Where do you want to be in five years?

In some ways, this is an outdated question because change is about the only thing you can count on in the workplace. Certainly high-tech companies are lucky if they can anticipate six months ahead, let alone have five-year long-range plans. You can share your career goals, your commitment to your career, and your ability to handle change. Explain that you have taken change seriously with a plan to accumulate multiple flexible skill sets to ensure yourself for success and a job five years from now. You can then add a more traditional answer projecting a career path which will illustrate your understanding of the profession and the forecasts for the industry gleaned from your research and informational interviewing. The Princeton Review web site has Career Search at *http://www.review.com/* which defines vocational areas and gives examples of what to expect at different years into your career. The standard reference is the *Occupational Outlook Handbook* at *http://stats.bls.gov/ocohome.htm*. It also projects what a career will be in the future.

4. What can you do for us? or Tell us about yourself.

This seems like the ultimate open-ended question, but you are really being asked, "Why should we hire you?" They do not want to know about your personal life. Your answer will depend somewhat on the placement of this question in the interview. If it is at the beginning of the interview, you should succinctly illustrate your strengths and how you accumulated them, including a little of your work history. You can also demonstrate your knowledge of the company, and that you are interested in learning a lot more during the interview. This will set the stage for the dialogue to follow. If the question comes at the end of the interview, you may want to start with a few questions that remain in your mind about the company or the job. Then you have a chance to pull together the best of the interview and add anything important that wasn't covered. Summarize your skills, traits, and experience and then illustrate, as specifically as you can, how they could be used to help the company solve problems and attain its mission and goals.

5. Choose three adjectives that best describe you. Why?

This isn't necessarily one of the most frequently asked questions, but it is a popular one right now, and we think a very good one. The preparation for it will be used in your answers whether the question is asked or not. First write down some adjectives that come to your mind immediately, then check your MBTI/Keirsey profile and Interest Sheet from the Career Interest Game for additional adjectives. Think it over and choose three that are genuine and also sell you for the job. And be sure you are prepared for the follow-up question, "Why?"

The **close of the interview** is very important. Just as the first twenty seconds determines the first impression of you, the close or your exit can determine the lasting impression. It is entirely appropriate for you to ask what the time frame for the hiring will be and if there will be a second interview. Don't ask questions about salary. Do say you would like the job or that you are very interested and look forward to a second interview. Most people do not do this; if you are interested and say so, it may be a distinguishing factor for you. If you are disappointed or relieved to have the interview over, try not to reveal it in either words or body language. Leave with the same confidence and self-assurance with which you entered. Look the interviewer in the eye, smile, shake hands, and be genuine. Whatever you would naturally say when leaving someone will be just fine and will help you to be remembered as a real person rather than one of the interviewees.

Part of the close for the interview is the follow-up thank you letter. Right after the interview, quickly write down your impressions and any specifics that you want to remember. Also write down anything that you feel you forgot to say or ask in the interview. When you get home, type a thank you letter that is both a business letter and a personal note of appreciation. Honestly express what impressed you in the interview, anything about the company and position that particularly interested you and why, and any additional information that might support your candidacy. Again, say that you are very interested in the position and feel qualified to make a significant contribution. Most importantly, sincerely thank the interviewer for the time spent with you.

DIFFERENT TYPES OF INTERVIEWS

Knowing what to expect in different types of interviews will also help you to be more prepared. **Directed interviews** are often used for screening purposes by personnel departments and are impersonal in nature. They involve a definite series of questions within a given period of time. Do not be surprised if the interviewer uses a checklist. These interviews are difficult to turn around because the interviewer is so focused. It is important not to take this kind of interview personally. It is not a reflection on you. Try to remember that this is the way this company conducts initial interviews. Make it your goal to present yourself well enough to make it to the next round.

Nondirected interviews are loosely structured, and the interviewer acts more like a moderator. You are more likely to encounter this kind of interview in the second or third interview. You will be asked broad and general questions which give you an opportunity to show your personality and how your work style and goals fit in with the company. This format gives you a lot of control so it is important to mentally remind yourself of your agenda. This is an interview with a great deal of give and take. Information is shared; a real dialogue takes place.

Stress interviews are not frequently used but it is better that you be prepared for them in the event that you encounter one. The point of the interview is to make you uncomfortable and to test how you handle stressful situations. The interviewer may utilize silence, criticize your resume, ask for a creative idea and then say she doesn't like it, challenge you on anything you say, or ask you a number of questions without giving you a chance to answer them. Make a sincere effort to overcome the objections and antagonism by maintaining a calm composure. Try to respond in a positive way by selling your skills, experience, and assets. A sense of humor along with confidence will go a long way to help you get through a stress interview.

Group interviews can feel like a stress interview but are most often used to save employees' time and make a number of people in the department feel involved in hiring a new employee. They are becoming more common because of the focus on work teams. What they are looking for is to see how you would fit in with the group, what your leadership abilities are, how you solve problems, and how you interact with others. The main thing to remember is to establish eye contact with more than one person when answering a question and to look at everyone, not just the person who may seem to be the leader. Try to establish some rapport with each person so they will all remember you when it is time to make a decision.

The **telephone interview** is being used more and more, and in the future, it is clear that you will be interviewed computer to computer. You should have a file of information for every position you have applied for. Have them handy, so that you can find them when the call comes. Again, preparation is the key. Usually telephone interviews are initial interviews and used for screening purposes. Your goal is to try to stand out, show that you have done your homework, and that you are a serious candidate.

CORPORATE CULTURE

There is a myth that plain hard work will get you ahead. However, if you are in the wrong culture, all that hard work will not make a lot of difference. The culture of an organization is its personality. It is made up of values and beliefs that are usually reflective of the owner, president, or founder.

Understanding the culture of an organization before you work there is a very difficult task. According to Ellen Wallach, "Organization culture is like pornography; it is hard to define, but you know it when you see it." However, here are several suggestions that should help define it and determine how you function in it.

Always keep the corporate culture in mind when you are networking, informational interviewing, and in the interview itself. Keep your eyes and ears open for comments regarding support for professional growth, the benefit package, rate of turnover, leadership styles, employee morale, the style of dress, typical length of the work day, attitude toward the work/family dilemma, and the ease and frequency of internal communication. If you haven't been able to assess the corporate culture through your interviews, here are some concrete suggestions for your investigation.

Call the public relations department and ask them to send you some material about the company. What kind of impression do the materials give you? What kind of image is being presented? Does the information seem forthright or withholding? Are people in the organization featured, and in what way?

Find out the name of the CEO and learn everything you can about her. Conduct an Internet search using her name and find out if any articles have been written about her. You can also ask the public relations department for a press kit. Press kits usually contain biographical material on the CEO.

Trust your initial impressions. When you walk into the reception area, are you made to feel welcome? How does the receptionist respond to phone calls? How do the employees interact with her? Is the attitude one of respect or indifference between employees? How are the employees dressed: casually, professionally, or a combination? Ask to talk to people who work there or have worked there. Also speak to customers or clients. You will be dealing with a lot of soft information. Study the values espoused by the organization. What are the corporate goals? Do they reflect values and goals that you can support?

Ask for a tour of the company that includes the cafeteria and staff room. This will provide an additional opportunity to see and feel what it might be like working there. Trust your gut. If you get one message from the physical environment and yet someone is telling you something very different, you need to do a little more investigation.

Don't confuse corporate culture with the mission of the company or organization. Often career changers think that working for a nonprofit will ensure working with nice people, a kind atmosphere at work, fair reviews, and an absence from the bottom-line mentality. Nothing could be further from the truth. In fact, some of the most abusive work environments we have heard about were nonprofit counseling centers. Another was an organization that planned conferences for famous authors of self-help books, many of which covered stress reduction. The irony was that this company would not allow its employees to take lunch breaks! As we mentioned before, the manner, competency, philosophy, and leadership style of the head of the organization is a much better indication of corporate culture than the mission of the company.

Defining the right organizational culture for you is much more of a challenge than defining the right job. Your progress in a certain organization will certainly depend a great deal on your compatibility with corporate culture. You will be rewarded for "fitting in" as much as for what you do. Carried to its extreme, this is often how incompetent people get rewarded by an organization. But in your case, you are looking for that environment that reflects your values and allows you to do your best work.

David G. Jensen, of BioOnline, shares many of his articles in full text at *http://www.bio.com/hr/search/articlelist.html*. We suggest you take a look at "Your Stay or Leave Equation" and "Birkenstocks or White Shirts —Which Is Right for You?" Jenson's advice is definitely appropriate for all career fields.

SALARY NEGOTIATION

The best indicator for success in salary negotiation is the degree of homework you have done in determining competitive salary levels for the position you are considering. You may have already been inquiring about salary ranges in your research up to this point, which is terrific. But if you feel you need more salary information, the Internet will be a big help. Here are a few sites.

1. Extensive salary survey information from professional surveys for forty career areas can be found at *http://jobsmart.org/tools/salary/*
2. Salary ranges and related earnings information about 25 professions are at *http://pw1.netcom~tomb/recruitment/salaries.html*
3. WageWeb: Salary Survey Data Online, salaries for 150 benchmark positions at *http://www.wageweb.com/*
4. The *Wall Street Journal* Career Center's Industry by industry look at salaries compiled by the *New Business Employment Weekly* at *http://careers.wsj.com/*

But even with the Internet you may need to be a detective and do some snooping. We coach clients to call the human resource department of a similar company, and ask for the person in charge of compensation. If the compensation person isn't there, ask for his name, so that when you call back later you will ask to speak to Mr. Compensation. When you reach the compensation manager, honestly say, "I am applying for x position at another company in your industry and am wondering if you would be willing to give me the salary range for that position." Most often, they will give it to you. Or you can call a similar company and ask to speak to the person in the same position. When you reach the person, in your sincerest voice, say, "I am applying for a similar position in another company and am trying to research appropriate salaries. Would you mind telling me the salary range for your position?" Always ask for a range so that you don't put that person on the spot.

There are also excellent salary surveys for every profession done by wage and salary compensation specialists or consultants. These surveys contain the information that compensation managers use to determine salary ranges in their own institutions. These surveys are as detailed as the following: executive secretary in the high-tech industry in the 128 corridor or fourth-year psychiatric social worker in a teaching hospital in Boston. You can sometimes access this information through professional associations or a major business library.

The dialogue you had with your employer in the initial interviews will in part determine the success of your salary negotiation. For example, you can't be a passive interviewer and then expect to negotiate the salary. Negotiation involves a good dialogue in which you clearly articulate the skills and experience you have to contribute; this will establish your value, and money follows value.

Before going into the interview in which you will be discussing your salary, make a complete assessment of living expenses. Determine what

your salary range is. Have hard figures in mind for the minimum you would be willing to earn and for your ideal salary. You should also be thinking about your preferred benefit package because benefits can equal up to thirty percent of your salary. They can include medical and/or dental insurance, pension plans, vacation, stock options, tuition reimbursement, commissions, bonuses, and sick leave. (Some forward thinking companies even have wellness days!) Other kinds of benefits are professional memberships, credit cards, transportation and mileage reimbursement. Be sure that you understand the compensation package and any options from which you will have to choose before settling on a salary and accepting the job.

Ideally, the employer will offer you an excellent salary or give you the salary range that would be acceptable and you will accept the higher figure in that range. Even if the salary is perfect, it is generally advised that you not take the offer on the spot. Say that you would like to think about it overnight and will get back to him tomorrow.

However, if the scenario is not so perfect, you may be pushed to state what you want for compensation before the employer will show his hand. Respond with, "I understand the salary range for this position in similar companies is $???? to $???, and I assume your salary range is competitive." If you are caught off guard and don't know the competitive salary range, try saying, "I'm sure your company's salary policy is competitive. What is the range for this position?" If the employer agrees with the range you give, or if the range he states is in sync with your personally determined salary range, you will probably verbalize your approval for your ideal salary figure within the stated range. If the salary offered to you is way below your minimum acceptable salary, you will be faced with either declining the offer or entering a negotiation process. This is your choice, and it is fine to walk away if that is what feels right for you. On the other hand, it is okay to ask for money, and experience shows that those who ask for it usually get it.

If you really want this job, you should calmly say that the figure is not in your acceptable range but that you are very interested in the position and hope that the two of you can work something out. Site the reasons for wanting more money. It may be that you were making more in your previous job and/or that you feel that what you would contribute to the company is well worth a higher figure. Again say, "I hope we can work something out. We both seem to want the same thing; you would like me to come on board, and I very much want to work for you."

Assuming that your previous experience of give and take with this person continues, the employer will probably make a counter offer or enter into a dialogue. Some possibilities for compromise are foregoing a six-month review in order to start at the higher salary figure, working out a signing bonus, negotiating a more favorable benefits package, or more stock options. After talking for a while, either one of you may want to have some time to think over the possibilities. Thank him for his willingness to discuss the options, tell him that you very much want to work out a settlement acceptable to both of you and that you look forward to his call. You have done all you can at the moment and will continue to prepare for that phone call.

For more information on the art of salary negotiating, take a look at these web sites:

Wall Street Journal-Articles on All Aspects of Salary Negotiation
http://public.wsj.com/careers/resources/documents/
cwc-jobhunt.htm
David G. Jensen's Cautionary Advice
http://www.bio.com/hr/search/negotiation.html
How to Get a Better Than Average Raise
http://www.hardatwork.com/Escalator/raise.html

A FINAL WORD

The purpose of interviewing is to gather information about the world of work and to present your knowledge and skills that qualify you for your life work objective. The dialogue that takes place during the interview will provide realistic feedback on the marketplace. It is okay to recognize the limits imposed by the reality of the work world, but don't give up on your core definition. Trust yourself and the direction you decided upon as a result of careful deliberation. What is the essence of what you want? What is your purpose? What are your short- and long-range goals? To what degree does the current opportunity allow you to fulfill your vision? Is this the place for you to take the next step in fulfilling your life work objective?

BOX 9.2 SAMPLE INTERVIEW QUESTIONS

Individual Needs and Commitment to Employer:

Tell me about yourself. (Why should we hire you?)
Why are you interested in this company?
What interests you about this position?
What is your greatest weakness? Your greatest strength?
What do you know about our company?
Where do you want to be in five years?

Professional Qualifications:

What jobs have you held? How were they obtained and why did you leave?
What qualifications and unique qualities do you have to succeed in this job?
What unique qualities do you bring to the workplace?
What have you done that shows initiative and willingness to work?
What areas of training and experience have recently developed?
How would you rank yourself in terms of computer and Internet literacy?

Interpersonal Relationships and Adaptability:

What do you think determines a person's progress in a good company?
Do you prefer working with others or by yourself?
Can you take instructions without feeling upset?
Have you ever had any difficulty getting along with other people?
What experience have you had working in teams?
Describe your experience supervising other people?
How do you manage excessive demands in your job?
How do you handle stressful situations or a stressed employee?

Behavioral Questions Specific to Your Profession:

How would you write a marketing plan for this scenario?
Here is a computer program. Show me how you would debug it.
Demonstrate how you would you design a three-fold brochure for sales.
How would you go about writing copy for a special feature on health?
Here is a financial report. How would you go about evaluating it?
Sell me this bag of chips.

Additional Questions:

What did you like least on your last job?
Tell me about the best boss you ever had. The worst.

What are your professional goals?
What have you done to improve yourself professionally in this past year?
Just what does success mean to you? How do you judge it?
What is the greatest problem you have overcome?
What do you consider your greatest achievement?
How much money do you want when asked early in the interview?

Objections:

You are too old, You are too young.
You do not seem to have any of the qualifications we are looking for.
This seems to be a career switch.
You are over-qualified.
You lack the educational requirements.

BOX 9.3   QUESTIONS TO ASK YOUR INTERVIEWER

Regardless of the type of position, you must be prepared to ask intelligent, informed questions that reflect your interest, knowledge, enthusiasm, and experience.

- Could you review the job description and/or duties? (make sure you understand what is expected.)
- Who would I be reporting to? (If someone other than the interviewer, ask to meet them.)
- Could you show me where this department fits in the organizational chart?
- Why is this opening available now?
- What do you think are the most important qualifications for the position?
- Is there a system for performance reviews? How frequently?
- Is the company anticipating major changes in growth or direction?
- What kind of training do you offer?
- End some of your answers with questions back to the interviewer. The topic will depend on the question; remember to make the interview conversational and a dialogue.

10

A New Beginning: Your Next
Life Work Transition

"Online, by experiencing the fluidity of the self, we can
experiment and explore every side of ourselves, including the
shadow side. We can play."   *Jeff Zaleski*

Congratulations. You have just completed our process for finding your
life work as a form of self-identity and self-expression. You have engaged in a unique process preparing you for the twenty-first century by
combining serious personal inner reflection and using the Internet, the
ultimate culture of change. The outcome can be experiencing your authentic self in fulfilling life work and at the same time making change a
natural part of your life.

In the process you have gathered strength from spiritual reflection
and the power of technology. You have gained an appreciation of how
you learn and what motivates you. You have also gained an appreciation
for life-long learning, a tool that prepares you for the future and positions you to be proactive in sorting out the possibilities for opportunity
in life and work. While doing so, you added skills and attitudes necessary to lead instead of just manage change.

There is momentum built into the process presented in this book.
Finding your true north and getting in touch with your spiritual core is a
fluid rather than static process. It assumes change and that you are interested in keeping up with your evolving self. Likewise, the culture of
the Internet is also fluid, moving and changing. Even being willing to
use the Internet means that you must automatically learn to roll with
and adapt to a moving target. You start **naturally** expecting change, and

acquire a sense of confidence that you will be able to go with it. Merging a spiritual journey with a journey in cyberspace is an excellent preparation for the change that is forecasted for every facet of our lives. The two even have similarities in vocabulary, for example, search, explore, and journey.

In addition to helping you accept change as a natural part of your life, our process has also given you concrete information about yourself and the world of work. You know the who, what, why, and where of your mission and purpose and you know the who, what, why, and where of the area of work that you have chosen. You also have the tools to use the powerful capability of the Internet to find, research, and secure the work that you love. Right now, you are feeling very confident because you have been through a healing and rich learning experience. We wish you joy and fulfillment in your transition in work whether it be a new job, a new profession, a better working environment, building your new business or cutting back—deciding that what is enough for you is less rather than more.

The skills you have learned in this process are life long learning skills. The shock, dismay, sadness, and fear you may have felt when you started this process will not happen the next time you need to make a transition in work. You will know that you can revisit our tutorial and go through the exercises that were most meaningful to you for establishing your True North. Or you may find that a different combination of exercises will be helpful to you in a new transition. You can return to Part III to select the exercises that will be most helpful and go to our web site, *http://www.lifeworktransitions.com* for free printouts.

You will also know which developmental models described in Part I were most comforting, inspiring, and insightful for you. And you will know that the step-by-step process and the Internet sites for success in Getting the Lay of the Land, Verifying Your Interest, and Applying for and Getting the Job in Chapter Seven will renew your confidence for engaging in and completing the job search process. You can also take comfort that our Internet site will have new up-to-date sites listed for all the areas covered in this book.

When the call for change comes to you, whether it is in response to some shift in your environment, or from an inner desire to express or be more than you are now, return to Part I and reflect on the models that have been your guides. Bridges remind us that for every ending there is a new beginning. With our four-part model you were introduced to the concept that you had the answers inside of you to find and create meaningful life work. The theory of Abraham Maslow introduced the knowledge that you could experience self-actualization through your work. As a result of understanding the nine stages of career development you probably can better name and resolve some of the vocational development issues that you are currently facing and that may help you move on. And last but not least, your body may be crying out to you to get your attention, from some stress-related symptoms. Pay attention.

If you find yourself reluctant to change, be kind to yourself and try to understand why you feel that way. Endings are always difficult because of the loss involved and the sadness we experience. In order to shift your response to change, acknowledge and address the importance of having your basic survival needs met. The necessity for taking personal responsibility for embracing your life work, requires a solid enough financial, emotional, and spiritual foundation. Perhaps you are willing to give up the comfort of belonging that comes with your current situation to risk assuming increased self esteem you know will come from making a change.

The beauty of Maslow's hierarchy of needs, is the basic assumption that the lower needs must be met, in order to achieve the higher levels of functioning. You may have been thrilled at the idea of experiencing self-actualization through your work. By accepting and expressing your inner core and choosing to develop the skills and talents that result in "full functioning," you bring your higher self to your life work. The insight provided by this motivational model can help you accept the idea that change can be natural and harmonious.

Our four-part model can help you accurately assess the kind of change you want to make in order to be more self-actualized through your work. Return to your personal mandala, and reflect on what you have been doing. Review the skills and knowledges and prioritize those that produce less return, and redesign your skills portfolio. Then reexamine your environment. Would you rather be partnering and collaborating with others on different kinds of projects to realize your true self? Who would you really like to be connecting with and serving? And finally, are you committed to your sense of purpose, or are there new concerns and opportunities calling to you? By reviewing your core, you will find the area of your life that needs your attention in order to begin the transition process. The core information from your personal mandala calls you to always be doing your true work.

In order to further your growth while increasing your commitment to change, we are going to review the nine stages of career development.

The first three stages of the model are a reminder of when you moved from reliance on external authority to the awareness that a process existed to help you make decisions. When your career began you might have believed, "Ah, this is it. I've found my niche." Then something occurred to make you aware of the possibility that a "wrong" decision had been made. Perhaps this book came to you when you were open to the possibility that there was a process that could be substituted for the authority you had previously held dear. And so this journey began.

During the next three stages, which simulate the neutral zone described by William Bridges, you can transform the chaos into creativity as you began to realize there are multiple "good" decisions and that you are truly free to experiment. You can experience yourself as a good decision-maker who is capable of resiliency, and you possess the innate wisdom to make a course correction when necessary. And finally, your awareness of the chaos of free choice forever ends the illusion that someone else is in charge of your life or your work (or your life work).

And now you long to continue your true life work as an extension of your career development. You want to experience the integration of self and career role as one and the same. You know that work must allow you to express and be all you can be. The commitment you experience is to yourself and the full expression of the value-laden criteria shown in your personal mandala. That is how we truly learn and grow and stay alive to that which is best within us.

And finally, let us review the energies of the seven chakras and get centered, as you prepare to lead change. Where do you feel most alive? Look at the questionnaire in Part One and discern where the blocks to your creativity might lie. When you are performing your daily activities with sincerity and commitment you are experiencing self-actualization. When you are connected from the first to the seventh chakra you are able to live a life of values, ethics, courage, and humanitarianism. Are you fully present in the moment, while using your best capacities? Do you feel inspired or guided by some higher purpose? Are you committed to following through on the next phase of this upwardly spiraling journey?

Having previously reviewed the first three motivational needs, you understand that your basic needs for safety and belonging must be met for change to occur naturally. The need for independence, freedom, achievement, and prestige connect to the corresponding energies of the first through the fourth chakras. In order to create a truly authentic life, we must develop the appropriate use of personal power. This activity is reflected in the fifth chakra, the center of will power. When you have found your voice and are following your dream, use your personal power to create and learn the important issues of self-control, rather than control over others. Exercising your will is truly about learning to surrender and accept what is.

By developing insight and intuition you can see beyond the visible and are able to reconsider your beliefs. The sixth chakra center runs the power of the mind and thus carries tremendous authority. The pursuit of truth and the ability to be self-reflective enhances your openness to the ideas of others and encourages you to learn from your experience. And finally, you won't be afraid to explore the deeper questions such as "Why was I born?" and "What is the deeper meaning of my life?" As you do so, you will develop more of your faith and spiritual awareness. When you are doing the work you love and love the way you are doing it, you are fully present to yourself.

If you want to pursue the models further, consider the following questionnaire. In your next transition, ask yourself these questions.

1. Do I feel suspended in an unfamiliar space without any roots or security?
2. What physical symptoms am I experiencing? Headaches, stiff neck, chest pain, stomach upset, pain in the posterior?
3. Are my security needs being met?
4. Do I wish someone else would just tell me what to do?
5. What part of my current or last job was the most distressful: the people, the location, the structure of authority, or the tasks and responsibilities?
6. Is fear commonplace in my work environment or industry?
7. Am I angry or bitter because of a lack of acknowledgment and recognition?
8. Am I having conflict with upper management because I think my ideas aren't being heard?
9. Do I want to be more of who I am in my vocation?
10. Do I want a position where my mission and purpose in life is fulfilled?
11. Do I feel excited about the next steps, have clarity about my values, and feel a sense of anticipation?
12. Am I questioning the very substance of my being?
13. Do I love what I do on a daily basis?

14. Am I discouraged over the fact that my degree did not lead where I thought it would?
15. Am I lacking the skills needed for most of the available jobs?

These questions reflect the insight and theory espoused by the five models presented in this book. If you answered yes to the most of the fifteen questions, review all of Part I. If you checked questions 1, 6, and 11, reread the information about William Bridges "Transitions." If you checked 2, 7, and 12, reread the chakra information formulated by Carolyn Myss. If you checked, 3, 8, and 13, take some time and consider Maslow's Hierarchy of Needs. If you checked 4, 9, and 14, go to our web site and read the entire text of Bob Ginn's "Nine Stages of Career Development." If you checked 5, 10, and 15, you are in the right place. Go to our web site and print the exercises from Part III; they will soon get you back on your True North.

What does the future hold? Create a new mandala that will help you reposition yourself in the world of work. Use this to screen out irrelevant information and focus on that which will bring you closer to your new position and place, using the tools you have learned to navigate the Internet.

We hope you have been able to play with the Internet to pursue your personal interests and needs as well as visit the career sites we have introduced to you in this book. The information is limitless, but so is the fun.

Having acquired the skills to navigate the Internet and manifest the intranet of your personal mandala, you are prepared to engage in the twenty-first century. As we near the conclusion of this project, we are clear that the rapidity of change brought about by technology will forever change the way we work. According to Alvin Toffler, author of *Future Shock* and *The Third Wave*, "Electronic commerce is going to radically reduce the cost of an enormous range of services and products and change the entire relationship of the society to the nature of work."

The Internet is the source of the change in the relationship between society and the nature of work. With the skills and knowledge you have acquired you need not fear the vastness of cyberspace. There is a myth that you can get lost on the Internet. Not so. You can always turn it off, and when you return, go to *http://www.lifeworktransition.com* and The Riley Guide. To relax a little you can go to Dilbert at *http://www.dilbert.com* and then, take a break. The Internet is manageable.

We hope you'll enjoy connecting with others on the World Wide Web. Research any topic that mirrors your beliefs. Whatever the reason or the need, the possibilities that exist on the Internet are infinite. And if it isn't there now, it will in the near future. In fact, maybe you'll be responsible for putting information on the Net, through a forum or list. Or you post a resume and from that get hired. It is possible you may start your own business and use email to connect with potential and new clients, to be followed soon after with your business web page.

The potential of this medium for connecting with the marketplace is infinite. As long as you know your criteria, your "true north," and that you can always turn off your computer, you will never get lost. The clarity of purpose and value illustrated in your personal mandala will help you verify the quality and relevance of information you gather. This medium provides tremendous opportunities for learning, partnering, and collaborating. According to Justine and Michael Toms, in their book *True Work*, "often it is the technology of the age that reflects the unfolding of a new consciousness. The Internet and the World Wide Web are an outer expression of what's taking place inside each of us—the recognition of our singular place and connection with the whole. The paradox is that we live in a time of great alienation as well."

We have done our best to promote sites on the Internet that are free and accessible to the public. Our personal favorites and standbys for Career Search are:

Ideas for the Future: The Global Ideas Bank:
  http://www.globalideasbank.org
Search Engine Tutorial: Search Engine Watch:
  http://www.searchenginewatch.com
Comprehensive Tutorial on Using the Internet: UC Berkeley
  Library Internet: A Tutorial: *http://www.lib.berkeley.edu
  /TeachingLib/Guides/Internet/FindInfo.html*
Meta Career Site: The Riley Guide:
  http://www.rileyguide.com
Overall Career Service Center: JobSmart:
  http://www.jobsmart.org
Comprehensive Assessment: University of Waterloo Career Center:
  http://www.adm.uwaterloo.ca/infocecs/CRC/
Assessment Test: The Keirsey Type Sorter:
  http://www.keirsey.com/frame.html and then
  http:www.doi.gov/octc/typescar.html

Interest Inventory: Holland Interests Game:
http://www.esc.state.nc.us/soicc/planning/c1a.htm and then
http://www.missouri.edu/~cppcwww/holland.shtml
Skills Analysis: Bowling Green Career Center:
http://www.bgsu.edu/offices/careers/process/competen.html
Goals: Top Achievement:
http://www.topachievement.com
Industry Review: Hoovers:
http://www.hoovers.com
Definitions of Vocations: Occupational Outlook Handbook:
http://stats.bls.gov/ocohome.htm
Relevant Vocational Information: America's Career Infonet:
http://www.acinet.org/acinet/occ_sea1.htm
Specific Job Titles: Human Resources Development Canada:
http://www.hrdc-drhc.gc.ca/JobFutures/
Salary Information: Wall Street Journal:
http://careers.wsj.com/
Professional Associations: Associations Online:
http://www.ipl.org/ref/AON/
Professional Journals (Online): News Directory.Com:
http://www.ecola.com
Company Research: Researching Companies Tutorial by Deb
Flanagan: *http://home.sprintmail.com/~debflanagan/index.html*
Resumes: Ten Minute Resume:
http://www.10minuteresume.com/
Cover Letters: CareerLab Cover Letter Library:
http://www.careerlab.com/letters/
Job Fairs: JobWeb:
http://www.jobweb.com
Job Posting Site: The Monster Board:
http://www.monster.com
Interviews: Career City:
http://www.careercity.com/content/interview/index.asp
Maps to the Interview: Yahoo's Map Service:
http://maps.yahoo.com/py/maps.py
Salary Negotiation: Hard@Work:
http://www.hardatwork.com/Escalator/raise.html
Advice: BioOnline's David G. Jensen:
http://bio.com/hr/search/search_1.html

We hope this journey to know and express your unique talents in response to critical needs in society has been enjoyable and rewarding. Since you have been exposed to the issues involved in vocational growth and development, you should have a better understanding of yourself as you learn to anticipate and lead change. Remember you can always get up-to-date information, or tips, to help with future change from our web site *http://www.lifeworktransitons.com.* You can also let us know how this book has helped you. Tell us your story and let us know about changes in your life work. What better way to emphasize that both this book and life work transitions never conclude . . . they just open up new beginnings for all of us.

Appendix: Web Sites

These sites are accurate as of July 7, 1999. Any changes since that date will be available and updated regularly at http://www.lifeworktransitions.com.

PART I Putting Your Spirit to Work in the 21st Century

http://www.nzdances.co.nz/journal/benefits.htm
http://www.gbod.org/quest/bookreviews/transitions.html
http://www.gwi.net/chutch/when.htm
http://www.globalideasbank.org
http://www.Year2000.com
http://www.flownetwork.com
http://www.maslow.com
http://www.cfil.com
http://myss.com

PART II Beginners Guide to the Internet

The Best Collection of Sites Relating to Job Search
http://www.rileyguide.com

Bookmarks
http://www.learnthenet.com/english/html/17bookmark.htm

Search Engines
http://www.yahoo.com
http://www.infoseek.com
http://www.altavista.com
http://www.aol.com/netfind/

Tutorials for Learning the Internet
http://howto.yahoo.com/
http://www.go.com/Help?pg=SearchTips.htm
http://www.lib.berkeley.edu/TeachingLib/Guides/Internet/FindInfo.html
http://searchenginewatch.com
http://www.cnet.com/Content/Features/Dlife/Habits/

Examples of Endings

http://www.avid.com
http://www.redcross.org
http://www.stanford.edu/

Logging In

http://www.nytimes.com/
http://www.careerpath.com

Navigating a Site

http://www.monster.com

Email

http://www.emailaddresses.com/
http://home.voyager.co.nz/email.htm
http://www.learnthenet.com/english/section/email.html

Practice

http://www.doi.gov/octc/intro.html

PART III   Finding Your True North: Creating Your Personal Mandala

http://www.ccl.org

Chapter I   *Telling Your Story*

http://keirsey.com/frame.html
http://www.doi.gov/octc/typescar.html

Chapter 2   *Defining Core Competencies*

http://www.academicinnovations.com/report.html
http://keirsey.com/frame.html
http://www.jist.com/adapt.htm
http://www.adm.uwaterloo.ca/infocecs/CRC
http://www.bgsu.edu/offices/careers/process/competen.html
http://www.adm.uwaterloo.ca/infocecs/CRC

Chapter 3   *Redefining Your Self: Passions, Preferences and Purpose*

http://www.esc.state.nc.us/soicc/planning/c1a.htm
http://www.missouri.edu/~cppcwww/holland.shtml.

Chapter 4   Goal Setting: Creating a Life Worth Living

http://www.smc.qld.edu.au/goals.htm
http://www.topachievement.com/

PART IV   Putting Your Spirit to Work in the Marketplace: Making the Connection

Chapter 6   Exploring the Wide World of Work Through the Internet

Explore What's Out There

http://www.businessweek.com/
http://www.adweek.com/
http://www.bls.gov/news.release/ecopro.toc.htm
http://www.carmelmiddle.org/olclass/math/jobs.html
http://stats.bls.gov/ocohome.htm
http://www.equimax.com

Temporary

http://www.dbm.com/jobguide/misc.html#temp

Industries

http://dir.yahoo.com/Business_and_Economy/Companies/
http://galaxy.tradewave.com/galaxy/Business-and-Commerce.html
http://home.sprintmail.com/~debflanagan/industry.html

Assessment Tests

http://keirsey.com/frame.html
http://www.doi.gov/octc/typescar.html
http://www.missouri.edu/~cppcwww/holland.shtml

Career Fields/Vocational Areas

http://www.uhs.berkeley.edu/careerlibrary/links/career.cfm
http://www.yahoo.com/Business_and_Economy/Employment/Jobs/
    Career_Fields/
http://jobsmart.org/tools/career/spec-car.htm
http://stats.bls.gov/ocohome.htm

Job Titles

http://www.review.com/birkman/
http://www.review.com/career
http://www.careerpath.com/

http://www.usnews.com/usnews/nycu/work/wo4find.htm
http://www.rileyguide.com

Professional Associations

http://www.ipl.org/ref/AON/
http://www.yahoo.com/Business_and_Economy/Organizations/Professional

Magazines and Journals

http://www.ecola.com/
http://dir.yahoo.com/News_and_Media/Magazines/

Educational Requirements

http://altavista.com
http://www.harvard.edu
http://www.umd.edu

Research Specific Organizations and Companies

http://jobsmart.org/hidden/coinfo.htm
http://www.hoovers.com
http://home.sprintmail.com/~debflanagan/index.html
http://www.rileyguide.com

Chapter 7   Using the Internet to Set Yourself Up for Success

GETTING THE LAY OF THE LAND

Industries

http://www.Hoovers.com
http://www.fuld.com/i3/index.html
http://businessdirectory.dowjones.com/

Vocational Areas

http://www.acinet.org/acinet/occ_sea1.htm

Specific Job Titles

http://www.hrdc-drhc.gc.ca/JobFutures/
http://www.review.com/career/
http://www.uhs.berkeley.edu/careerlibrary/links/occup.cfm
http://stats.bls.gov/ocohome.htm

Professional Associations and Journals

http://www.ipl.org/ref/AON/
http://www.shrm.org/hrtalk/
http://www.lib.uwaterloo.ca/society/overview.html

Forums, Lists

http://www.liszt.com
http:///www.n2h2.com/KOVACS/

Specific Organizations and Companies

http://www.excite.com
http://www.dogpile.com
http://www.yahoo.com
http://home.sprintmail.com/~debflanagan/index.html
http://www.rileyguide.com
http://www.jobhuntersbible.com
http://www.dbm.com/jobguide/employer.html

VERIFYING YOUR INTEREST

Informational Interview

http://www.quintcareers.com/informational_interviewing.html

APPLYING FOR THE JOB

Newspapers and Journals

http://www.careerpath.com
http://www.ipl.org/ref/AON/
http://www.yahoo.com/Business_and_Economy/Organizations/professional
http://www.ecola.com
http://www.libraries.rutgers.edu/rulib/socsci/busi/busejour.htm
http://www.lib.uwaterloo.ca/society

Homepages of Companies

http://www.amcity.com
http://dir.yahoo.com/Business_and_Economy/Companies

College Password Job Site

http://www.jobtrack.com

Job Fairs, Real and Virtual

http://www.careermosaic.com

Reviews of Job and Resume Posting Sites

http://www.jobhuntersbible.com
http://www.nbew.com/weddle/index.htm
http://www.careerxroads.com

Top Ten Job Posting Sites

Monster Board	http://www.monster.com
Career Builder	http://careerbuilder.com
Career Path	http://www.careerpath.com
America's JobBank	http://www.ajb.dni.us/
Job Options	http://www.joboptions.com
Headhunter.Net	http://www.headhunter.net/
Career Mosaic	http://www.careermosaic.com/
Career Web	http://www.careerweb.com/
Hot Jobs	http://www.hotjobs.com
NationJob Network	http://www.nationjob.com/

Sample of Industry Specific Job Posting Sites

Non-profits Community Career Center	http://www.nonprofitjobs.org/
Human Resources Society for HR Management	http://www.shrm.org/jobs/
Social Work NASW Jobs Online	http://www.naswdc.org/
Medicine Doc Job	http://www.docjob.com
Accounting AccountingNet	http://www.accountingnet.com/
Software Engineer Jobs.Internet.Com	http://jobs.internet.com/
Education Chronicle of Higher Ed	http://chronicle.com/jobs/
Park Service Nat'l Pk Service Careers	http://www.nps.gov/pub_aff/jobs.htm
Advertising Adweek Online	http://www.adweek.com
Telecommuting Telecommuting Jobs	http://www.tjobs.com/

More Niche or Industry Specific Job Posting Sites

http://www.dbm.com/jobguide/jobs.html

Job Posting Sites in Your Area

www.dbm.com/jobguide/jobs.html

Time Saving Web Sites

http://www.javelink.com
http://www.careerindex.com/

Chapter 8   The Resume and Cover Letter: The Perfect Introduction

http://www.lifeworktransitions.com
http://www.10minuteresume.com/
http://eresumes.com/
http://www.damngood.com/jobseekers/tips.html
http://www.dejanews.com
http://www.10minuteresume.com

http://www.eresumes.com/tut_asciiresume.html
http://www.careerxroads.com
http://www.nbew.com/weddle/index.htm
http://jobsmart.org/internet/reseval.htm
http://www.dejanews.com
http://jobsmart.org/tools/resume/res-what.htm
http://www.damngood.com/jobseekers/tips.html
http://www.careerlab.com/letters/

Chapter 9   Winning the Interview

Interviews

http://www.careercity.com/content/interview/index.asp
http://riceinfo.rice.edu/projects/careers/channels/six/Interview/text/
     The.interview.html
http://www.review.com/
http://stats.bls.gov/ocohome.htm
http://www. bio.com/hr/search/articlelist.html

Salary

http://jobsmart.org/tools/salary/
http://pw1.netcom.com~tomb/recruitment/salaries.html
http://www.wageweb.com
http://careers.wsj.com/
http://public.wsj.com/careers/resources/documents/cwc-jobhunt.htm
http://www.bio.com/hr/search/negotiation.html
http://www.hardatwork.com/Escalator/raise.html

Chapter 10   Your New Beginning

http://www.dilbert.com

If You Could Only Go to One Site . . .

Ideas for the Future: The Global Ideas Bank:
http://www.globalideasbank.org

Search Engine Tutorial: Search Engine Watch:
http://www.searchenginewatch.com/

Comprehensive Tutorial on Using the Internet: UC Berkeley Library Internet: A Tutorial:
http://www.lib.berkeley.edu/TeachingLib/Guides/Internet/FindInfo.html

Meta Career Site: The Riley Guide:
http://www.rileyguide.com

Overall Career Service Center: JobSmart:
http://www.jobsmart.org

Comprehensive Assessment: University of Waterloo Career Center:
http://www.adm.uwaterloo.ca/infocecs/CRC/

Assessment Test: The Keirsey Type Sorter:
http://www.keirsey.com/frame.html and then
http:www.doi.gov/octc/typescar.html

Interest Inventory: Holland Interests Game:
http://www.esc.state.nc.us/soicc/planning/c1a.htm
http://www.missouri.edu/~cppcwww/holland.shtml.

Skills Analysis: Bowling Green Career Center:
http://www.bgsu.edu/offices/careers/process/competen.html

Goals: Top Achievement:
http://www.topachievement.com

Industry Review: Hoovers:
http://www.hoovers.com

Definitions of Vocations: Occupational Outlook Handbook:
http://stats.bls.gov/ocohome.htm

Relevant Vocational Information: America's Career Infonet:
http://www.acinet.org/acinet/occ_sea1.htm

Specific Job Titles: Human Resources Development Canada:
http://www.hrdc-drhc.gc.ca/JobFutures/

Salary Information: Wall Street Journal:
http://careers.wsj.com/

Professional Associations: Associations Online:
http://www.ipl.org/ref/AON/

Professional Journals (Online): News Directory.Com:
http://www.ecola.com

Company Research: Researching Companies Tutorial by Deb Flanagan
http://home.sprintmail.com/~debflanagan/index.html

Resumes: Ten Minute Resume:
http://www.10minuteresume.com/

Cover Letters: CareerLab Cover Letter Library:
http://www.careerlab.com/letters/

Job Fairs: Career Fairs
http://www.careerfairs.com/careerfairs/default.htm

Job Posting Site: The Monster Board:
http://www.monster.com

Interviews: Career City:
http://www.careercity.com/content/interview/index.asp

Maps to the Interview: Yahoo's Map Service:
http://maps.yahoo.com/py/maps.py

Salary Negotiation: Hard@Work:
http://www.hardatwork.com/Escalator/raise.html

Advice: BioOnline's David G. Jensen:
http://bio.com/hr/search/search_1.html

Bibliography

Career Planning and Life Work References

Boldt, Laurence G. *How To Find the Work You Love*, New York: Viking Penguin, 1996.

———. *Zen and the Art of Making a Living: A Practical Guide to Creative Career Design*, New York: Penguin Books, 1993.

Bolles, Richard and Victoria B. Zenoff. *The Quick Job Hunting Map for Beginners*, Berkeley, CA: Ten Speed Press, 1977.

———. *The Three Boxes of Life: And How to Get Out of Them*, Berkeley, CA: Ten Speed Press, 1981.

———. *What Color is Your Parachute?*, Berkeley, CA: Ten Speed Press, 1998.

Campbell, David. *If You Don't Know Where You're Going You'll Probably End Up Somewhere Else*, Resources for Christian Living, 1990.

Crystal, John, and Richard N. Bolles. *Where Do I Go From Here With My Life?*, Berkeley, CA: Ten Speed Press, 1980.

Figler, Howard. *The Complete Job-Search Handbook*, New York: Henry Holt & Co., 1995.

Gilman, Cheryl. *Doing Work You Love: Discovering Your Purpose and Realizing Your Dreams*, NTC/Contemporary Books, 1997.

Hayes, Kit Harrington. *Managing Career Transitions: Your Career as a Work in Progress*, New York: Prentice Hall, 1996.

Jackson, Tom. *Guerrilla Tactics in the New Job Market*, New York: Bantam, 1992.

Jackson, Tom, and Ellen Jackson. *The New Perfect Resume*, New York: Doubleday, 1996.

Lakein, Alan. *How to Get Control of Your Time and Life*, Signet, 1976.

McMeekin, Gail. *The Twelve Secrets of Highly Creative Women: a Portable Mentor*, Conari, 2000.

Montross, David H., Theresa E. Kane, and Robert J. Ginn, Jr. *Career Coaching Your Kids*, Consulting Psychologists Press, Inc., 1997.

Sher, Barbara, and Annie Gottlieb. *Wishcraft How to Get What You Really Want*, New York: Ballantine Books, 1986.

———, and Barbara Smith. *I Could Do Anything If I Only Knew What It Was: How to Discover What You Really Want and How to Get It*, New York: Delacorte Press, 1994.

Tieger, Paul D., and Barbara Barron-Tieger. *Do What You Are: Discover the Perfect Career for You Through the Secrets of Personaity Type*, Boston: Little, Brown, 1995.

Toms, Justine, and Michael Toms. *True Work: The Sacred Dimension of Earning a Living*, Harmony Books, 1998.

Wood, Orrin G., Jr. *Your Hidden Assets*, New York: McGraw Hill Professional Book Group, 1982.

Yate, Martin John. *Knock 'Em Dead*, Adams Media Corporation, 1997.

Leadership and Self-Development

Bennis, Warren, and Burt Nanus. *Leaders: Strategies for Taking Charge*, San Francisco: Harper Collins, 1986.

Bridges, William. *Transitions: Making Sense of Life's Changes*, Reading, MA: Addison-Wesley, 1980.

———. *Creating You & Co.: Learn to Think Like the CEO of Your Own Career*. Perseus Books, 1998.

Boyett, Joseph, and Henry Conn. *Workplace 2000*, New York: Dutton, 1992.

———, with Jimmie Boyett. *Beyond Workplace 2000*, New York: Dutton, 1996.

Buechner, Frederick. *Wishful Thinking: A Seeker's ABC*, San Francisco: Harper Collins, 1993.

Csikszentmihalyi, Mihily. *Flow: The Psychology of Optimal Experience*, San Francisco: Harper Collins, 1991.

deCastillejo, Irene. *Knowing Woman: A Feminine Psychology*, Boston: Shambala, 1997.

Fox, Matthew. *The Reinvention of Work*, San Francisco: Harper Collins, 1995.

Frenier, Carol. *Business and the Feminine Principle*, Boston: Butterworth–Heinemann, 1997.

Gawain, Shakti. *Creative Visualizations*, New World Library, 1985.

———. *Creating True Prosperity*, New World Library, 1997.

Grossman, Rogers, & Moore. *Innovation, Inc.*, Wordware Publishing, 1987.

Hakim, Cliff. *We Are All Self-Employed: The New Social Contract for Working in a Changed World*, San Francisco: Berrett-Koehler, 1994.

Hall, Douglas. *The Career is Dead—Long Live the Career: A Relational Approach to Careers*, San Francisco: Josey-Bass, 1996.

Handy, Charles. *The Age of Unreason*, Boston: Harvard Business School Press, 1990.

Herrmann, Ned. *The Creative Brain*, Lake Lure, NC: Ned Herman Group, 1991.

———. *The Whole Brain Business Book*, New York: McGraw Hill, 1996.

Hillman, James. *The Soul's Code: In Search of Character and Calling*, New York: Random House, 1996.

Hyatt, Carol, and Linda Gottlieb. *When Smart People Fail, Rebuilding Yourself for Success*, New York: Penguin, 1993.

Keirsey, David, and Marilyn Bates. *Please Understand Me*, Prometheus Nemesis, 1984.

Knefelkamp, Lee, C. Widick, and C. Parker. *Applying New Developmental Findings*, New York: Jossey-Bass, 1978.

Maslow, Abraham. *Toward a Psychology of Being*, New York: John Wiley & Sons, 1968.

———. *Religious Values and Peak Experiences*, New York: Viking PR, 1994.

Myss, Caroline. *Why People Don't Heal and How They Can*, Harmony Books, 1997.

———. *Anatomy of the Spirit*, New York: Random House, 1997.

Noer, David. *Healing the Wounds*, San Francisco: Jossey-Bass, 1993.

Nouwen, Henri. *Reaching Out*, New York: Doubleday, 1986.

Ogilvey, James. *Living Without a Goal*, New York: Doubleday, 1995.

Perry, William G. *Forms of Intellectual and Ethical Development in the College Years: A Scheme*, San Francisco: Jossey-Bass, 1998.

Progroff, Ira. *At a Journal Workshop*, New York: JP Tarcher, 1992.

Ray, Michael, and Rochelle Myers. *Creativity in Business*, New York: Doubleday, 1988.

Ray, Minzler, and World Business Academy. *The New Paradigm in Business: Emerging Strategies for Leadership & Organizational Change*, New York: JP Tarcher, 1993.

Seivert, Sharon. *Working From Your Core—Personal and Corporate Wisdom in a World of Change*, Boston: Butterworth–Heinemann, 1997.

Spangler, David. *The Call*, New York: Putnam, 1996.

———. *Everyday Miracles*, New York: Bantam, 1996.

Whitworth, Laura, Henry Kimsey-House, and Phil Sandahl. *Co-Active Coaching*, Palo Alto, CA: Davies Black Publishing, 1998.

Wakefield, Dan. *The Story of Your Life: Writing a Spiritual Autobiography*, Boston: Beacon Press, 1990.

Zukav, Gary. *Seat of the Soul*, New York: St. Martin's Press, 1990.

Internet References

Crispin, Gerry, and Mark Mehler. *CareerXRoads*, New Jersey: MMC Group, 1998.

Kent, Peter. *Poor Richard's Website: Geek-Free, Commonsense Advice on Building a Low-Cost Website*, Lakewood, CO: Top Floor Publishing, 1998.

Raymond, Chet. "The F2F Challenge: Can a Body Meet a Body Coming through the Wire?" *The Boston Globe Magazine*, May 28, 1999.

Riley, Margaret, Frances Roehm, and Steve Oserman. *The Guide to Internet Job Searching*, Illinois: NTC/Contemporary Publishing Group, Inc., 1998–99.

Ryan, Michael E. "Job Hunting and Hiring on the Web," *PC Magazine*, May 25, 1999.

Smith, Rebecca. *Electronic Resumes and Online Networking*, Franklin Lakes, NJ: Career Press, 1999.

Zeleski, Jeff. *The Soul of Cyberspace: How New Technology is Changing Our Spiritual Lives*, San Francisco: Harper Collins, 1997.

About the Authors

DEBORAH L. KNOX

Deborah L. Knox has been a pioneer leader in the field of Career and Life Work Planning for over 20 years. Her career includes work in government, higher education, corporate America, grassroots community efforts, and start-up organizations. She received her early training from John Crystal, co-author with Richard Bolles of *Where Do I Go From Here With My Life?*, and formed Crystal Associates of New England in the early 1970s to introduce this model program for career and life work planning success.

Deborah was an early contributor to other model career programs locally (Continuum and The Women's Center at Lasell College) and nationally (Worcester Area Career Education Consortium, one of the first public/private partnerships funded by the Department of Labor and HEW). She conducted a major study for Operation A.B.L.E., "New England Employment Opportunities for Older Women Workers" in 1990.

In 1980, Deborah established her own career coaching business, Deborah L. Knox & Associates in Newton, Massachusetts. She combines an interest in and study of psychology, spirituality, Eastern Religion, and early religious traditions. With every client, she is interested in leadership development and provides a solid coaching orientation to helping them achieve self actualization.

Deborah is a colleague of the Creative Problem Solving Institute at the State University of New York at Buffalo and a featured speaker at professional association meetings locally. She is a consultant at Polaroid Corporation and has contributed to training manuals on career development as part of Polaroid's Career Transition Program. She has conducted workshops at adult education centers and held teaching positions at Radcliffe College and Boston University.

Deborah directed a professional women's organization, Women West of Boston, during the mid to late 80s. She was the first Program Director of the Boston Chapter of International Association of Career Management Professionals, formed in 1993 and now serves on the board. She was a founding member of a unique collaboration for professional development, the Individual Career Counselor's Consortium, and is a member of the Holistic Career Counselors Consortium. She completed the Advanced Training from The Coaches Training Institute in 1998. She has her B.A. from Elmira College and has done graduate work in the field of adult education at Boston University.

SANDRA S. BUTZEL

Sandy has had a long-standing interest and knowledge in the sociology of work, career development, and education. In 1984, she applied this knowledge as the Internship Coordinator for the Women's Center for Continuing Education at Lasell College. In that position, she secured paid internships for over 200 re-entry women and assisted Deborah Knox in teaching a career development course. This experience culminated in a collaboration with Deborah to write *The Unicorn in the Market Place.*

Sandy founded her own independent career counseling practice, Decisions for Positive Change, more than ten years ago and has counseled men and women of all ages in every stage of career development process.

From the very beginning of her practice, she has had a computer in her office and introduced her clients to the wonders of technology. Ten years ago, many clients were exposed to word processing for the first time and were encouraged to try it for themselves. Sitting side-by-side at the computer, writing a resume became not only an exercise in building self-esteem but also a lesson in understanding how a computer worked. Many clients were inspired to take their first computer course and therefore made themselves "computer literate" and more marketable in the workplace.

With the arrival of the Internet, Sandy began introducing it to her clients. They saw and experienced the magic and mystery of the Internet as just another source of information accessed with only a click of the mouse. Sandy not only used the Internet with clients for research but also as an intuitive tool to help clients think out of the box. Employing her theory that "for every idea, there is a universe of work," she literally showed that idea to clients graphically with the Internet.

Sandy feels that one of the most rewarding by-products of her practice has been the development of a large sharing referral network among her clients. She perceives that same sharing spirit on the Internet and takes pride in helping her clients access this remarkable resource for information and connection.

Not only does Sandy model using technology to her clients, she also models a sense of life/work balance. In addition to her private practice, she is also a Trustee of Whittier College in California, a Trustee for the Newton Free Library in Massachusetts, an Appointee to the Telecommunications Advisory Board in Newton, Massachusetts, a Director of the Pomroy Foundation, and has spent years in leadership positions in the League of Women Voters. She holds a B.S. and M.S. in sociology and psychology.